GAY CHRISTIAN MOVEMENT (GCM)
BM 6914, LONDON WCIN 3XX
01-283 5165

Jeremy Seabrook

A Lasting Relationship

Homosexuals and Society

Allen Lane

First published in 1976

ALLEN LANE
Penguin Books Ltd
17 Grosvenor Gardens, London SW1
ISBN 0 7139 0911 0

Typeset in Monotype Ehrhardt
and printed in Great Britain by
Ebenezer Baylis & Son Limited
The Trinity Press, Worcester, and London

Contents

5

Preface

Five years ago I went to Blackburn to talk to the people who live there, because I felt that the place where people live is perhaps one of the most crucial sources of personal identity. My feeling proved in large measure mistaken. The town seemed to be only a ghost-town of a community. True, many of those I met were haunted by nostalgia, bitterness and regret for a time when to be a Blackburnian meant something deeply significant. I received the impression that most people, especially the young, no longer received any really important clue as to who they were from the place where they were born or had lived for a very long time. The memories of communal life, of a shared predicament, had become a kind of myth. The place no longer fed them a sense of belonging, no longer served as a definition of who they were. To have been born in Blackburn – or any other town and city – has been reduced from a position of central importance in people's lives to being merely an incidental detail.

It was not by chance that, five years later, coming to talk to gay people about themselves and their sense of identity, I had a strong sense of an attempt being made, through sexuality, to restore what people had mourned so elegiacally in their changed Northern industrial town: a shared situation, a community of assumptions, beliefs, attitudes. The rhetoric of gay liberation is the language of nationalism, the identity of a *location*, although that location is now internal, a place of psychic belonging, which has replaced the kind of identity bestowed by place of birth in previous generations. The old identity implied not only place, but an economic function too: Blackburn meant textiles as Nottingham implied lace, Doncaster coal, Sheffield steel; but with the removal of the intense awareness of place – and it was conditioned by knowing where we stood in relation to the process of *production* – we have had to look elsewhere to find out who we are. We have turned inwards, to characteristics which will restore to us a feeling of communality, to reduce the sense of being stranded and robbed of identity. It is not surprising that sexuality should be one of the strongest sources of meaning that individuals can find within themselves; and it is in this way that the once un-thinkable aberration which homosexuality was considered to be has become a means of furnishing us with some of the things that were stolen from us by the loss of belonging to a place (even if those claustral and oppressive cities did supply us with a transient and only limited identity). And the gay community is a place – internal but ubiquitous – where individuals try to retreat from a society that exaggerates the differences between individuals, the uniqueness of their predicament, their isolation from one another, in an attempt to find again something to share with others.

In order to contact the individuals who describe their life in this book, I have used a varying approach; ranging from advertisements in papers to personal contact; the mediation of friends and acquaintances, organizations for gay people, clubs, pubs. In this way it has been possible to talk, not only with people who regularly use pubs and clubs, but many of those who would never be able to acknowledge publicly their sexual orientation. It does not claim to be exhaustive or totally representative; and it restricts itself to the social life of male homosexuals. The aim of the book is to look at more general areas of social change and see how they influence the lives of a substantial minority in the population; and to assess whether these changes increase or diminish for us the chances of leading lives that are happy and fulfilled.

JEREMY SEABROOK

The author and publishers are grateful to *New Society* for their kind permission to use the material appearing here under the title 'A London Meeting of the GLF'; this was originally published in *New Society* under the title 'The Gay Companions'.

Most homosexual men are anxious that the stereotype of the homosexual should be effaced, and that people should be accepted 'for themselves', without reference to their sexuality. That stereotype is nearly always qualified as effeminate, mannered, emotionally volatile, unstable, predatory and promiscuous. In one sense, the need to obliterate this caricature is no longer relevant; the irony being that in many particulars the stereotype of what used to be regarded as an inadmissible aberrancy has become a perfectly acceptable image of 'straight' society. It turns out, in retrospect, that the homosexual subculture – aristocratic in inspiration, upwardly mobile, self-indulgent – was in the forefront all the time, and the life of the homosexual community only foreshadowed a way of life that has become available to a far wider range of the population, following the emergence of a more generalized consumer society. Homosexuals, because of their anomalous position in the economy, always had the potential as prototypes of consuming man. There is no longer any need to abolish the caricature, just as there is no longer any compulsion to retain it. The subject is becoming a matter of indifference to the society which says 'Be what you are, find yourself, be true to your identity', and the cries of liberation are lost in the universal carnival.

It may be that formerly, because of the shame and secrecy involved in being homosexual, individuals had to signal their sexual orientation through codes, mannerisms and inflexions that congealed into the popular stereotype; this meant that only the bravest and most determined would enter the subculture, and that many people must have been deterred from giving expression to their sexual needs. The model for being homosexual must have appeared very repellent to many of those who knew they preferred their own sex, and it is certain that until very recently the sexual life of most gay people was furtive, inadequate and repressed. And while there are still many who are victims of this process, whose lives are corroded by guilt and fear, for the most part these people are of an older age-group, live in small communities, or occupy more traditional areas of society – conservative working class, traditional lower middle, where the absolute nature of maleness and femaleness is a basic datum of the view of the world.

The homosexual world itself illuminates the changes that have taken place in a much wider social context. These changes are not revolutionary, as some militant gay groups claim, and they are not necessarily personally liberating, although they certainly are for some people. On the contrary: it seems to me that the new openness about homosexuality is simply part of a process that stems from a minor deviation in the course of capitalism, which has been able to create such an abundance of things that the only real problem is how to dispose of them.

The material plenty of the West has created a quite new kind of human being. The spread of goods and services on such a spectacular scale has altered patterns of belief and life-purpose, has radically modified the individual's concept of himself, has substituted (however short-lived and illusory it may be) security for subsistence. But because we are still haunted by images of an antique and secular poverty, we have been incapable of a really rigorous critique of the social consequences and ideological shifts that have followed such enormous increases in production and consumption. We have been so dazzled by the scale of our achievements that we have failed to take into account at least two fundamental questions. We have assumed that the availability of such a wide range of material things somehow puts out of court any discussion of their provenance, and renders irrelevant any idea of the morality of the machinery that dispenses them; and, on the other hand, we have not closely monitored what effect an indefinite extension of over-saturated markets actually produces on human beings: the perpetual renewal of hopes, desires and dreams, the ceaseless stimulation of needs and wants, the avidity for happiness that consoles itself with satiation, the aspiration towards fulfilment that settles for endless having and getting. It is out of these processes that the new human being has been born: the homosexual community has fallen victim to this inexorable development, and in fact, represents a heightened or caricatured version of it. In the gay world the influences of the new economic necessity are more naked in their exploitative barbarism. It illustrates to what extent we have failed to impose our will upon the society we live in; blind helpless tropisms that we are, bending submissively to whatever is demanded of us, whether it be that we remain impoverished and unrewarded labour, or insatiable consumers of endlessly replenished perishables in the name of some unidentified but pervasive beneficence.

It is perhaps possible to show something of these changes through the individuals upon whom they work; but only partial and fitful insights can ever be gained by such a method into broad social and economic movements and their repercussions on morality, belief and ideology. People's account of themselves – however tendentious and one-sided – often shows that what we have come to regard as private dramas, individual experiences, incommunicable tragedies, form part of far wider social and economic processes.

Bill Wexford, sixty-two

Bill lives in a terraced house in a Midland town; it is a poor house, with a mud-stained fanlight over the door, a dark passage covered with brown oil-cloth, an unused parlour with a dusty moquette suite. He lives in the back room, where a coal fire burns and sheds its ash across the buff-coloured tiles; there are two chairs with wooden arms and dull crimson moquette seats; embroidered chair-backs have been washed so many times that the different coloured silks have frayed, and the pattern of daisies is only a ghostly reminder of the elaborate work it once was. The whole room speaks of his mother's absence; and she died more than ten years ago. A wedding photograph stands on the sideboard, face half-hidden under a huge hat, framed in leather, with a leather strut to make it stand up. In the hearth a jug of spills, a scattering of half-consumed red and blue strips of wood on the mantelpiece. There are built-in cupboards in the recesses at the side of the fireplace, painted brown, with doors secured by knobs that manipulate a strut of metal behind the cupboard doors. There is a dusty vase of plastic flowers on the shelf beneath the cupboard, some anemones dim with dust, and next to them an enlarged photograph of Bill's mother taken not long before she died: an old lady, a back garden, sunshine on a trellis of neglected roses. *Radio Times* open at yesterday's programmes lies by his chair, and a mug has stuck to the hearth, where some cocoa has spilled. A row of books on the shelf beneath the cupboards, books on fishing, a Home Doctor, an encyclopedia, some *Readers' Digest*s, a knitting pattern. A 1930s clock, like a blister, on the mantelpiece, ticks slowly, and a Labrador dog lies on the worn hearthrug. On the wall there is the metal stump of an old gas-jet. Ecru lace curtain at the window, its fine mesh having caught the dust from the room and the street. A threadbare carpet scattered with ash which has fallen from Bill's cigarettes and dimmed its already faded pattern. Bill is slight and balding, with a stoop and a pleasant, anxious face; his eyes are bright blue and mobile, never resting for long on objects or faces.

'Well, I'm getting on for sixty-two now, so I don't know as it matters all that much. I ain't had a life to speak of. I ain't been mis'rable, mind you. I ain't had no life of me own. And I don't want you to think I'm blaming anybody for it. I was just the one as stopped at home and looked after our old lady, and that's all there was to it. I had four sisters, they all got married, and then suddenly, there I was on me own, left with the old gal. I've always been one for being on me own. "Bill don't need no women round him," she'd say, "he's got a mother and four sisters, that's enough for anybody to be gooing on with."

' 'Course you must remember, this is gooing back a few years. I was born in the war; and I know it's a shocking thing to say, but do you know when the happiest time in my life was? It was in the Second War. I went to Egypt, Italy, that's the only time I had any pals.

'I never thought of myself as being anything out the ordinary. I left school in 1930, I wasn't stupid, only me mother being a widow, she needed the money. She used to do a bit of outwork in the little back bedroom, the sound of the treadle gooing used to wake us up about six in the morning. I don't think we realized what a life she had. I went in the boot and shoe, damn lucky to get a job. I never thought about women. I'd never been all that struck on 'em, but it never occurred to me I wasn't interested in 'em, that way, like a man should be. All the blokes at work were always gooing on about their wives, how they hated women, mouthing the odds, chosping and chattering . . . There was one old boy at work, he wasn't married, he said he'd sooner be wed to a shroud than a petticoat. And I never thought I was any different to that. Because at that time there was a fair few blokes never got married. Nobody thought anything of it. In them days you could say "My Mam's me only sweetheart", and that sort of thing. If you said that today, what would folks say to you? "You must be a bloody queer." It just never happened. Well, you read about it in the Sunday papers, indecency and all that sort of thing. I remember thinking "Oh, how shocking. Isn't that terrible?" I never thought one day I might finish up like that as well. Not that I have, I ain't bin in the papers, only I could've been . . . I don't know how to tell you what it was like. Before your time. People just scratted for a living, you thanked God if you went to bed with a full belly, you thanked God if you'd got a bloody bed to go to.

'It was definitely gooing in the army that woke me up. I liked being with blokes. Even when I started work, they used to take the piss out of you when you was young, but I liked even that. Used to send you on some bloody fool's errand, send you to a shop for three penn'orth of cobbler's pork; bread that meant, only being a green-horn you used to goo and do it and make yourself look a fool. I liked their company. In the army it was better, you all had to muck in, like. I liked to watch them. Only still the penny never dropped. We used to lark about a bit, and when we was together, sometimes we used to play about with each other like. Only it always meant more to me than it did to them. They used to forget about it after you'd finished, but it used to prey on my mind. I used to think about it, and if there was blokes I liked, used to imagine things, me and him, being together . . . Then one day, this chap and me, we used to just, you know, pull each other off, rubbing up we used to call it, and he had this book of sexy photos, all these women with big bums and looking over their shoulder and sticking out their tits, and I said "Put that away." And he said "Why, what's the matter with you, you ain't a nancy boy are you?" He came from London, and it was just the way he said it, made me realize everything. I said "No, course I ain't." But that knocked me for six. Just coming out the blue like that. I was twenty-seven. Aah.' Bill falls into a long re-flective silence. He takes up a bottle of pale ale that has been stand-ing in the hearth, removes the crinkled top with a rusty bottle opener, and pours it into a jam-jar. He notices that I am looking at the jar, and grins. 'Bloody cheaper than glasses. They don't last five minutes. I break glasses, too clumsy. I've got one, I give it to visitors. Not as I have many of them.'

'After he said that to me, I just kept out of his road, although I really liked him up to that time. I felt I couldn't face him, because he knew the truth about me.

'When I got back home, I more or less carried on the way I had before. My old lady was getting well on in her sixties by then, I more or less kept house for her. She kept on putting me bit of grub in front of me, making the beds, doing her bit of washing and shop-ping, keeping the place clean. She used to say to everybody "My boy'll never leave me." I'll be honest with you, I used to hate her sometimes. Then afterwards I used to feel sorry, because she was such a good old gal. Always got a pile of clean washing on her arm, steaming, while she held the pegs in her mouth and pinned them up on the line, peering into the stoopot to sort out the best bits for me. It broke my heart. Boot and shoe had had it after the war, so I got meself a job driving a lorry for a timber firm. That took me away a fair bit, but I never thought of leaving home after that. I felt so ashamed of meself, of what I was, I thought the only thing was to make out it wasn't there. I worked meself to death. I used to drive eight, ten, twelve hours at a stretch. Of a weekend I'd goo down to the pub sometimes, I knew I was safe there, only married men. I went fishing a bit on me own. I never had nobody, not for sex, right from the war till 1969 when the old lady died. She left me this little house. I'd got a good gooing-on . . . I've always been a saver. I was brought up to be thrifty; the old lady used to say "The poorhouse is the grave of working people." She scratted and saved and bought this house off the landlord in 1935; got it for a couple of hundred pound; and she got that by slavery; she was a slave; she sat ther in a pinner and her old hat, sitting after the light had gone and she could hardly see to do the work . . . So I'm bin left comfortable. I could retire if I wanted to, but what would be the good of that? What would I do? Sit and watch meself get older. Nobody wants you at my age, I don't kid meself. You want to remember that, boy. You want to make the most of yourself.

'Two of my sisters are dead. Grace had a cancer, died last summer. I've got a sister in Cloutsham Street, and another lives out Kettering way. I come home of an evening, I get meself a bit of tea. I still ride me old bike, only that ain't the pleasure it used to be. You goo down a country lane and you're lucky if some bugger in a great car don't force you into the ditch . . . Used to be a real pleasure, goo as far as Clifford Hill, bit of bread in your saddlebag, bottle of pop . . . I still do me 'lotment, only I'm got that in such a perfect state, I don't know what I can do with it . . . The old lady used to come up of a summer afternoon, used to sit out in an old garden chair under the apple tree . . . But time, oo, it hangs that heavy. I sometimes don't know what to do with meself. Sundays are the worst. I goo up me sister's for a bit of dinner, help her wash up. Then her and Albert fall asleep about three o'clock, and I come away, never say ta-ta . . . I don't want to sit there with people who are sleeping . . . Then when I get home I know I'm in for the night. I'm got a dog, Labrador. Bitch. Nice. But them ole evenings, they goo on for ever . . . Sundays . . . I sit and think about what it was like when

we was kids. Sunday School, our old gal dressing us up nice . . .
She used to wash all us kids out the same bowl, boil the kettle on the
fire and wait for it to start singing . . . We had a little enamel bowl,
and we used to let her wash us, we just sat there while she did it . . .
She soaped the flannel, hands then feet, me and the girls together . . .
We never thought nothing of it . . . Then we put our feet in our
lap for her to cut our toenails . . . Then she picked up the bits and
burnt them . . . and we watched 'em burn in the fire . . . You know
what they did, they crossed the water with their finger, like that
[makes sign of cross] if they washed somebody else in it, I don't
know why. Some old wives' tale I 'spect . . .

'When I started work I worked up Henry Street, and I walked
home for me dinner . . . She used to say "Get this poultice across
your chest and you won't be done so bad!" A pudden, boiled pudden
in a cloth, or a stoo . . . My dad died in the war, just after I was
born. He never seen me, and he always wanted a son . . . She hung
on to me, our old gal, for grim death . . . And I suppose I hung to
her . . . Only she knew she'd die first, well she didn't know, but
that's what you expect, isn't it . . . She was in her ninetieth year
when she died . . . I think to meself "Yes, it's easier for them as
pass on than it is for them as get left behind." When I get fed up I
tell meself "Only a few more years, and I shall be with her again."
So I don't get upset. Just a bit depressed like . . . I've had a good
life in some ways. Good health. I had her as a companion right till
I was fifty-five, so I had her with me the best years of my life. Only
I've never had anybody to share things with, a partner. Perhaps I
should've had a wife. I've always been keen on me home. Not so
much lately, I haven't bothered since she passed on. She died in her
sleep. You can believe it or believe it not, but when she got to the
latter part of her time, she was always up by six o'clock, winter and
summer, said she never needed the rest; and it were a Sunday
morning, and I had a bit of a lay-in, and I woke up about ten, and
I thought hullo, it's quiet. And before I opened that bedroom door,
I knew she'd gone. I'd got a premonition. Before I opened that
door I said to meself "Bill, my duck, you're on your own now."

'I expect there was others like me. Only you never got to know
them. You daredn't talk about things like that . . . I wouldn't have
opened me mouth about it, not at work. I thought I was the only
one like it.'

The vigour and power of the old woman speak through him. Her presence is felt beyond the physical objects that recall her existence. She has imposed herself ineffaceably on her son. It really is not an issue whether homosexual men are excessively influenced by their mothers, as is often believed. There are men who remain untouched by the most forceful viragos, while others perhaps flee to the shelter of quite inadequate and weak mother figures. Perhaps certain natures find themselves in a conjunction that favours certain processes; but whatever happens, it is too unpredictable and variable to lead to facile generalizations about mother-domination.

What is clear from the experience of Bill Wexford is that the upbringing to which he was subjected effectively blocked the way to any ready acknowledgement of his sexual needs; but how far this was present in the working-class culture, and how far a product of an extremely vigorous family influence, it is difficult to say. The two seem to be virtually inextricable. Where the family stops and something called 'society' begins is an elusive and fugitive line of demarcation. It seems that the family itself only carries out the delegated ordinances of the culture; like rent-collectors for absent landlords, exacting tributes and imposing demands which do not originate with itself, the purpose of which it does not understand.

Bill saw no possibility of a relationship with another man. In his society there were men who were married and men (a fairly small minority) who stayed at home. Virtually no one in a small community left the home of his parents to set up a *ménage* that was not based upon heterosexual monogamy, even if they lived in what then passed for sin. If people were not married, this fact was always known, possibly through the network of oral communication, but it did seem that people in such a closed community were equipped with a mysterious sensory mechanism that enabled them to detect all deviations from rigorous orthodoxy. They just knew – those women with their watchful eyes and doubting mouths, those men with their look of distrust and their unshakeable certainty – that the whole thing was a swindle, but that if they weren't going to get away with it, neither was any other bugger.

The kind of repression of which Bill was a victim is still there. The efficiency of the socialization process depends upon its power to extinguish the individual by the force of its values, customs and beliefs. Bill says that working-class people used to deny that homosexuality existed in the working class. It was a product of decadence, an affliction of the rich and leisured, and indeed was often adduced in argument as proof of the corrupting influence of money. This belief heightened the sense of outrage of the poor, gave substance to their view of the immorality of a system which robbed so many people of the chance to do more than subsist. Perhaps this is why among the more traditional segments of the working class the sense of shame is most tenacious. It appears to them to be more than an aberration: it is also a betrayal.

In one sense the perception that to be homosexual was a result of privilege was correct. Or rather, it would have been more accurate to say that it was a privilege to be able to give expression to it; a privilege that is now being extended to social groups for whom formerly the question of their happiness, fulfilment or sexual identity would have been an unthinkable luxury.

However, a more general awareness of the existence of homo-sexuality doesn't help some individuals to relate it to their own experience and needs. The word, the concept – like the stereotyped images it evokes – has a repelling and contaminating power which makes people recoil and say 'That can't be me.' And even many of those who are quite aware of the phenomenon and know homosexual individuals can remain in complete ignorance of their own relation-ship to it until late in life. There is a wide divergence in the factors which awaken people's consciousness of themselves in all areas of their lives, including the sexual. Just as some people discover that they believe in God or could easily be Communists by chance, sometimes as the result of casual conversation or random encounters, so others discover their sexuality in their mid-forties, or on the verge of retirement. I spoke to a man in his early sixties who claimed to have had no sexual relationship in his life, and who discovered that he was attracted to young men. He said it was like becoming aware of his body for the first time; but not in a pleasurable way. He said it was like discovering two corpses: the self he had never been, and the self he was.

Charles, late fifties

He lives in a flat in South Kensington in a baroque palazzo, crowded out with *objets d'art*, curios and antiques; an eighteenth-century tombstone is a coffee table, the walls are totally covered with en-larged prints of his favourite cities; so that you can choose between a vista of the Île St Louis, the waterfront of New Amsterdam, the Pantheon in Rome; there is a salon which is like a loge in the *opéra-bouffe*; velvet drapes looped with gold and thistle-shaped tassels, *baignoires* in red plush, a gold-studded *causeuse*. There is a mingled scent of incense and pomanders; Arab blankets cover the floors, the work of nomads with whom Charles feels he has great affinities; he calls himself one of life's nomads. He is corpulent and wears rather tight and silky clothes; a lilac silk coat, high heels; he wears a toupet and a little rouge on his cheeks, to which he refers deprecatingly as soon as I arrive, '. . . the ravages of time. But at least I have recipro-cated, I have wrought my own ravages upon time in my modest way.' He is arrogant with a grand manner, and gestures that describe elaborate arabesques; he holds his head up to disguise his double chin, and this adds to the sense of hauteur. His nails are manicured and well polished, lanceolate and long. He is mannered and camp – he maintains designedly so. His demeanour merely exaggerates what is already there. It is, he says, a kind of distancing self-consciousness, a way of protecting himself against the world. He talked about the 'arbitrariness of things'. 'You don't think I sur-round myself with all this paraphernalia because I like it, do you?'

CHARLES: 'My dear, I loathe myself. I always have done. I've always conducted my life with periods of debauchery alternating with the most profound penitence. Quite genuine penitence. I am a deeply religious and spiritual person, and I've always resented as the vilest of temptations the peccadilloes to which I am prone. And alas, prone is what I have so often been, whether in ecstasy or remorse. I'm quite incapable of reconciling these two aspects of my life. I can only assume that God intends that I should suffer, per-haps for my arrogance, which is nothing short of overweening . . . I find it very humbling. When I'm feeling especially pleased with myself for having achieved something – which, heaven knows, isn't often these days – I might be walking along Sloane Street, and suddenly I see an angelic youth, one of the *angeli musicanti* of Melozzo da Forli, and I'm totally enthralled, and my knees turn to jelly, and – well I don't now – but in the past I used to follow the young men whom I found irresistible. And there are so many of them. Fortunately, as one gets older, one can control one's instinct to give chase . . . How many times have I not been deflected from some errand by a beautiful face or a pair of legs or the curve of a body? . . . It is a mercy that I have never had to rely on earning a living. I am in fact nominally an antiquarian, but that's only because of my family's conscience; and I leave the running of the business to friends and associates, who of course rob and expropriate me like pirates. But if I had been obliged to earn my daily whatever, I should certainly have been dismissed a hundred times, purely for having been waylaid by beauty and youth, which have lain in ambush for me all my life. That has, I feel, also been part of my punishment. I realize that I am privileged, and that many of those to whom I have found myself in thrall have been quite the reverse. I've been generous to them naturally. It would be unthinkable not to have been. This has led to some singularly distasteful situations, such as those in which the wretched youths feel obliged to simulate extremes of passion in return for quite modest rewards. Not to speak of the times when I have been threatened, physically, by those who imagined that they could extort from me material gain, when I had already given them so much. I would say to them, "You may beat me to pulp if you are so moved." I've always quite enjoyed the idea of being beaten, although when it comes to it I'm a frightful coward. And it always worked. I've never been molested in any way.

'I am impregnated with a strong awareness of social class, as indeed, I believe most of my generation are . . . I sometimes think that if I had felt the urgency of some occupation, I would have been less inclined to succumb to temptation. But as it is, I've been a dilettante of beauty and physical form. In the flesh, you understand. I'm not trying to ennoble it by specious reference to art, as some of my friends are inclined to do. I'll tell you something that will interest you. I used to detest working-class youths when I was myself young, mainly I think because they seemed to be either too full of carbohydrate or skeletal and rickety. I could never understand where Oscar discovered his young men. But the welfare state has been accompanied, I do assure you, by a quite stunning improvement in the physique of the mass of the people. And for that I am profoundly grateful, although in principle it remains a matter of the greatest indifference to me whether the working classes remained in their slums, or whether they inherited the earth, as now appears to be the case.

'I am guilty of the most subtle refinements in my taste . . . The shimmer and iridescence of the hair where the pubic hair stops, for instance. Pubic hair itself is, in my estimation, a deplorable obscenity, although I've never actually said so to the Almighty . . .

And I loathe blemishes. Sometimes I have taken home an adolescent flawless of feature, only to discover that his back was disfigured by positive craters of the most purulent acne, and I've had to send him packing. Lamentable though such conduct is. It's bad enough to pluck them off the streets – a bit like stealing rosebuds from somebody else's garden, but then to dismiss them is even more unpardonable. And the other thing is the extreme perishability of the commodity of youth and freshness; I don't mean simply that it fades, but that one is soon thoroughly sated by it; and indeed it becomes more of an irritant as soon as one is able to establish that it is accompanied by an almost total absence of intelligence and conversation, as is almost invariably the case.

'I've never had a relationship that lasted. I mostly dispose of them after a few weeks at the most, and go through this ghastly expiation process. I'm Anglo-Catholic as you probably guessed, and I do find it an immeasurable consolation.

'I don't like the way I am. I don't enjoy the experience of being dependent upon people whom I fundamentally despise. But I need their youth and beauty, I need to absorb it in great draughts; like any other addiction, I suppose. I am extremely well connected, as I expect you gathered, but all that means as little to me as the fate of those in whom I've been so profoundly but briefly interested. I couldn't number them. There must have been thousands during my lifetime. I've been in love hundreds of times, but however intense, it has seldom lasted more than a few days at most. Except of course, for a boy at school when I was seventeen, and he was fourteen. And that I managed to sustain at a high pitch for at least a year; which is the closest I've ever come to constancy; a state no doubt exacerbated by the total unavailability of the youth in question. Contrary to what is vulgarly believed about a public-school education, I spent my school years in a state of total celibacy, which was only partly compensated by the religious ecstasy into which I frequently fell. There has always been a strong correlation between my sexuality and my faith; which is not to derogate from my faith, which, I repeat, is very real and very important to me. In fact, it is only in terms of my belief in God that I can make any sense of my sexuality, and its attendant difficulties and unhappiness. Otherwise, I should most assuredly have blown my brains out long before now.

'I don't think I'm interested in Gay Liberation. I don't think

I've ever had any problem in that direction. When I was at Cambridge I had my first sexual experience, and when I came down I more or less gravitated towards the world of the rather privileged smart homosexual artistic and literary people. Yes, I suppose I am a snob, but that is abundantly made up for by my needs of youth . . . I don't know what homosexuals did who were not in the same social circle as myself. I don't suppose they did very much at all, poor things, shop assistants and factory workers. I never thought about it. You must understand, that most of the young men whom I've known were not homosexual. At least they denied that they were, and I was never interested enough to pursue whether they were lying.

'I do understand what you mean about homosexual being an occupation in itself. Perhaps I should put occupation homosexual on any forms I'm asked to complete . . . I don't agree that the removal of guilt would help in any way. I think conscience is the last bulwark against anarchy . . . It hasn't stopped me from doing precisely as I choose, but at least I feel badly about it afterwards.'

Warm evening in the road; late patches of sunlight through the leaves of the lime trees. The street lamps are being turned on; a woman walks a dog on a lead past the stuccoed villas. Otherwise silence. The air is scented with syringa and lime. Charles stands on the doorstep, holding his hair in place against the warm breeze. He gives a little wave as I turn the corner, fingers folding one by one over the palm of the hand, beginning with the little finger.

In many ways he supports the idea of what homosexuals are: it was perhaps the privileged position of upper-class people which helped them to avow their sexuality first; and this acted as a model for those in more modest condition; out of the imitators of the rather aristocratic manner, the rudimentary homosexual subculture was born.

There is a certain homogeneity among homosexuals who formed the subculture in the first half of this century. The subculture was characterized by leisure, privilege and aristocratic/artistic pretensions. It was upwardly aspiring, snobbish; and although, like Charles, it may have wanted as sexual objects people from other social classes, it incorporated and re-socialized them, initiated them into its customs and rites, which were essentially *haute bourgeoise* in style. There was something conformist in the deviancy. There

21

were very limited ways of being homosexual. For those who could not accept the style and manner of the subculture – or would not be accepted by it – secrecy or repression were the only alternatives. There could scarcely be a greater contrast between the younger homosexuals and most of those who admitted to their homosexuality in the 1920s and 30s. It seems that to declare oneself enjoined upon individuals a certain predetermined way of being: whether society expected the style, the manner, the baroquery, or whether these evolved as a defiance, as an extension of the heroics needed to ignore the social opprobrium and emancipate oneself, it is difficult to say. Those who overcame the bitterness of repression and shame and who participated in the social life of their peers seem to bear a remarkably similar imprimatur. Of this style which undoubtedly fed the caricature, Leo was perhaps the most extravagant exponent I have met.

Leo, sixty

Flamboyant, loquacious and theatrical, he is now sixty; an illustration of *nomina* being *consequentiae rerum*. Leonine, with imposing grizzled hair and so commanding a presence that when he speaks, even the intake of breath causes people to fall silent and wait eagerly for the wisdom inhaled so meaningfully from the air and distilled in such authoritative and irrefragable modulations. He admits to being profoundly egotistical. He is intolerant, proud, and is not accustomed to have anything he says called into question. For this reason – as he himself says – he has always surrounded himself with his intellectual and social inferiors, so that he might glitter by contrast. He has always sought sycophants and admirers: a great spoilt child. He sweeps in large parabolic movements through life: his words, gestures, movements all describe perfect arcs in the air. His face is rather fleshy: his hair, sometimes coloured a shade of ash-blond, is kept in place by a permanent wave, piled up at the front. He sometimes looks a little like a miniature of Marie Antoinette. He wears two or three rings on each hand with gleaming jewels, a *breloque* on a gold chain over his stomach, a plain gold bracelet. He wears a sort of doublet pinched in at the waist, which redistributes some of his flesh, a blouse with a *jabot* and *guipure* lace at the cuffs. He has been quite well known as a travel writer, and is a culinary specialist in the dishes of the Eastern Mediterranean. He despises the Western Mediterranean as a barbaric place dedicated to the cultivation of the olive and the grape, the two most tedious seeds the Almighty saw fit to distribute on the face of the earth. This doesn't prevent him from spending several months each year in Italy: he has an apartment in a palazzo near the Piazza di Spagna, which he fills with friends and admirers and acquaintances. He doesn't consider himself primarily as a homosexual; and indeed, his relations with the avowedly eccentric crowd around him are marked by a proper – even prudish – sense of correctness. Until his relationship with Jean-Paul, he claims not to have had any deep feeling for anyone for twenty years. (Sex, he says dismissively, oh that's nothing, you can have sex with anybody, but to have a relationship takes consummate skill and a great deal of care.) In the early fifties he says he had a relationship with a woman, a passionate love-affair in fact, and she committed suicide. After that he found it psychologically impossible to live in England. It had always been a climatic and culinary hazard, and after this experience it became out of the question. His only other relationship had been when he was in his early twenties, with a young man whom he'd met at university; and that had never come to anything physical but had run its course in an atmosphere of literature, abstraction, speculation about the soul, gossip and travel; and had been played out in sublime moments on the North African coast in the stifling heat of the sirocco, long afternoons in the shade of fig-trees, cool terraces and stifling quaysides in Mediterranean fishing ports.

He met Jean-Paul in the summer of 1972. He had been properly introduced, by a woman-friend who had been able to vouch for the respectability of the young man and assured Leo that if the young man found himself penniless in Rome, it was no more than youthful carelessness, and if he would be so kind as to accommodate a perfect stranger for a few days, she would write to his mother and inform her of the boy's plight.

'The moment I saw him, I thought of some archetypal myth about the god sent down in disguise, you know, Philemon and Baucis, something like that, where nobody recognized him and all turned him away . . . Like Jesus Christ, I suppose, it's only a recrudescence of the same myth . . . Anyway, when I saw him, I said "That boy is a god . . ." He was dreadfully scruffy, quite ungod-like. He had been mixing with a horrible crowd of people,

playing guitars and begging and probably being quite promiscuous –
I expect they were students. It seems that everybody is a student
these days, unless they do anything so dull as studying . . . He wore
blue-jeans, cut off at the knees, and ancient sandals, and a denim
shirt which was torn and indescribably grubby; his face was dusty,
his hair tangled and looked about ten shades darker than it was –
which turned out to be the colour of corn of a ripeness you don't
see in England, a kind of auburn rust-colour. He smiled, and was
dreadfully apologetic, and in fact, the moment I saw him, I think I
was aware of a peculiar kind of magnetism, a sense that my destiny
and his were to be inextricably bound together. I was courteous to
him, and offered him a bath and some clean clothes – of course mine
were several sizes too big for him, but I had a young friend – quite
heterosexual – who had been head boy of one of the more well-
known public schools, and he was staying with me, so I was able to
give Jean-Paul some clean clothing. He was a very strange boy. He
was going to stay for a few days, until he could get back to Geneva;
but in the event he was with me over a month. Thirty-two days to
be precise. The first evening, after dinner, he said impulsively "I'd
like to go out with you for a walk." So we went to the Borghese,
and then to a café, where we sat until it closed; and then we sat on
the Spanish steps until dawn, just talking . . . It appeared that he
believed in mysticism and considered himself to be on some kind of
journey. I don't understand it really; but I was aware that he was a
very spiritual creature, quite free of any taint of vulgarity . . . He
was very gentle. One night he said to me "You're hypersensitive,
Leo." We spoke a mixture of Italian and English, because although
my Italian is excellent, my French is virtually non-existent . . . I'd
never had anyone so . . . beautiful take an interest in me for years.
When I was younger, I do assure you it was different and I took great
pleasure in keeping them at bay, because they were for the most
part rapacious and insensitive, and I knew I would have exposed
myself to untold damage if I'd committed the folly of letting myself
go . . . But with Jean-Paul, I felt something that had been submerged begin to awaken . . . It was a kind of spiritual cleansing.
Because you know my real problem is trying to keep myself sheltered
from the ugliness and cruelty of the modern world. I'm a very moral
person, very puritanical in a way, which is belied by my apparent
articulateness . . . Words come easily, but my emotions are hidden
beneath them . . . Inside there is something very austere about me,

and I assure you I abominate the so-called permissive society and the promiscuity of the world of the homosexual . . .

'Well, for a few days we became inseparable, and I began to feel I was really falling in love with him. He seemed to delight in my company, because I am a quite amusing *raconteur* and I have a certain *savoir-vivre*, and although he was of good family – my friend was as good as her word and allayed my fears on that score within two days, there was a cable from his mother in Geneva – he was socially somewhat callow . . . I noticed that he returned all the time to his mysticism. He belonged to a sect I'd never heard of, and I'm afraid I sort of dismissed it. He said he was destined to follow some spiritual pilgrimage which hadn't been fully revealed to him, and he sensed that I was one of the landmarks on the way. Then one night he took the initiative, and he put his arms around me and said "I think you're falling in love with me." I was absolutely dumbfounded. I couldn't deny it. I almost began to believe in his mystical powers. I felt a deep sense of panic inside. He said "I've renounced all physical demonstrations of affection. That is why spiritual relationships are so important to me, and that is why I can touch you like this and yet remain remote." Well, it didn't take any great degree of insight to realize that was a danger signal. But unfortunately, I was involved, dreadfully, and I'd gone along with him in a rather irresponsible way – showing my admiration, buying him things, taking him to expensive restaurants. I told him that he was to make himself at home and that he must stay as long as he wished.

'I had arranged to go to stay with friends in Greece towards the end of August, but of course I stayed on . . . He used to talk to me endlessly; in the middle of the afternoon when it was so hot, I was only aware of his beautiful voice which merged with the warmth, it was like a physical caress . . . I thought "Well, I will simply let this relationship grow and develop as it may . . ." But after a time we seemed to come to an *impasse*. By the end of the second week our conversations became repetitive and a little boring. I tried to get beyond this spirituality, and found nothing. Or rather I couldn't get through it. It was so full of abstractions and vaguenesses, transcendence and references to wholeness and completeness and being and becoming. It became tiresome. I thought, I imagined that because he was so young he'd never been involved in a relationship before. And, accordingly, I treated him very gently. But he always managed to turn the conversation from any expression of emotion.

25

And then he asked if he could bring friends to the apartment. Well I said yes, of course; but it wasn't long before the whole place was full of them. I don't know who they were; they were inferior types, do you know what I mean? Some of them very dubious indeed. No, they weren't dubious, they were very clear. And I thought "Well, if he prefers that kind of person to me . . ." And of course they stayed for meals, and they slept there, and the whole place threatened to become a shambles . . . This continued for about two weeks, and then I said to him "Jean-Paul, I think this has gone quite far enough. I do not propose to turn my home into a hospice for the homeless and outcast of Rome." And he became very angry and we had a violent quarrel. I will not describe the scene that passed between us; he talked to me in terms that were breathtaking in their vulgarity. No matter how good his family was, the fellowship of low companions had corrupted him. He was in fact the only truly corrupt human being I have ever met.

'I should have turned him out there and then. But in fact, he said he needed me. What would you imagine if a person told you he needed you? . . . I suppose I deliberately blinded myself to the awful things he had said, and I took his request to stay as an admission of what I had suspected all along – that he had no relationships on other than the most superficial level. And I said he could stay, as long as he sent away his legions of hangers-on . . . Which he did . . . And we spent an evening which I can only describe as the happiest in my life. We had a sublime meal, and drank rather a lot of wine, and I felt, oh so rejuvenated! We were rather silly. And then he told me how lonely he was, and how he yearned for a real person to relate to. I told him that I'd thought his spirituality rather nonsensical. He said that it was genuine, but that it also served as a screen behind which he could conceal his lack of real human attachments. I felt very sorry for him, and we lay for a long time on the sofa with my arm round him; and there was an apocalyptic thunderstorm outside, which made it all seem so much more sublime. About midnight, he said he felt wretchedly tired and he actually shed a few tears, and said he'd never met anyone as kind as me; and that he'd like to retire for the night. I said Goodnight to him, and sat for hours in my salon, just thinking. There was nobody else there that night for some reason. I think it was because I'd arranged to be away in Greece at that time, and, anticipating my departure, everybody had left . . . And then, at about four o'clock,

I could bear it no longer. I thought "I will just go and look at him sleeping." I certainly had no intention of asking to be invited into his bed, or anything like that . . . And I crept down the corridor, and *piano, piano*, opened the door. And what I saw is what makes me believe that he is the most corrupt and depraved person I have ever known. On the pillow were two heads. He must have gone out and picked somebody up, in a bar, in the street, who knows. You can imagine the turbulence of my spirit at that sight. I managed to compose myself. I said nothing. I simply crept out in horror. The next morning he came in to breakfast as if nothing had happened. Evidently the youth had been shuttled out at a conveniently early hour. He sat down and looked at me with his pale troubled eyes and I said "I'm going to Greece, Jean-Paul. I want you to leave today." Not a word of explanation. I refused to discuss it. He pleaded; he was abject; but that only made things worse. To have gone out like that after an evening of such gentleness and tenderness, to me it was incredible that a human being could commit such an act of treachery. The most degenerate *scugnizzo* would have shown more sensitivity. After the conversation we had had the preceding evening . . . It debased all the things I felt to be finest in my nature. I felt smirched. I just couldn't get rid of him quickly enough. I told him that I didn't want to hear from him again, and that if I were in his place I should learn to distinguish authentic feeling from its counterfeit among the people he frequented . . . I tried to indicate the shock which the delicacy of my nature had undergone, but I don't think he understood. All lost on him, I suppose. He wept. But as I then realized, tears were only part of the extensive armoury with which he laid siege to people. I wrote to the Marchesa who had originally introduced him to me, and said that I thought she was deceived in him; and she wrote me back a very cool letter, saying that she was never wrong in her judgement of people. And since then our relations have remained rather strained. We're both too well-bred to allow it to come to a rupture over a youth we both scarcely knew, but in fact that wretched young man almost destroyed a friendship which I value far beyond anything he could offer, and which will outlast any of these infatuations . . . He was so very beautiful.

'I've written it all down, for publication, posthumously, in far greater detail than I've been able to tell you . . . I think my self-respect was badly wounded. Not vanity – I am vain, I know that, but I feel the deepest pride I have in myself was hurt . . . Not only that. I've always thought, being an artist, that I had some understanding of the vagaries of the human heart. And I was quite simply wrong . . . You'll understand that, of course. It is rather demeaning to have to learn lessons of that kind at my age. One scarcely emerges from them with one's dignity enhanced; and as one gets older and a little more obese and a little less lovable, one needs all the dignity one can muster, I do assure you . . .

'I'm so much more wary now. I shan't ever fall in love again, if it can be called love, what I felt for Jean-Paul. I am so sensitive that if I am rebuffed or hurt in any way I withdraw to an extraordinary degree. I have many consolations; many friends, good company and conversation. I'm not lonely. But I shall never give myself again, in the way that I feel I squandered what is most precious within me upon that wretched young man.'

One of the traditional models offered to gay people by the subculture was that of tragic hero: a great love disdained. When I saw Leo a few months after he had talked to me, he had almost forgotten Jean-Paul, and said 'Oh don't mention that wretched creature's name to me.' He had met someone else. '*Al cor gentil ripara sempre amore.*' Love is an endogenous disease; and in gay people, perhaps for lack of an externally imposed structure, because of the absence of acknowledged institutions to regulate the affections, it seems closer to the surface, more readily released by the appearance of a new individual; and is more readily consumed than in straight society. The courtship rituals are brief and compressed, and there is an acceleration of conventional time-sequences, in which love can be kindled, flare up and die within a few days. It is the reverse of courtship: sex first, then, if it's interesting, a relationship second. Many older gay people say that as a defence against their own feeling of vulnerability they learnt to suppress their emotions, and in fact seem to have led lives of considerable emotional repression, even when achieving all the sexual satisfaction they needed. Many who spoke to me seemed petulant and angry at those who have betrayed them, deceived them, exploited them. They have been preyed upon, used, disregarded; and saw themselves as an injured party, giving and selfless; and if they appear bitter or distrustful, it is only what the malevolence and insensitivity of others has wrought.

It is impossible to distinguish between the homosexual condition and the social condition of homosexuals: at many points the conjunction is so complete that neither generalizations about homosexuals nor society can be tested. It is not that there is anything substantially different in relationships between gay people from those between male and female; but without the constraints, the received models of behaviour, the culturally predetermined path of true love, the homosexual has had more often to improvise; and it is perhaps this that throws into clearer view processes that are common to everybody; only they are taking place within a compressed time-scale, and in a place that most would regard as dislocated from reality, although at the same time it is a heightened, theatrical, selfconscious intensification of reality that makes it so disturbing and relevant to heterosexual society.

Kenneth Jameson

A bungalow-*chaumière* on the outskirts of a Surrey town, hidden from the road by a high holly hedge. A concrete path leads to a rough-wood varnished door, with a black metal knocker, a little stiff from recent rain, so that there is a risk of striking the black percussion knob sharply on the back of one's fingers. On a length of wood just inside the porch '*Pace a chi entra, saluti a chi parte.*' A fanlight over the door, a settle in the hall. The dining-room opens to the right, and through this access is gained to the sitting-room. In the dining-room which is cluttered and contains a great deal of bric-à-brac, a picture of Mr Jameson's great-grandfather, and a sonnet written to him by William Wordsworth on the final passing of the bill to abolish slavery in March 1807. Inside the salon, some stephanotis is burning, and the smell pervades the whole house, which is baroque, tepid and veiled; so that the whole atmosphere is a mixture of a kind of ecclesiastical sensuality and secular comfort. The dining-room table is late Victorian, drop-leaf, and upon it stand a china Virgin and child, a brass candlestick, and a cyclamen with pink blooms fading like dying butterflies; all of which adds to the sense of religious celebration. There is a dresser against the wall with built-in shelves, in dark wood, and ornamented with rows of Meissen and Delft plates. A vegetarian lunch has been prepared – salad and potato, cheese and onion pie, and passion fruit tart. Kenneth is recovering from a bout of overslimming caused by vanity and resulting in malnutrition. All over the house are

Kenneth's paintings: he shows me his latest. It is a water-colour of Christ blessing a male prostitute. In the sitting-room an olive-green carpet is covered with scattered white mats. There are two large buttoned leather armchairs and a brocade sofa. The wallpaper has a pale olive damascene pattern, and the curtains match. There are many paintings on the walls, some collages in a primitive child's book illustration style, and a lot of *objets d'art* – more Meissen plates above the picture rail, lacy Spanish fans on a buffet; there is an *etagère* and a *chiffonnier*; some photographs, including a picture of a dead woman in a purple cloak holding a crucifix. The gas-fire, boxed in walnut, is protected by a polished brass fender. On a *pouffe* a biography of John Clare; a stand with plants depending from hooks at angles to it – stepmother's tongues and spider plants and ferns. Adjoining the lounge there is a conservatory where Kenneth sleeps, winter and summer, a high bed with a floral eiderdown, which looks out on to soaking lawns, mossy tree trunks and the green flame-shaped conifers; hedges of holly and yew; in spite of the winter sunshine there is a slightly glaucous feeling, as though the whole room were submerged, silent, peaceful, remote. The house is called Elim, after the first oasis which the children of Israel came to when they went out of Egypt. The name of the house has already led to at least one caller wanting to know what time the services started.

Kenneth is overwhelmingly kind. He lives more retired from the world than ever before. He says that his relationship with God is the only real enduring relationship. That is not to say that he has renounced physical contact; it is simply that the opportunity presents itself less frequently than formerly, and now that he is in his sixties, he no longer feels the same insistent need. He is dressed in a black zip-fastened jerkin, corduroy trousers and wedge-heeled fashionable shoes. He wears two large rings, a gold bangle and a gold watch. He is warm and effusive, and calls me 'dear heart'. He is psychic and reads the Tarot, although he gives away all the money he receives from the Tarot to charity or to individuals. He subscribes to many charities.

KENNETH: 'I came here for a fortnight, and I've stayed twenty-one years.'

He met the previous owner of the house, and she invited him to stay for a couple of weeks when he was suffering considerable nervous strain. She became ill, and he stayed to nurse her; an indisposition that lasted more than ten years, until her death. Her nephew lived with her, and then he, too, died, and Kenneth inherited the house.

'I don't think she ever really loved me; at least, not until the last year of her life. And then she did seem to cling to me . . . I've always had more women in love with me than men in my life. I've always attracted women. I've never had reciprocal love from someone I could love too. As a matter of fact, I detest the whole homosexual, "gay" thing. I detest the word gay. I think it's so wrong to categorize people in that way. I think all people are ambisexual, and by these absurd labels, one so reduces the life of individuals . . . Being . . . whatever it is makes life so much more rich and rewarding than that makes it sound. That doesn't mean I haven't had my share of it; and of being in love. But always, it seems, with the wrong people . . . But I do have my religion, and my painting and my writing, although that seems so leaden these days: it's so much more laboured than it ever used to be. The years the locusts have eaten, God has given back to me.' He smiles, a radiant, gentle smile. 'I have a lot of friends. I like people. I could see, as soon as I opened the door to you, that you had come to me in a spirit of love. I can tell with people. As you know, I read the Tarot, and the influences of the Virgin, the Sister, the Earth-Mother are in you. I can tell . . . I spend a great deal of my time in prayer and in meditation. I am considering a book about Christ and the Tarot. Whether it will ever get written . . .' He shrugs, a resigned unsorrowing shrug. 'I feel so tired sometimes . . .'

'I was born in Kingston upon Hull. My father was unfortunately a drunkard, although my mother was middle-class in origin. I suppose we'd come down in the world somewhat because of my father's unfortunate failing. And when I left school I had to go to work in a shop. I knew of my desires at a very early age. At the age of six I can remember having been sexually interested in an uncle. I remember going and sniffing the seat of a chair where he'd been sitting. And I think it was like this all through my adolescence. There was a boy next door. He went to Grammar School, and I didn't, and he had a friendship with a man who worked in the boating pool. And I know that I longed to do whatever it was they did, but never dared. He initiated me into masturbation. Then, when I was about sixteen or seventeen, I used to go and stand on the Corporation pier, and underneath, I knew there were men doing all kinds of things, but I kept my eyes on the horizon, no doubt looking for some non-existent sailor, and all the time wanting to do things I had no means of putting into practice. Then, at the age of nineteen, I was sent to Italy, to learn the business of some relatives of my father's who were quite well-off. And that's where I first learned something about sex, because of course I fell in love. You see what I mean – Mediterranean men will take part in sexual activity with men, just because it's a natural thing to do, not because they're gay or anything. I mean, that's why the ancient Greeks knew about these things, and we who are supposed to be so much more civilized – ' he shrugs in mild despair. 'Anyway, I wanted him, Nino, to come back to England to live with me. But Mussolini wouldn't allow anyone to leave the country, so we had to get a forged passport; and anyway, there had been an assassination or something at Marseilles, and they checked all the passports, and of course it was discovered that his was not authentic, and of course he fell under suspicion, and I had to part with him. That was heart-breaking. Eventually he did get out of Italy and he came to live with me in London. I don't know whether he was homosexual really; I know that I kept him, and what's more I had to go on the streets to do it in the end. I know that sounds a bit melodramatic, but it was absolutely true. There was a pub not far from Piccadilly Circus, and I used to go there with the intention of being picked up by men . . . Because otherwise I knew that I would never have been able to keep Nino. A lot of the men I picked up, nothing ever happened. They often just took me to a hotel room, and some of them simply hugged me. I think they were moved as much by curiosity as by anything else. Australians, South Africans, people like that. But he left me in the end, just the same You can't really tie people to you in that way.

'I've been an actor. I wasn't considered a very good one at the time, though today, with the wider range, and less stress on things like enunciation and formality, I think I would have been considered much better. I was never any good at movement. I've been so many things – actor, writer, painter. I had a certain amount of success with my first book, and then the publishers commissioned my auto-biography; but then for some reason rejected it when it was completed. I was taken up for a time by the Sitwells, I knew people like the Farjeons, Binkie Beaumont, but you know how it is . . . I somehow never really sustained things. Perhaps I've been too diffuse with my talents. Anyway, when the publishers refused to publish, I did a stupid thing. I sued them, because I was hurt by their rejection . . . In the end it was settled out of court, but it wasn't very pleasant, the whole business. I worked for five years, writing stories for women's magazines. I don't think anyone can write that kind of thing for longer than five years. You become too repetitive. They wanted me to deal with subjects that broke away from the happy-ever-after, a woman in love with a much younger man, even abortion, things like that. Because they were trying to free themselves from some of the old taboos. At that time I could write very effortlessly.

'I used to hold parties here, for CHE, London main group as well as the local branch. But people will steal things. I suppose we all need so much love, don't we, but there are some people who steal things, presumably because love is lacking in their lives. I don't mind, only it's so boring when they do. So, lately, I've been inclined to withdraw even from that. I used to go to London a great deal, but even that has fallen off. It's so difficult with the trains, and getting to theatres, and it's impossible to get home again. So I lead a life of retirement, not in the work sense; but a much more secluded existence than I've ever been used to.'

Late afternoon; the striations of cirrus that blurred the sunlight earlier in the day have thickened, and only thin green spaces appear between the violet-grey clouds. Beyond the holly-hedge the home-going traffic strings chains of red tail-lights in one direction, yellow in the other. Kenneth stands in the porch and waves; the wind moves his pale hair, and sways the dark flickering conifers; a dry rustle in the holly.

Corresponding to a yearning for an ideal (future) love, there exists in the life of many older gay people a past perfect love, often referred to in the most elegiac and sometimes hyperbolic terms. 'It was too beautiful to last', 'I was a fool, I let him go', or 'He broke my heart and left me'. It takes on a retrospective lustre, and by contrast with it, no future relationship will ever be the same. People claim they are 'dead inside', or that 'he took all the love that I had to give in this lifetime'. It is part truth, part pose, part defence. But the phenomenon appears with great frequency: it is a justification against an empty present and uncertain future; a refuge and an assertion that they were once irresistible, essential to the life of another person. It is often accompanied by folkloric detail, which recurs in various guises: 'He locked me in a hotel bedroom and took all my clothes away and said "You are my prisoner, I want you all to myself." ' It often took place in a foreign country, on holiday perhaps; at least distant in time and place. It is part of the elaborate defences against the vulnerability that isn't to do with social shame. People whose affective lives are often reduced to brief affairs and one-night stands need to feel they have the ability to inspire fatal and absolute passions. But it is an idea that doesn't bear too close a contact with the love-object, and always seems to flourish at a remove from it. It is rather like those unhappily married people whose consolation is the thought of the man or woman they should have had. 'I threw myself away on the wrong one.'

James Skeffington, late fifties

A small town in Dorset, eighteenth-century and Regency main street, with houses washed in pastel colours. Sunny day in March suggesting summer; many evergreens give the illusion that there is no winter here, and only through the gaps in the houses through which the beech woods can be seen is there any hint that it is still winter; with the wet though newly greening grass and the long puddles reflecting strips of fallen sky. On the outskirts of the little town there is an early Victorian inn that has been converted into a house: the walls washed white, the daffodils against the wall; silence, the crying of rooks; the churchyard near by creaking with yew, the Norman church tower furred and green with moss and stained with saffron-coloured lichen. Already bright diminutive stinging nettles appear in the ditches, the crocuses in the gardens are opening their spindle-shaped heads to the sunshine. The house is surrounded by a high creosoted fence, and beyond, the new buildings of a cramped private estate. 'I've got two law-suits on at the moment,' says James. 'They've cut down a wood to build a bloody estate.'

Inside, two rooms have been made one, a large chimney breast removed and rebuilt so that it forms a partition though not a separate room. Outside, some of the remaining trees form an erratic lattice against the sky, rattling like bones as evening falls and the sky turns to indigo. Mr Skeffington refers to himself as gay; he is dressed all in blue – shirt, sweater, blazer, with the red triangle of a handkerchief in the breast pocket. His white estate mini is dim with splashes of the winter's mud. 'I can't clean it. I've about as much strength in my arms now as a boy of eleven or twelve. War wounds. I was wounded in the Dieppe raid, had half my neck blown away. My central nervous system is totally impaired. I'm only half the human being I used to be. I'm fit, physically sound as a boy of thirty-five; but I've got the nervous system of a man of eighty. I've probably got no more than five years left. I've been having blackouts, getting more and more frequent. It's as if someone had hit me on one side of the face; then on the other; then at the back of the neck and on top of the head. I'm out cold. One of these times I just won't wake up. I've had concussion five times in my life. The first time was when my father – he had very rigid ideas on virility, his idea of teaching a boy to swim was to throw him into a pond about twenty feet deep – he put me on his mare, ferocious creature, sixteen hands high. I was about ten, I suppose. I'd had a pony called Peggy which I used to ride. Anyway, one day he put me on top of this black mare, got a groom to hold her while I got on, and then brought down the long riding crop he was holding on her back. I think I held on for about two hundred yards, and then I was thrown. I was concussed for several days. It was his idea of making a man of me. He was a gentleman farmer. You don't hear the term very much now. We had a thousand acres near Blandford, and a further thousand in another part of the county; two hundred acres of the home farm, Manor Farm. I suppose my father was the local squire. We came from a very ancient family, records go back to the fourteenth century, Enfield in Middlesex was our area originally, Enfor the name, something of hell; it was changed in the seventeenth century in deference to an admiral who had money and with whom we were connected by marriage.

'I went to a local public school, not a very good one. I've always felt I was the most ill-educated person I know. Everybody now seems to have ten O-levels, four or five A-levels. I always wanted to be a doctor; but there was a Latin master who told me I was no good, I'd best forget it. And until that time I'd always been very good at Latin. But his judgement seems to have influenced my life considerably. I left school at sixteen, went back to the farm. I hated it. I never had green fingers or anything. I remember walking round, with the clayey earth sticking to my feet, and it always seemed to be raining. I stuck it three months, and then I went in the Navy; mainly to get away from the dismal prospect of an eternity of mud and rain. I wanted to be an architect; and my father took me to the local architect. I showed him some of my drawings, and he said "These are nearly all ships, you should be a naval architect." That's how I came to go into the Navy. It was, incidentally, how I got introduced to homosexuality. I was seventeen the first time I got fucked; although there, it was a kind of physiological necessity: there was no feeling, no emotion. It wasn't until some time later that I learned about love. I fell in love, which is, I suppose, the way most people learn about it. I went to London to study, and I got in with a very doubtful crowd. The homosexual world is full of people whose principal activity seems to be bitching and backbiting. I think that's what happens to homosexual people if they don't know love. That is one of the great dangers. A frustrated bitchiness, then it turns to transvestism and all the rest. I think I'd like people to know that gay people can be manly, courageous, as honest and straightforward as anyone else. I'm a real man in every way. I can drive a car, ride a horse, shoot a gun; although now I am anti blood-sports, when I was a kid, I used to have a Lewis and go out with my father shooting. I've loved and I've been loved. In fact, as I've got older, I've known more love, and had more sex too, if it comes to that. But I think you have to have other centres of interest to your life, a strong character, a vigorous personality; and that's what a lot of homosexuals lack. I find a lot of young people need – not exactly a father figure, but more of a favourite uncle . . . I've three on the go at the moment. One I'm in love with, one who's in love with me, and one other, whom I've been trying to taper off. I've left Simon £3,000 in my will, so he can stand on his own tiny feet. Actually they're rather large.' (Laughs.) He picks up a nine-teenth-century Wedgwood vase. It has Simon's name on the bottom. 'A lot of my things are marked for whoever will inherit them . . . I like giving. Not just material objects, but affection, love, if you like.

'I don't know about the causes of homosexuality. I've thought of my own situation. There are certain events that stand out that may have been contributory factors. When I was very young – you'd better not start eating yet, what I'm going to say is rather dis-gusting – we had a nursemaid, my brothers and I. And one day she came into the room, not wearing any bloomers or anything;

and to give herself some strange sexual thrill, she sat on my face. Cunnilingus I believe it's called. I can remember the smell, it was absolutely disgusting . . . Then I suppose I was close to my mother in the early years; I was always aware of a certain softness in me, which I think my father sensed too; and up to a point had the sensitivity to respect.

'In London I fell in love for the first time. A BBC producer, very gentle and kind, who taught me a lot emotionally . . . Unfortunately a friend of his, to whom I had at some point given my home address, saw fit to write home to my family, telling them I was queer. The letter was received by my older brother, my father having died a few years previously. He sent me a cable, ordering me to meet him; in London, near Cleopatra's needle. And I was called loathsome, disgusting, an abomination. That did shock me. It was the only time I've been really ashamed of being gay. At that time I used to visit places like the Running Horse, places in the West End; but it was a lugubrious period, the nineteen thirties, what with the legal position, the furtiveness, the threat of blackmail and everything.

'Yes, my father had died when I was sixteen. He was killed on an electricity-generating plant on one of the farms. My mother was distracted, and went completely to pieces. She sold most of the land for £4 an acre, and although it was the time of the depression, we had paid £14 an acre for it. Not only that – she simply threw everything away. We had some ships made out of mutton bones by prisoners taken in the Napoleonic Wars – there are some in a shop in Jermyn Street I noticed recently; and I'd made them all new rigging and so on, and she'd simply thrown them all away. The result is that I've absolutely nothing belonging to my father. I remember being furious at the time. At sixteen or seventeen, one can be very unforgiving. So that's how one lost all one's money.

'When I was shot up in Dieppe – cannon took half my neck away. I was brought over to Newhaven, and spent some time in hospital. There was a voluntary worker who used to visit the hospital, and we became great friends. She was the wife of an art critic, and she offered to take me to her home to convalesce. She agreed to take me to the hospital daily to have my dressings done and so forth. She said "My nephew is staying with us at the moment. He's on leave from Montgomery's Intelligence Staff." And when I arrived, I rang the bell, and the door was answered by Matthew – or [mentions the name of a well-known film actor] as he came to be known. And we just looked into each other's eyes and that was it. In spite of my injuries – and I wasn't a pretty sight at the time. It didn't seem to matter . . . We were together for twelve years. It was without any doubt the most significant relationship in my whole life . . . But in the end our lives diverged, he went into the glare of publicity and the life of the film world . . . We still meet from time to time, have two or three days entirely to ourselves. He was very loving, considerate, tender. That lasted until 1954; and in a sense it stands as a luminous centre to my life, around which the lesser constellations of my relationships have always revolved.

'I moved into this house only recently. Previously I had a Queen Anne House, at the other end of the town. Sold it to a Judge. This is very small, but it's quite enough, and I'm trying to make it habitable. I've had to get rid of so much stuff, antiques . . . As you can see, I collect glass and china. This goblet is 1780, this is a Victorian imitation . . . Would you like some wine?' I feel nervous about the goblet. 'There's some Pommard or some Beaune. The Beaune I opened last night. It's good. Let me try . . . Mmm . . . Dry, but the Beaune is softer . . . You don't mind a cold collation? My woman hasn't come in. The chicken is delicious. I cooked it last night. This one I had sent up from the town, it's all right, but not the same . . . Do you like chicory? . . . There's a cheeseboard of Port-Salut, Boursin à l'ail, Stilton . . .

'Of course I regret that I didn't have a proper education. It's been a constant thorn in my side. But I have been very successful as a yacht designer. I used to be able to draw to two-thousandth of an inch, but I doubt now whether I could draw to half an inch. I make of my life what I can. I have parties, about once a month; dinner parties, perhaps twice a week. There is a young man who comes here, his own parents don't seem interested in him. I don't know what he sees in me, now that I've got too much tum and my hair's going white . . . He was fucked when he was twelve, he's been used by homosexuals for years, without the least sense of being cared for. That's what I've been able to give him, I've been able to treat him as a human being, with consideration and concern. He means a great deal to me. He's a very intelligent young man, and incredibly attractive.'

Simon is present for dinner. Flax-coloured hair, slight regional accent; he wears a dark suit and sunglasses, talks very carefully, and is a little like a child being allowed to stay up with the grown-ups for a special occasion. He is polite, attractive, smiling, almost too good to be true. James looks at him from time to time, in a hesitant way that says he can scarcely believe his good fortune. Simon doesn't know yet what he will do. He would like to act, to write, to travel, to meet people. He hasn't yet decided how best to employ his talents. He claims to be a Socialist, against the conservatism of James, who says that he is a Liberal; but the discussion is without passion – it is in a sense the only legitimate way of asserting himself against the concern and care of his patron; any other area of divergence would be inadmissible, and so it takes on a specious ideological character. Simon has no interest in the life of his parents, who, he feels, have failed him; and he looks upon James as an idealized adoptive parent.

Three months later Simon had left him. 'I knew it couldn't last. I didn't know it would end as soon as this. I think he's gone where he can get better pickings. He's fallen under the influence of very doubtful people. Somebody who runs a call-boy ring in Portsmouth.'

Fred Grayson, early sixties

Lives alone in a room in a Midland city; in a poor, mainly immigrant area, crumbling brick, immigrant-dominated, villas called Jasmine House and Vine Cottage with brickwork picked out in red and white; a few well-maintained spinsterish houses, bays draped with ghost-white lace, hydrangeas in the garden, doors varnished. Chapels, schools, disused factories gape bleakly across the area, superseded disciplines that have lost their power, like ancient stern founders of dispersed families. Some of the windows are splashed with dust and mud, curtains rudimentary drapes that hang ragged and uneven at the glass; fleur-de-lys railings rusted, plaster oakleaves weathered away, a tympanum of a parable wasted to two dimensions. Fred lives in the attic room of a house that has been turned into a number of flats; cheap, white doors with plastic handles, a neutral, carpeted public area. Fred has filled his room with small objects, plastic flowers, dolls, small ornaments, so that it resembles a boudoir and less of a rather bare bed-sitter, despite the candlewick counterpane on the double bed and the large 1930s wardrobe.

'I was born under a lucky star. I'm a Taurean – headstrong,

thrifty, thrusting sort of people . . . Are you Gemini? . . . Oh no, Taurus? . . . Really? You don't look like a Taurean. No, I'd have said Gemini.' I assure him my birthday is mid-May. 'I did a course in Astrology, I've done courses in all kinds of things – Astrology, Elocution, Dramatic Art, Creative Writing, Journalism . . . I've written poems and articles, published in America, of course; nobody would touch them here . . . They were too advanced, out-spoken. Wouldn't do here at all.

'I'm psychic. I always have been, although in recent years I've not been so much involved with it. My mother had a healing, a faith healing, that is, when I was thirteen, and that made a very deep impression upon me. I believe that the spirits govern our lives in many ways – not the spirits of the dead who are earth-bound, but all these murders and bestial acts that one hears of, I believe that people who commit them are possessed by demons, evil spirits. I've always been a Christian Scientist, emphasizing the "Christian", you know. Often I lie awake at night and pray that there'll be a way through all this turmoil and strife in the world . . . Because when you look at the frightful mess everything is in, it can't help but trouble any thinking person . . . Let me see your hand, I can read palms too. Your left hand is what you're given, and your right hand is what you make of your life, how you use your talents, or whether you squander the gifts everybody is born with. Yes . . . Your life line's quite good . . . You've got some money coming to you in later life. You'll never want, I can at least assure you of that.

'I say I'm a Christian Scientist; I'm not sure that I believe in spiritualism itself, because they can sometimes be at the mercy of evil spirits, and it isn't too wise to meddle like that, indiscriminately. The mother of a friend of mine had a message, in the middle of the night. She had a message that her daughter had been taken ill. This woman lived in Plymouth, and the daughter lived some five or six miles away. So she got up and walked – no cars, no buses. She walked the five miles, and of course, when she got there her daughter was asleep, the whole family. The daughter was inclined to disbelieve it. She said "What on earth are you doing here?" Her mother said she had received a message that she was ill. Malicious spirits, you see; and that's how people's acceptance can be under-mined.

'But I suppose you want to know about my homosexuality . . . Well, I've never been anything else. And I've known myself since

I was very young. My father worked in the Admiralty. I got on very well with him, no problem there. But I had two sisters, and my mother used to make such a fuss of me . . . I don't know whether that has any influence on the way you are.

'I've had some marvellous times, the people you meet, being like this . . . I mean, celebrities, show people, you can meet anyone, being queer. I like men with muscles, good strong men. A lot of people I meet are bisexual, they're the ones I feel sorry for. I mean, they don't seem to be able to make up their mind. They can be very hypocritical. If you see them in the street with their wife, they can't acknowledge you, they pretend you're not there, look straight through you. It must be terrible to have to lead a life like that . . . They come here sometimes, and then they have to rush off back to their wives, tell them they've been working late, all excuses. And do you know, people like that, they're all take, take, take. They never give. Never do they come and say "I've brought you a little present, a cake for tea", even. I suppose they save that for their wives, because they feel guilty and want to make it up to them afterwards. But I'm always giving. Perhaps that's my nature, I'm always giving. But this I do know: I know that homosexuals are the most inconstant, fickle, untrustworthy, lying, thieving lot, and they all ought to be stood up against a wall and shot. Including myself.'

JS: 'Surely you don't feel that, really?'

FRED: 'I've been badly let down in my life. That's how I've found them generally. Although I've been lucky. I'm lucky here, I've got my own place. Most people aren't so fortunate, they have to do it in the toilets. The way some of them behave, in this town, it's disgusting . . . I know one man, a solicitor he is, handsome man, about fifty, lots of silver hair, he's in there very often, practically undressed . . . I mean, it's people like that who get the rest of us such a bad name. They don't seem to care what they do or where they do it. And they are often people with responsibility, a position, they should know better . . . A policeman could come in at any time . . . There are really some disgusting things that go on in those places . . . It's still the place where most people like me have to meet. Where else can you go? In a car or in the toilet, and that's about the limit of it. Because, I don't care what anybody says, we are still such a small minority when all's said and done. There aren't many of us . . . And you have to be so careful with people in towns like this. They might be all right to your face, but behind your back – that's what you have to wait for to find out what they really think about you. Gossip. Especially women, they're the worst. I can't stand the touch of a woman. Ugh. There is something about it that just revolts me.'

JS: 'Why do you live here, in a town like this, if you have no real friends, relatives here?'

FRED: 'I keep on the move. I've lived in sixteen towns now. That's how you get new experiences . . . Although, of course, they're not really new, but they're new faces . . . I don't know, I think the older and uglier I get, the more people I seem to have sex with . . . I had somebody here this morning before you came, and I shall probably have somebody later on this afternoon . . . Perhaps as you get older, you don't care so much what people think, and you get hardened to things, and so you let people know if you like them, where when you're young you get all frightened of people saying no, or insulting you.

'I've never lived with anybody. They'd disturb my routine too much. I don't know why I'm like it, but I can't bear mess and muddle. I know. You might say "A home is for living in", but if anybody upsets my routine and my way of doing things, I get really uncomfortable . . . I don't want anybody intruding on my way of doing things – I don't mind you being here, just for a short while, because when you're gone I shall be able to tidy up after you . . . But to live with anybody, it would drive me mad. I like nice things. You should have seen this flat before I cleaned it . . . I like to go round junk shops, second-hand shops. I love finding bargains. That vase and all those flowers, I got them very cheaply. You have to be careful. Fortunately I was left a little money by my parents, but it doesn't go very far these days. I can't afford holidays now.

'The neighbourhood isn't very nice, actually. Prostitutes, blacks all round, as you can see . . . I have had black men, I had a student when I was in Reading, his organ was that long.' He spaces out his hands like a fisherman boasting of a catch. 'Before that I was in Northampton.' He shakes his head. 'Too small. When I was there I had to have a new set of front teeth. I was afraid that would spoil my sex life. But no, not a bit of it . . . No, as long as I can go on getting what I need I'm all right, and as I say, there doesn't seem to be any danger of it stopping.

'Once I was in Swindon, and the police were after me because we'd been caught in somebody's car, and I got the summons and all the rest of it, and my friend in Brighton who's psychic wrote to me out of the blue and said "Something is worrying you, but don't give in to it, it'll all blow over." I thought "Huh, what does he know about it?" But do you know . . . I never heard another word . . . Whether the other fellow was somebody who wanted to have it all hushed up or not I don't know, but it died a natural death.

'I've had some wonderful times in my life. One of the best was when I lived in Southampton, and I got to know a lot of people on the big liners, you know. Very sophisticated, cosmopolitan. I've had lots of jobs, of course. I think the best one I got was when I answered an ad in the paper in Bristol. The job was in a Surgical Goods shop. People used to come in and ask the most intimate questions. I got to know all the secrets of their matrimonial life, and there was I, a crusty old bachelor, offering them advice on all sorts of sex matters. I loved it. I was in my element. And I had a little area at the back of the shop, the things that went on there were nobody's business . . . I've had enough experiences to fill a book. But as for living with somebody, having them on top of you all the time, upsetting your little routine, trying to change your little ways, oh no, I couldn't put up with anything like that.'

He comes down the stairs to say good-bye, a slight figure in carpet slippers and a waistcoat-cardigan. Grey drizzly afternoon; children coming out of school; saris, trousers, jewels brilliant against the nineteenth-century industrial murk; coloured silk splashed with mud.

Mr Litvinoff, sixty

Mr Litvinoff is a nervous greying man; slight, dark-rimmed glasses with a face that has been marked by the misery and shame that have accompanied him all his life. His parents were bakers in North London, and he was brought up a Primitive Methodist. His father deserted his mother when Henry was seven, and his mother managed to keep the business going and bring up the two children alone. She was a strong and forceful woman, with fierce ideas of morality and propriety. Henry had a grammar-school education, and then went out to work in a shop. He ultimately made a career in catering with a merchant banking company. In 1945 he married a woman who had tuberculosis; and he nursed her through her last years, until 1956.

He married again about 1960 a woman half Polish half Rumanian/ French, who had been in the resistance in the war, and who already had a family of her own. His first wife had one daughter from a previous marriage. He has no children. He fears that if he had, the weakness which he feels has permeated his whole life might perhaps have infected them in some way; although he enjoys the company of his step-children, and they give him a sense of rejuvenation. When I was at his house, one of his wife's sons came in; a seraph of twenty, a university drop-out, working as a labourer and hoping to become a professional musician. His step-father addressed him in a rather facetious and dated slang, which somewhat embarrassed the youth, and he did not stay in the room for long. As soon as the boy came in, Mr Litvinoff deflected our conversation into areas of innocuous generality. He is a man who is deeply ashamed of what he regards as an anomaly irreconcilable with the morality and values of his upbringing. He dealt with it in a curious and rather ambiguous way, by marrying women who already had families of their own, and by at first marrying someone with a terminal illness: it gave him a ready-made structure which he hoped would place him at a remove from his transvestism and homosexuality; would give him a purpose and an alibi. Perhaps he believed in the redemptive power of self-sacrifice; however true any of these things may have been, he is still a man haunted by a sense of misplaced gender, by an awareness of the impalpability and inexpressibility of the things he most deeply longs for.

Mr Litvinoff lives in a block of ex-industrial dwellings in West London; the flats were converted, by knocking two workmen's dwellings into one over twenty years ago, anticipating the widespread upgrading of so much erstwhile working-class accommodation in London. The street itself is in pink brick, Gothic and cavernous; access to each flat is by flights of flinty steps set in deep, narrow stairwells. The flat inside is rather like the apartments of European cities: a lot of ornaments, heavy buffets altar-like and sacramental, ornate drapes. The flat is high and narrow: looking down, the street is reminiscent of Milan or perhaps Vienna. There is a pine table with a bench that backs against the window. I drink coffee from a mug with Capricorn on the side; in the centre of the table there is a heavy china fruit bowl that contains three diminished soft apples, a shrivelled satsuma and a banana. *The Times* and the *Daily Express* are unopened on the table. Mr

Litvinoff has been doing *The Times* crossword. A partition in the long room divides the kitchen area from the sitting-room.

MR LITVINOFF: 'I think I'm what is called a fetishist. I like black things, black material, underwear . . . I think I can trace it back to a memory I had when I was only three or four. It was during the First War, and someone came to the house, a man, a cousin of my mother's, I believe. He was in the Navy, and was wearing one of those black oilskins. I think I was woken up to see him as being a very heroic and impressive figure . . . I can remember screaming and screaming in fright; and I remember him saying to my mother "You shouldn't have woken him up." Symbolic almost. I don't know whether that was the starting point of it . . . As there are, I've discovered, so many like me, I don't suppose they can have all been through an experience like that. You just don't know, do you? . . .

'My sister was several years older than I was, and I remember when she was about nineteen I was about twelve or thirteen, and I used to dress up sometimes in her things. It used to amuse her . . . she laughed. I didn't of course realize at that time what was happening to me . . . I was very much under female influence all my life, sister, mother, aunts . . . Anyway, it left me with this desire to – not to be a woman exactly, but to assimilate myself to an image of femininity . . . an image, oh, how to describe it? . . . the Nordic Junoesque type of beauty, broad shoulders, Amazonian . . . a rather masculine kind of woman, a certain sexual ambiguity . . . Not Lesbian, though. Statuesque, classical . . . monumental . . . It is very strange to explain to someone who has not experienced these things . . . It is very much a fantasy, but one which I am compelled to exact sometimes . . . I do correspond to someone who has similar experiences, a man who is a historian in the South of England. I've never met him. I write to him as Joanne, and of course I'm Henriette in my fantasies. There's always something unobtainable in one's desires, something elusive. I find that by writing them, it is an enormous help. It acts as a kind of catharsis, although there is always something inaccessible at the core . . . I find that I'm quite interested in the image of Suzie Wong, you know, the perfect doll-like diminutive creature . . . But it's always this earth-mother, goddess, Venus-like woman, Cybele, Hera, dominating all-pervasive, that one tries to merge one's identity with.

'I do dress up; in order to have sexual relations with my wife. My first wife of course knew nothing about my tendency, but this one, I told her before I married her . . . I think at first it intrigued her, it made life very exciting. I wear a black nightie or something, in order to be successful. That was all right . . . But now, well, we go off our own ways sometimes, and turn a blind eye . . .

'For years I was haunted by the most dreadful guilt about it . . . I think the established religion has been of no help to me as I fought my way through the terrible complexity of what I was searching for, with its moral imperatives and impossible demands. It took a great deal to acknowledge what I really wanted. It was all so furtive. I know it is being brought a bit more out into the open now, but it's still such a subject for sniggering and scandal. And one is constantly open to blackmail, of course. While I was with my first wife, I had to go out to prostitutes and so on. There is a group now, called the Mackintosh Club; I know it sounds like a subject for terrible jokes, but it is at least a way of opening up the whole issue, and for that we have to be grateful.

'Don't think it's the Danny La Rue kind of dressing up. That's asexual essentially, antiseptic. I've never really seen the point of that. I think that's why he's so popular. In the last analysis the image he projects is sexless, harmless. It couldn't offend anybody. Don't get me wrong – I don't want to be a woman; it's only this impalpable image of femininity that is a kind of obsession. I'm attracted to men sometimes, not conventionally pretty, but epicene. In a way, what I yearn for is a kind of amalgam of both sexes . . . Perhaps you can best understand it if I give you this poem: it tries to embody the way I feel about this feminine image that haunts me.

The Amazonian Queen

'Hippolyta, thou hast no peer!
I hear thee call in accents clear,
While the world sleeps.
Cross chasms of uncounted time,
From mystic grove in distant clime,
Thy influence seeps
To hold my eager mind in thrall,
And fain I would before thee fall
Prostrate: adore
Magnificence embodied, such

E'en Oberon might fear to touch
Thy robe, before
Permissive grace thou might'st bestow.
How then may mortal hope to know
Thy bounteous gift?
When, fearful lest thy beauty's blaze
My captive senses should amaze,
I dare not lift,
Above thy arched feet my sight.
Hippolyta! Resolve my plight,
My thirst assuage;
Within the solace of thine arms,
Where springs the fount of all thy charms:
My form engage,
Entwine, in ecstasy so rare
That, ever soaring upward where
The systems wheel,
Our flaring passion will star-guide
Thy patient suitors, who abide
Thy call. Reveal
Thy fertile presence then, O Queen,
To those, who nightly on thee dream;
Their darkness thus thou canst illume,
If thou thy ancient rule resume!'

*

The experience of Bill Wexford was probably that of a majority of
homosexuals, especially in the working class, until very recently.
There was simply no admissible outlet. I remember, as a child, going
to Great Yarmouth for holidays, and reading with troubled fascination the graffiti on lavatory walls. 'Bum pal wanted', 'Chap wants
mate for bum fun'; crude and puzzled invitations in indelible pencil
to meetings behind the bandstand or under the pier at 11.30 p.m.
on Saturday, 17 August; a clumsy attempt to incorporate something
unspeakable into the normative and acceptable; a desperate consciousness of a situation that could not be faced; reality bursting
the limited categories of working-class experience. I remember
wondering what it all meant, and resolved half-heartedly to hide and
spy on some of these nocturnal assignations; although by that time
we were already asleep under the candlewick boarding-house

counterpanes, and the tables all set for breakfast with marmalade in cut-glass bowls and butter collecting a deposit of dust particles from the air.

The bachelor who stayed at home to look after his mother was a dim recognition of certain irregularities, but it was sanctioned – even sanctified – by the idea of renunciation and the importance of motherhood in the matriarchal hives of the streets. When a society blocks outlets to the expression of certain needs, these often deform themselves – like homosexual 'marriages' that are caricatures of the institution they try to assimilate to; in this way, those who live these experiences are absolved from the pain of feeling themselves deviant. This seems to have been one of the principal functions of the public lavatory – a way of reconciling the unacceptable with the most basic human needs; and these act as a convenient mask, even in the mind of the individual involved, for other purposes. Even today many working-class homosexuals say things like 'Well it's the only place for people like us to meet.' Many of those who can admit to their homosexuality are isolated from alternative means of self-expression.

Anybody caught by the police in a public lavatory is bound to say he was using it for a legitimate purpose; and even sometimes convinces himself that such was his intention in going there in the first place. But around it, there did – and does – cluster a whole way of life, which in turn gave rise to a body of folklore, a 'culture' almost.

'I used to spend hours in the cubicles on the sea-front at Blackpool. I even took a book with me for the times when there was nobody interesting around. The cubicles were made with wooden partitions, and there were knots of wood that had been pushed out, so you could look through into the next compartment. If somebody nice came in who started wanking, you could put a note under the dividing wall. There was one bloke, he had tape recordings of police messages that came over the radio, and if anybody old or ugly came in, he used to play these recordings of police messages, and the bloke used to pull his pants up like lightning and get out. And then he'd wait for somebody who was more acceptable to him.'

'Pulling down those old wooden lavatories is a crime against gay people. I knew somebody who used to do everything through holes in the walls – he even used to fuck people through them. He never knew what they looked like or who they were.'

'I remember as an adolescent going into the lavatories at home and

48

there were stories people had written on the walls, fantasies that expressed something quite deep about how people really felt. There was one from somebody who had made a kind of confessional of the lavatory, and written all his "crimes" there, what he had done to young boys, and how he needed to be punished.'

'There was something closed and self-contained about the place; deep subterranean caverns of mystery and excitement. The place was beneath the pavement, which was covered by those thick glass tiles, which transmitted a strange artifical kind of daylight. I met a sailor who took me into one of the cubicles, and that was the first experience I ever had. I suffered afterwards. I felt so guilty and ashamed, it was unbearable. I thought my parents must be able to read on my face what I'd been doing.'

'One day, I'd had a row with my boy-friend, and I felt really low. I always go cottaging when I'm feeling really suicidal. And I went out for a few drinks and started doing the rounds. And I finished up not far from home in this little very dimly lit place, that had only three stalls. And I went and stood in the middle. And eventually two other people came in, and one stood on one side of me, and the other stood on the other. And I felt all very excited, you know; and then I looked. And on one side of me was my boy-friend, and on the other was his ex. I think we just had a laugh and went home for a drink.'

It is impossible to assess what proportion of homosexuals even had recourse to the brief and furtive possibilities of 'cottaging' (a reference perhaps to the Arcadian architectural style of many public lavatories in parks). Such meetings sometimes led to the formation of long-lasting relationships. It is still a widely used way of meeting people, although it is felt to be only one of many outlets, given the range of alternatives. Like any culture once established, the traditions of the homosexual world are tenacious and conservative; and there are many who will dilate on the joys, the excitement and danger of cottaging, which are felt to give it a sense of reckless adventure, in contrast to the more conventional meetings in pubs and clubs, which are either felt to be tame, or attended by rather predatory and ritualistic conventions. 'It's very basic and elementary. Besides, some people like to inspect the goods before they get them home. If you know what you're looking for, you might as well be honest, and get what you want.'

It is very difficult for individuals who have achieved what they thought was some kind of balance in their lives, by 'coping' with their homosexuality – whether by repression or by channelling it into other areas, sometimes after an excruciating process of self-denial, self-mutilation almost – to see the emergence of groups of people who can admit to their gayness without shame. It seems to make retrospective nonsense of their struggles. It is not surprising that many older people are embittered and resentful about their past, and envious of the young, whose lives seem so much more full of opportunity for self-expression than their own has been. There are some people whose spleen against the young – a natural enough process in many old people anyway – is exacerbated by the personal self-refusal, which to them has been such a triumph over what they could see only as impossible circumstances. It has its counterpart in the jaundiced and grudging vision of the victims of an earlier industrial society, for ever saying that the young don't know they're born, have got a big eye-opener coming to them, ought to have a strap soaped and laid across their arse; not realizing that the young have been socially fashioned for a quite different purpose from that which drove them into factory and mill fifty years ago. Among older gay people this is expressed in terms of 'It's disgusting the way they dance together in public'; 'You never used to touch each other in public in my day, that was something for the privacy of your bedroom'; 'They'll be doing it like dogs in the street next'; 'Can you wonder at the epidemics of VD there is about'.

But the change is a gradual one; and many individuals are caught in its mechanisms, poor mangled human sacrifices, torn between the values transmitted by parents and teachers, and the cajoleries of the new beguiling culture of self-fulfilment, tormented by conflicting imperatives. Refugees, exiles between cultures, a whole generation of spiritually displaced people; and nowhere is the process more sharply illustrated than in the lives of homosexuals, ground between the values of their childhood and the exigencies of a changed social function.

Keith McCallum, forty-one

The curator of a museum, he lives in a flat in a villa in North London, meticulously clean and orderly. There is a denuded public area of white doors, and even inside his flat the style is austere, cool and sober. A patterned carpet, a three-legged occasional table, a dresser; a dining area, an electric fire on the wall, with a single candlestick on either side of the shelf formed by the top of the fire. A vase of daffodils is the only object to disturb the symmetry and order of the room; and even they seem to turn their strident trumpets in a concerted direction. Mr McCallum indicates the extinguished grey coil of the fire on the wall. 'We're told we must conserve energy. You're not cold, are you?' He is small and nervous, and wears rimless glasses, a purple shirt, carpet slippers; noiseless, self-effacing, almost a sense of having so little place in the world that he passes through it leaving no trace, everything undisturbed.

Mr McCallum is surprised by my appearance, and for some time doubts my good faith. He interrogates me very closely about my intention, and says that he had hesitated a long time before talking to me.

He was born in a small industrial town in Scotland, in the mid-thirties, and grew up on a rather bleak council estate, which in itself seems far removed from his appearance and manner now, which suggest academic precision, and far removed from the white-painted villa where he lives, which evokes small fixed incomes, gentility, hydrangeas, cats.

'My parents separated before I was born. They then came together for a time, before finally separating again just after my sister was born, a year after myself. I was over thirty before I saw my mother again. What I did not realize was that the woman I grew up to call mother was in fact my grandmother. My father lived in the same house, and I must have been very naïve not to have realized that they were not like married people in any sense of the word. They had different bedrooms; but I suppose a child doesn't speculate on things like that. My grandmother had seven children, and, at least at the outbreak of war in 1939, they lived at home, my aunts and uncles, although of course I was never aware of the relationship. They were all rather coarse, noisy people. I always felt myself apart from them. And it was a very curious thing – when my grandmother died, and I went to get a copy of her birth certificate, I realized that she had been illegitimate herself. So I wonder if my own love of culture, of reading and music and theatre, came through her in some way. Certainly no one I knew as a child was interested in such things.

But however that may be, my grandmother was a fine woman, although she could hardly read or write. She was barely literate, but she was very straight and firm and held herself well, dressed well. She was a very devout Catholic. I was myself for a very long time. In fact, it is only in recent years that my faith has weakened; at the same time as I began to acknowledge my homosexuality. I did make an attempt to join a monastery, Carthusian; the Trappists, the most enclosed and strict order of all. I had been for retreats to a monastery in Scotland when I was younger, and I spent some time in a monastery in the Midlands when I was contemplating a permanent retreat from the world. Unfortunately they rejected me. Whether they sensed that I had this tendency, I don't know. But they said they thought I might be too unsettling an influence. And it was soon after that that my faith began to decline.

'I am homosexual, but I have never, never given any expression to that tendency, no action, nor word, even. I have recently made myself known, but to a young woman. If I were heterosexual, I should expect to remain celibate until I had chosen a partner, to whom I should remain true for the rest of my life. And I see no reason to behave any differently because of the fact of my homosexuality. So when I say I'm a homosexual, it is in that sense only. If I had been born at a different time in a different place, who can say what kind of a person I might have been?

'I think it is true to say that I do regret it now. But I am the product of the kind of situation in which I grew up. You must remember that I was brought up by my grandmother, and she held to the ideas and values of her own generation. There is perhaps something anomalous in my situation, in that I was brought up reflecting the morality of a generation earlier than I perhaps should have done. But even so, life was very limiting at that period in the part of Scotland where I was brought up. Most people worked in the foundry. I can remember most of the people I knew coming home from work with dirty faces from the ironworks . . . There was never a book in that house, although the house always seemed full of people. They were always coming in and bringing their friends, and no matter who came, the meals always seemed to stretch. My mother – you realize that when I say my mother I mean in fact my grandmother – performed the miracle of the loaves and fishes very often.

'I have been terribly lonely. I'm not saying that in a self-pityingly

52

way, although I have done that too. I've been very solitary and isolated . . . The first time I left that house I was twenty-three or twenty-four. Although I found nothing whatever to interest me in that environment, I never left it until I was quite old. I was a rather small and weak child, and whether my grandmother over-protected me I don't know, but I always lacked companionship. And the result of all that has been that if I should die tomorrow, it would not make a scrap of difference to the life of anyone on this earth. And that is very sad.

'Of course it took me a long time to come to terms with my condition. It was a long haul in some ways. I was always aware of an attraction to boys when I was at school, but it was something one thrust out of one's mind. It is only recently that I've been compelled to acknowledge it fully, and that because of a young man with whom I've become more involved than with anyone ever before. I have had a feeling of attraction to men before, but never anything as sustained as this – four years now. He works in the same place – a different department, but every day we have lunch together, we go to the theatre and to concerts. He seems to be very much a heterosexual. He has a girl-friend whom he sees regularly, but whom he seems to show no great wish to marry, although he has bought a house in the country and is thirty-one years of age. He appears to enjoy my company, and always comes to call for me at lunch time; he comes into my department most days for a chat. He was recently in Northern Ireland, and he spoke to me on the telephone for forty or forty-five minutes. Now I wonder, did he talk to his girl-friend for as long as that? You see, if I were in his place, there is nothing I should want more than to marry her. Why does he hesitate? Is there something in him? . . .

'I've never made any secret of my lack of interest in women. Sometimes, when looking through a magazine, he will make some appropriately heterosexual observation about one of the photographs, and I make it quite clear that I am not interested. Is he, I wonder, aware of my interest in him? What does he think of it? Does he find it repellent? I wonder if the people at work speculate on the nature of my relationship with him? If they attribute to us a relationship that in fact does not exist? I wonder further, how he may feel about any such attribution? Whether he cares or not? . . . Of course, I could not risk talking to him in this way, for fear of jeopardizing what I already have of value. But it was not until the age of thirty-eight that I became so deeply emotionally engaged with another person . . . I think I am rather slow, but I am tenacious. I was once told that having been born under the sign of Capricorn that one exhibits many of the characteristics of the goat – stubbornness is certainly one of mine . . . I've a feeling that I shall live to be a very old man. Sir Compton Mackenzie, Pablo Casals, many of those born under Capricorn live to be a great age. So who knows what the next fifty years may have in store for me?

'I have a great love of peace. When I was twenty-three I was working as a booking clerk on British Railways; and I was sent as a relief for two weeks to West Perthshire. The countryside was so peaceful, so beautiful; it gave me that sense of peace which I so long for. Which is why I like this place. I can come in and shut my door and listen to music, which I love above all.

'I have always endeavoured to remedy my solitariness by being busy. I used to do some acting – indeed, I was sometimes out six or seven nights a week, rehearsing or performing. And I do still go to concerts or the theatre a great deal. I read much. I am, I suppose, in many ways, a simple person. I once inserted an advertisement in the personal column of the *New Statesman*, to the effect that I was interested in Wagner and the theatre and so forth. And I received a stream of answers, some of them, I may say, so outrageous that they went at once into the wastepaper basket. I reduced them to twelve possibles, and accordingly I made arrangements to meet them on successive evenings. Fortunately I arranged to meet them all at a club I belonged to – at the Arts Theatre – I say fortunately because, do you know, without exception, they were looking for promiscuous sexual partners. I would not, of course, entertain any such idea. I am not in any way typical of the vulgar idea of the homosexual. I do not mince and I do not lisp. I resent the way in which the caricature is accepted so generally. I did join CHE, but I attended two of their meetings, and really, it wasn't to hear about the sex life of individuals. It was dreadfully boring.

'I must say that when I opened the door and saw you, I had a shock. I didn't quite know what to expect. One places oneself so much at risk.

'In many ways I am self-sufficient. I've achieved more, materially, than I could ever have hoped. I enjoy my work very much. But I have always been alone.'

54

There seems to be a high correlation between people who are homosexual and a sudden disruptive mobility, broken cultural traditions, whether of class or race. The part of an individual's identity that derives from a well-defined role in social and cultural terms is often crucially bound up with sexual identity. This would seem to support the idea that absent/cruel/indifferent father or authority figures coincide with a homosexual orientation. There appears to be a high proportion of homosexuals among people released from the working class by the education process, but here it is impossible to distinguish cause from effect. Such people are haunted by the absence of the kind of certainty and security that used to be found in working-class culture – and it cannot be exaggerated, the absolute and authoritarian nature of that culture, and the way in which those nourished within it derived a sense of total meaning and purpose. It explained everything; it was a whole cosmology. Once the relativistic nature of social values has been learned by an individual, this knowledge, transferred to the point of destination of the socially mobile, operates as a corrosive force preventing a wholehearted allegiance to any new set of social values and attitudes. Many people from the working class carry a strong sense of having been bereaved, and walk sadly around absolute creeds and dogmas for a whole lifetime, like those souls outside Elysium.

The same is true of all those who 'escape' what appears to be a cultural identity destined for them.

Raoul Schwarz, thirty

Small, Cape Coloured in origin. A lively and attractive young man, wearing an Afghan coat over a navy-blue fisherman's jersey. He has almost no trace of a South African accent; and he is like one of those heroes of picaresque novels of the eighteenth and nineteenth century who, through the charitable caprice of an individual, is taken out of his environment and re-fashioned for a quite different life.

'I was born in a ghetto in Cape Town, District Six. It's the kind of place where when the ships came into port, the crew were advised not to venture. The place I lived in was a block, a tenement block. We had one bedroom. Ten children, seven brothers, two sisters I had. My father was a cobbler. I haven't seen my mother since 1960, when I was sixteen.

'Strangely enough, I had a happy childhood. I used to organize all the children in games and plays of various kinds, I enjoyed going barefoot, I was aware of a certain sense of freedom; when you're at a certain point in the social and economic hierarchy, you know you can't go any lower . . . I knew that I was homosexual from a child, although I was much older before I could put a name to it. I suppose I started being actively homosexual when I was about twelve . . . When I started work I was thirteen; thirteen, isn't it incredible! I suppose I should be thankful that such schooling as I received even taught me to read and write! I worked in a chocolate factory as a messenger when I first left school. After that I had, oh, quite a few jobs. Then, when I was fifteen, I met an English boy, and that encounter was one of the most significant influences on my life. Because of Apartheid, of course, we had to meet at night, on the beaches. It was very risky, but very exciting. That was the most important relationship for me; although I later discovered that he was quite Fascist in his social outlook. At the time I didn't investigate such things too deeply, they didn't have quite the primordial importance they ought to have. But he gave me £40, and I'd managed to save up a little money out of my £2 per week, God knows how; and I knew that if I took a migrant workers' ship from Mozambique to Portugal, I could travel steerage quite cheaply. I was motivated by a very strong will to get out. It was a matter of survival. I wasn't unhappy there as a child, but as I grew up I couldn't fail to be aware of the restrictions that lay in wait to limit and oppress my life as an adult. In the area where I lived there were about a dozen old queens, and they were tolerated . . . I think at that level of dispossession people are forced to be more tolerant of the – weaknesses, or whatever – of others. I was fifteen then; I never gave it a thought about where I'd go or what I'd do. I wasn't afraid. You only had to think of the alternative that was mapped out for you if you stayed there; and nothing, nothing could be worse than that.

'I got to Lisbon, and was picked up by a woman who was a prostitute. I looked younger than I was, and she took me home to her family, and they mothered me for a fortnight. This girl worked – as a prostitute – in Paris actually, and she was going back to Paris to her job, and so I travelled to Paris with her. They were very kind. I can't imagine what I would have done without them. And from Paris I took the train to England, and I've been here ever since.

I went at first to live with the family of the boy I'd met in Cape Town; but that didn't last too long, and I came to London and started looking after myself. There was a tremendous culture-shock, of course. In fact, even my English at that time wasn't too good. My parents spoke Afrikaans, and although they could speak some English, they preferred not to. So, in a way, I had to acquire a whole new personality . . . And that's what I did. I sort of re-worked my social education, by observing, by copying other people. At first there was an element of my watching to see which knives or forks or spoons other people used next, and then imitating them. But I think I was very lucky. The people I met were socialists, and not really inclined to go in for the elaborate rituals that so many rather grand middle-class homosexuals seem to go in for. I don't know what might have happened to me if I had fallen into that world. As I was so desperate to find new cues, new ways of being, I would probably have slavishly copied them. But you can't say, because you do have your own preferences as a person; your personality must fit in, temperamentally.

'It seems a terribly long way away, my childhood. It is. Geographically and temporally. I've been in my present job eight years. I work in a library and information-retrieval service. It isn't demanding. I can more or less work according to my own feelings. Nobody checks up on me, as long as I get the work done. I've become a quite different person from what I was, and what I should have been, if I'd remained in Cape Town. It's unthinkable. My intelligence would certainly never have been stimulated. I don't know what I'd have done there. Laboured at a level of near slavery, of course. But apart from that . . . I don't know what kind of relationships I would have had; I suspect the quality of them would have been less good; you don't have time to cultivate important and deep relationships in societies where you live scarcely above subsistence.

'I live with a friend with whom I have a good relationship. I don't look for promiscuous sex. Is that unusual? It is, I'm told it is. Of my friends, most of them are ordinary people; I've perhaps two or three gay friends, that's all. I think that sexuality is only a small part of one's life. I mean, the sex of the person you go to bed with is only important when you're in bed with him or her. I don't say that I rule out the possibility of all other relationships, but they simply don't occur. I haven't time. I don't go to clubs or pubs. I read a great deal, and I have a wide range of interests, from gardening to Wagner. I love opera.

'I feel I'm very well integrated into the society. I have fairly radical views, as you can expect, but I don't feel any lack of identity. Lack of commitment maybe. I feel I'd like to write. I have written, but I haven't shown it to anyone. I don't conceal the fact that I'm gay, and I don't flaunt it.

'I did marry. A lesbian girl, as a marriage of convenience. I spent two years in Australia; it was very old-fashioned, like England probably was in the nineteen fifties. If you had long hair, you were automatically a pooftah. And I met this girl, and we're very good friends. She said "Wouldn't it be a good idea if we got married?" I'm still South African by nationality, I suppose I ought to do something about that. It means you can't go to any Communist country, which is a bore.'

The lack of reference to received points of authority is felt by many people who are the products of mobility and change; but there is something more poignant in the position of the homosexual, who has the sense of social disinheritance heightened by an inability to flee into privatized roles of male/female, the fortress of the nuclear family; in a way all homosexual people are permanent orphans. Raoul echoes the picaresque struggles of many working-class individuals in this country in the nineteenth century; long journeys to the frontiers of the bourgeoisie, elaborate re-socializations, re-learning ways to be; the upwardly mobile image of the homosexual only reflected the image of social progression open to anyone born into the working class and motivated, for whatever reason, to get out. There was only one exit. Norman Blake, now seventy-eight, came to London from Stoke on Trent in 1916. He ran away from home when he discovered that a woman whom he had always believed to be a distant relative was in fact his mother; the victim of all kinds of cruelties in the interests of maintaining something curious called family honour; to which noble concept he was from birth a human sacrifice. He lived in lodgings in South London, and worked in a shop. Aware of his homosexuality, he spoke to no one for two years. He made no friends, and had no idea of how to give expression to his needs and feelings; was pervaded by disgust, shame, fear. It was not until he was nineteen that he made his first friend – not sexual partner – but simply managed to talk to someone waiting in the gallery queue for the theatre.

Being homosexual gives many people a sense of selfconsciousness, a feeling of the arbitrary nature of the processes which have fashioned them, and this self-awareness often extends far beyond the aspect of their sexuality. The random visitation of being gay derogates somehow from the importance of being anything else. In this sense, many homosexual people are constantly aware of all other possibilities, and this is perhaps a clue to gay humour: the play-acting, self-distancing, the attempt to anaesthetize pain by striking attitudes towards it. This is a process now accessible to many non-homosexual people, although it has been there a long time in gay culture – a feeling of dispossession, a loss of identity, of the nature of chance rather than necessity in the acquisition of values and identities. Again, one of the reasons why 'straight' society is fascinated by the phenomenon of homosexuality is because once again gay people could perceive through the contradictions and ironies of their sexuality something of the mechanisms of social and psychological dislocation that afflicts us all: we are all the anomalous and bereaved progeny of historical accident, passive and helpless victims of cultural contamination and a damaged sense of community. Of course in London such people are more readily found, being highly motivated to remove themselves from the source of their pain; and the range of alternatives offered by a metropolitan area can assuage the sense of loss. It is significant that gay liberation, which uses the rhetoric of nationalism and evangelism, is an attempt to restore a sense of total identity that has been lost in the dysfunction of the unwieldy and ill-understood machinery of social formation. Two people I met illustrated in spectacular fashion the nihilism that is the extreme form of the self-distancing camp attitude towards life:

Huguette,

a lesbian born of the rape of a French girl by an American Negro from the army; deported and sterilized by the Nazis.

'I've had a very violent life; as I suppose befits somebody who was conceived in violence; which is odd, because I'm a very peaceable person. I've always thought of myself as rather soft and certainly feminine; but because of my appearance, I don't know, people have always attributed the opposite to me. I was brought up as a kind of curiosity of nature; if I were young now I should probably enjoy myself more; but I was an object of the greatest interest to the girls in the little town where I lived. They would stroke my skin and see if some of the colour came off, and then wipe their hands on their blouse. I grew up feeling monstrous; and I suppose my mother kept me as a tangible symbol of the dreadful thing that had happened to her. Now that is not a very pleasant foundation for a relationship, and naturally I hated her. She used to look at me and say "Ah, if you knew what I had suffered." I did know, because she transferred it all to me. I suppose in a way that was why I stayed in Paris during the war. I think I almost willed myself to be deported; it was a kind of confirmation of the estimation of myself which I had received. I could refer to external authority again, which, after I'd left home I hadn't done. But on looking back, I realize that all the relationships I'd ever made with girls had been poisoned from the same source. I'd been an absolute bitch to them. I think I wanted to provoke them into confirming that I really was an unacceptable human being. Which, in the end, they invariably did. That is to say, I wanted them to confirm what I'd learnt about myself, but I desperately wanted them to deny it as well. And this they could only do up to a point . . . I provoked them into a situation where all they could say was "You're impossible, you're a monster, I don't want to see you any more." And I spent all my life in that abyss, having to re-live my childhood, and never, never seeing my way out of it . . . I can see it now. But I no longer have any human involvements, so I've no chance to put it into practice.'

Sharon, mid-forties

No less than Raoul or Huguette, he is a product of a broken culture, born in a working-class family in Huddersfield in the mid-thirties. His mother died when he was three, and his father abandoned him and his three brothers. He was farmed out to a series of separate and often-changed foster parents.

'I don't need to go in for all this gay lib rubbish. I think it's hysterical. By liberated, what I mean is, do you get all the sex you want? If the answer's yes, then you're liberated. Sex pure and simple. Well it's not very pure, but it's fairly simple. I think all

gay lib is is a lot of frustrated queens. I think it's up to every individual to liberate himself, like I did. Nobody's going to do it for
you. And believe me, if you can get rid of the kind of background
I had, you can reach for the moon.

'I started getting liberated when I was nine, in the flea-pit of a
cinema in the run-down bit of Huddersfield where we lived; there's
nothing but run-down bits of Huddersfield, but that's beside the
point. I was picked up by a man in the pictures, one of those men
grown-ups tell you not to talk to. Don't let them screw you, they
ought to say; but instead they say "Don't talk to them", and all the
while they mean something else, which gets you all interested and
worked up, so you've got to find out what it's all about . . . Come to
think of it, I didn't talk to him anyway.

'I was living with me Auntie [he pronounces it "Antie"]; she was
anti-everything, anti-life, anti-love, anti-sex. She once locked me
in a cupboard, in the living-room, nasty brown cupboard where she
kept all her wool and her bits of material for darning and patching,
and where all the mice came from, oh . . . I can't tell you the terror
I felt. And do you know what I'd done? I'd eaten some jam out of
the pantry. She said "I can't lock everything up out of the way of
thieves, but I can lock the thief up." She said "You can stay there
till you're sorry." I just howled and howled, I was suffocated . . .
I had these awful feelings that my bleached bones would be found
in a hundred years' time. She locked the door on me – it was where
she kept her rent money and everything . . .

'This feller, he had an allotment. I suppose he was about forty,
oh hell, that means he was the age I am now; only he seemed really
old to me. And he had one of these wooden huts where he kept his
tools; although the one I was interested in didn't live in a garden
hut . . . It was a bit uncomfortable, but I hadn't discovered some
of the interesting variations I've learned since, like doing it in bed.
I took to sex like a duck to water. I think if I was a woman, I should
have been a prostitute; no seriously, I think it's a very high calling;
to relieve the frustrations of humanity, I can't think of any better
work. Like nurses and that really, only nicer. I used to go down
there every Saturday afternoon. Antie didn't trouble where I was,
as long as I didn't get into trouble. I used to watch him digging;
he had brown arms, he was nice . . . I think I got fed up with him
in the end, and just stopped going down the allotment. He once
knocked on the door. He waited for me to come out of school,

but I didn't go with him after that. He wanted to buy me things. She went mad. She said "Are you his father, if you are, where the bloody hell you been all these years, and if you ain't, sod off."

'I never went to Grammar School because, well, I'd got a lot of other things to do than work. I let everybody know at school that I liked sex with boys. They all took the piss rotten at me, but it didn't stop some of them hanging about all furtive like after school, and saying how about coming down the park . . . Parks were very sexy places in my childhood, bushes rustling and all that . . . If Corporation Park could talk, my God wouldn't it tell some stories, all dirty ones. For the recreation of the working classes . . . Anyway, some of these big butch footballers who were first to take the piss, they used to hang round and say "Hey, Shar, how about coming down the park"; even used to take a bloody football, hypocrites, make out they were going to do a bit of footie. But I never betrayed them. I thought "No, you've got to keep your dignity." And that's something I've always maintained through life. I've always kept my dignity. And my God, have I been in some places where I could lose it . . . But I had a fantastic time, ever since I could remember. My life has been people; not what age I am, not where I was living, not where I was working, but who I was with. By the time I was fifteen, I was going to London almost every weekend, hitching lifts – that was an education in itself, sometimes all I had to do was go a few miles down the Leeds Road, and I'd got myself fixed up for the weekend. I've stayed in some marvellous places. Hotels, country clubs, yachts, liners, holidays, I've had some incredible holidays. My life's been one long holiday . . . When I went to London I used to spend the night with blokes who picked me up, I wasn't fussy where I met them, cottages, arcades, pubs. I bet I'm one of the few people who've had clap before I was sixteen. Twice. That was a bit embarrassing, because I didn't know what it was the first time, and in my innocence I went to my own doctor, and told him I had this pain in the bum. He tried to put the frighteners on me, but I never gave anything away. I wouldn't betray anybody. There's too many people in the gay world who'd betray Jesus Christ again tomorrow; they can be very treacherous . . .

'The day I left school was the day I left Huddersfield. Shuddersfield I used to call it. I went to London like a bat out of hell. Within a week I was living with the first person who said he would love me forever. That was the first time I ever heard anybody say that and the last time I believed it. In the gay world forever means till a week on Tuesday. He was a dancer, and I was very succulent at that age. I had some marvellous times with him. Parties; of course I wouldn't piss on them now, but at that time I thought This is living, really living. I discovered the pubs and then Amsterdam, Paris . . . I like everything, you see, I mean, I think I must be more sexed than a lot of people, because a lot of my friends are paired off now, you know, they stick with somebody they can't bear the sight of because they're afraid they'll get old and ugly and get left on the shelf. People who think like that are old and ugly already inside, however they may look. So they settle down in a nice garden flat in Croydon and dish the dirt about everybody else. But I'm still as busy, sexually, as I was when I was twenty. I should think I'm out five or six nights a week. On the seventh I rest. I stay at home one night a week, to show I can, to prove to myself I'm not a sex maniac. But if I go three days without sex, I'm a screaming lunatic, I kid you not . . . No, I'm not exaggerating. I can't go a week without sex; I'm not good at masturbation; I've never masturbated, as a matter of fact. I've never needed to. Mind you, in my more desperate moments I've been with some wrecks of humanity . . . Liberated, look love, I've had siph five times and I've lost count of the clap. Not to mention some of my other troubles, little local difficulties. I once spent a month in hospital having my sphincter sewn up after a little contretemps with a man from overseas . . . I said to them "Now I want a nice little chain-stitch" . . . I've had somebody from every part of the world, I'm not prejudiced, from Fiji to the Arctic wastes. No, I've not been there, they all come here if you wait long enough . . . I honestly can't think of a country in the world that I haven't had somebody from, except Red China. That's the only ambition I've got left. Sex is my life. I'm not obsessed. Well, perhaps I am, but everybody's obsessed with something. Better that than winning the pools, or playing the Stock Exchange. I've had a good career. Sex-wise. The other doesn't count. Work? I'm a barman, except that I wouldn't bar any man if his tool was big enough . . . I don't have time for friends. I've got friends, people who would shed their last drop of blood for me, but I don't go out visiting them in their homes and that sort of thing . . . There's no such thing as friends; everybody's out for sex, and those who go on about friends are just those who can't get it.'

JS: 'Do you think that even being liberated like you say you are, you might miss something?'

SHARON: 'Not if it's in pants, I don't.'

JS: 'Don't you think that you might become a slave to sex?'

SHARON: 'A slave to sex, oh yes please. I like it. That's me. A slave to sex. Well you can come and help me write my life-story; and that's what we'll call it.'

JS: 'Do you know what I mean though?'

SHARON: 'No I don't, I think it's rubbish.'

The conversation ended as some of Sharon's friends arrived. I saw him again in the same pub, about a fortnight later; much more depressed, less lively.

'I'm just depressed. I get depressed. When I think about my life, you'd be bloody depressed . . . What have I got? I've been taken up with people, you'd be surprised, but they don't want to know when they've finished with you . . . I went to the most fabulous dinner parties, champagne flowing like water, big houses in South Kensington, they promise you the earth, you make them laugh, then "Oh I'm sorry, I can't possibly see you . . . I've got people staying, I'm just leaving for America, I'm terribly busy." I know all their goddam excuses. I'm just a joke, that's the trouble. I'm just somewhere to put it when you're a bit hard up. Sodding hypocrites . . . I've got a diary full of names and addresses; and do you know, there isn't one I could ring and say "I feel low, let me come and talk to you" . . . I could get sex in any one of a dozen places tonight . . . But where's the big hand-outs when it comes to love?'

Being homosexual is full of paradoxes. Sharon at some levels is an aimless desocialized person; at others, acutely conscious of his origins, his class. He lives in a world apparently abstracted from the contingencies of time and social locus; one-night stands, random encounters, meetings without consequences. This world has its own values, beliefs and rituals, and is itself an attempt to escape the exigencies of class, economics. Coupled with the mourning for loss of identity there is an exultation in that loss – the flight into negation, mobility, exoticized hedonism, out of which the mutilated personality hopes to create a new self.

In this way the homosexual is no longer an outsider in the main flow of the culture. On the contrary, the homosexual has been a kind of pathfinder; a pioneer of the new kind of human being that has come into existence under the protective shelter of plenty. In one sense we have all become gay. The subculture of those homosexuals who dared to admit their membership of it originated in privileged areas of society – among the leisured and rich, who could buy themselves immunity from the moral obloquy that attended what was considered a dangerous deviancy. The subculture was well-off, self-indulgent and reached only a small minority of homosexual people. The tone was upper middle class with aristocratic leanings. It assimilated individuals from the lower reaches of society and more or less successfully colonized them. But because such people were leisured, because they were absolved from the need to raise a family and could divert their income to their own comfort and concern, the homosexual culture already showed incipiently many of the traits of what has come to be the consumer society. We have all become privileged and leisured. There is no longer any need for individuals to be frugal, self-denying and repressed. Quite the reverse, in fact: our survival depends upon concern with and expenditure upon our selves – not the body as labour, as a piece of productive machinery, but the body as sensory experience, the body as a mediator of fulfilment. The gay subculture has always represented a practical embodiment of this once dangerous doctrine, which is now enshrined at the whole centre of our culture. It is therefore scarcely surprising that so much of the guilt and shame should fall away among young people. The model for the consumer society already existed in the culture – aristocratic, leisured, self-indulgent – and the homosexual world helped to provide a concrete image for the evolution of consumerism; in the same way that what were once considered to be dangerous and very progressive models of education – with their stress on self-determination and self-fulfilment – have become institutionalized in processes that have helped to create the new human being that is Consuming Man; a quite new and unparalleled phenomenon, with its own values and beliefs, its hedonistic and ferocious care for itself, its mystical belief in pleasure, plenitude and enjoyment.

This society is still in a state of becoming; and indeed, in many areas it has scarcely supplanted the old culture based upon the disciplines of poverty, repression, insecurity. People who have lived lives of bitter self-denial are, understandably, unsympathetic to the changes that have led to the belief in the search for personal happiness; and, naturally enough, it is not easy to suggest to those who fret endlessly at their own sense and responses, like an old country-man trying to dislodge tenacious fruit from a grudging tree, that the joy and fulfilment which they seek to wrest from life may be as much a tyranny and an illusion as the impoverished and obliterating process of which the old bear so many cruel and ugly scars.

Edward, twenty-five

Born in Jarrow in 1949. He is an only child, born to parents of working-class origin. His father has twice in his lifetime been made redundant, and is a silent and introspective man, humourless and intolerant. Edward early in life became the focus for their un-satisfactory relationship, was appealed to to arbitrate in his parents' disputes, was drawn into the struggle of which he was the living symbol. From the age of seven or eight he remembers being forced to beg them not to separate, to stay together; he became the intermediary of their messages when they did not speak for days on end. For many years he has tried to forget the isolation and agony of his childhood. He is melancholic, self-effacing and em-bittered, deeply anxious and apologetic for his whole existence. Until well into his twenties he never doubted the version that he was offered by his mother of the struggle between her and his father; she invoked the cultural stereotypes of working-class male and female roles – she was the martyred object of her husband's tyranny, meek, self-sacrificing while he was selfish, thoughtless and intolerant. Everything she did annoyed him. If she sat knitting, the click of the needles annoyed him; if she drank cups of tea he became angry. She could do nothing to please. He showed no interest in his child; he drank; he escaped to the pub with his own father whenever he could, to be free of the constraints of the home. Edward's mother returned when she could to her own mother, in a country town in Scotland. In the summer she would take Edward for a month and they would both go raspberry-picking in order to earn some money.

'We lived in a sort of tenement till I was adolescent, and then we moved to a new council flat. I never had any friends. What mates I did have sort of melted away when I went to Grammar School, and the rest of them I lost when I went into the sixth form and we moved into the new flat. I had one friend, but I didn't see him outside school. I used to dread the weekend; everybody else lived for it, but when I went home on Friday evenings my heart used to sink; I was cut off from the outside world. My mother had no friends, she was isolated from her family. My father was one of thirteen, but they've all got separated somehow, they've quarrelled or they don't see each other . . . There's so many scenes from my childhood, if I start thinking about it, that keep coming back . . . I used to try and keep the peace between them, and then when I got to about fourteen I couldn't take it any more, I used to walk out of the house, and they gradually stopped. They don't talk about leaving each other any more. Once, I made arrangements for me mother to see a solicitor, but needless to say, she never kept the appointment.

'When I got to university, it was a revelation. I didn't realize people could actually enjoy themselves . . . It helped me a lot. The only thing was that I found out I could get on all right with people, I had quite a lot of friends. I had girl-friends, I had this girl called Janet, I used to have sex with her; it never really excited me, but I sort of thought it was the thing to do. Then I fell in love with this friend, and it sort of came home to me . . . I told him about it. He was very nice, we shared a flat, only he couldn't give me what I wanted. I think for about two months when I first knew him and he seemed to be responding a bit, I was happy. But after that . . . when I realized that he couldn't feel for me in the same way that I did . . . I suppose I got a bit mel. again . . . And that's the way I am. I left university and I did a Cert. Ed. I've been teaching for two years now; only I'm in Stoke, and I'd like to get out. I can feel myself getting so restricted. I've got friends, only most of them are married, and they try to get me together with girls I'm not interested in. I couldn't tell them about being gay. If you've got a relationship with somebody that's supposed to have been based on some sort of honesty, you can't revise it later and tell them you've been deceiving them . . . I need to get out. There's nobody who really knows me, who I can really talk to . . . There is one guy, he's thirty, he's doing a thesis but he's even more screwed up than I am. So that's not much use . . . These are things I've never talked about . . . I used to tell Colin a bit about my background, only he had a pretty awful childhood and we used to get into a rather pathetic competitive situation, where we didn't really listen to each other, but just poured out our own feelings.

'I have to keep in touch with me parents. They're proud of me. If I go home it's very sterile. There's never anyone there, except the two of them. They never go anywhere together. Me Mum goes to Bingo. People who decry Bingo, they don't know how awful the alternative is for a lot of people. She goes for the company, not because she wants to win prizes . . . Me Dad goes out for a drink, or he sits and has a glass of home-brewed beer, and then he'll go to bed at about nine o'clock. Up early. I've tried to get them to go away on holiday. No, we can't make the effort. All the trouble . . . We'd have to cross London, there's always some reason that's no reason at all for why they can't move . . . I keep on at them. I think they just do it now to test me, to see if I will keep on at them. So I do . . . But basically whatever it was that was going on between them just caught me up in it, and robbed me of my youth, and certainly I've never known what it is to be happy . . . I like to be on my own a lot. I need to be alone, I can't stand too much of anybody's company. I've got to do something. I tend to drift. Drift and dream. I have day-dreams, fantasies about having a lot of money, a big car, living it up, travel, you know. Very bourgeois. I used to be fairly left-wing when I was at university, but I've sort of lost interest since. I live very much inside myself, I'm hardly aware of what goes on . . . I hadn't really realized until just now how far I've been from the world outside . . . They won't go out for a meal, they won't do anything . . . Me Dad likes curry, because he was in India in the war, but I can't even get him to go out into Newcastle for a meal . . . He says what's the use. They don't talk . . . I indulge myself. I like a good meal, I buy things for meself. I sort of feel Oh well there's nobody else to spend it on, why shouldn't I . . . I've got a flat, at the top of a house. I want to get a lot of things for it, modern style. I have a car, mainly for getting up home in, the train is too slow for a weekend . . . I did music, and in a way that's been the worst thing that I could have done. It made me more introspective, more romantic and dreamy . . . It's been too much of a consolation for things which are inconsolable . . . It's made me put up with things that nobody should have to . . . I feel angry with meself sometimes. I'd like to do something different, make a radical change in my life . . .

'I've got to look after my parents. Their life has been so awful, they've had nothing. Their lives are so empty. I think I've got a duty to be good to them in their last years . . . Although ever since

68

I can remember they've sort of folded their hands as though their life was over.'

Edward has a constant, anxious frown, and his forehead is quite permanently creased with a kind of bewildered misery; he exudes a sense of depression; and yet he has a transforming and deprecating smile which reveals the kind of person he might have been.

He talked of his life as though it were a profoundly intimate and personal, incommunicable tragedy; shame and years of oppression made it an excessively emotional experience, even to discuss it. And yet his situation is a perfect illustration of what has happened to the working class. His parents, ambitious for him, encouraged school-work, which flourished in the emotional vacuum of his life, and they achieved their ambition for him. But the process of upward mobility was something the whole class was destined for in the wake of consumer society; the emotional severance has happened to a whole generation. And they believe it is a personal tragedy; like being gay; or whether it means divorce or isolation or a vague sense of lack of fulfilment, it is all felt to be part of an incommunicable personal grief, whereas it reflects simply the fragmentation of community, dispersal of families, loss of identity of a whole class; and because of the sense of shame it cannot be discussed; working-class people blame themselves for what they believe is their own responsibility. After all, is there not something called equality of opportunity and didn't we rise up by our own efforts? Did we better ourselves, or were we bettered? It is part of a huge epic process of social and economic change, this isolation and fragmentation; and as if that wasn't enough, because of the privatization of griefs and anxieties, we have taken on responsibility for something that this latest and most subtle evolution of capitalism has done to us. Just as Edward says of Jarrow – symbolic unhappy name – they have gutted it and rebuilt it, to get away from the clogs-and-hunger image. But alas, it is only the image the community has shed; the processes of which Edward is victim are the same processes as those of which his parents were victims: his father, oppressed by the threat of unemployment and dismissal and loss of earnings, disciplined, corrected, chidden by the employment structure, took home the authoritarianism and visited it upon his wife and son; and she was the victim of his oppression; and their son was the victim of the processes that have required the working class to do something other than be primary producers; the process that has transformed them, economic sorcery, from producers to consumers; and Edward unhappily does as the society bids him, seeking solace in goods, self-indulgent, regressive, unhappy society trying to placate the legion of murdered children which his generation is. It is unimportant how the individual tragedies are produced, or what the nature of the private suffering is; in this being homosexual is only incidental. But it is part of an ongoing process that is no less cruel than it was when our bodies were broken and our minds stunted in the employment of capital.

The deviancy of homosexuality was always regarded as a threat to the main culture; as though it might spread, contaminative, contagious, to affect the whole population, infecting the whole society with sterility: generations failing to replenish themselves. Most individuals feel close enough to the situation of homosexual people to feel this as a threat; there is something hedonistic, infantile, irresponsible in the gay situation, something beguiling, a prolonged holiday from life, the real business of living. And if it is these features which make the homosexual model an attractive image of a consuming society, it is the same features that posed such a menace to a society based upon frugality, discipline and self-denial. But in the strange game of sexual identity which the homosexual has always played with social and sex roles, the appearances suggest something that did not really exist. The subculture did not depart as far as was imagined from orthodoxy, and was in no way an undermining influence on the main institutions of society; it was too deeply permeated with snobbery, social aspirations, upward mobility to be a real threat; and many homosexual relationships faithfully reflected the beliefs and attitudes of a right-thinking morality and social and political beliefs; it adapted the institutions of the society, and that society could be seen, refracted, through the modified and deformed version of the subculture. If the homosexual world sinned against the society, it was through its social pretensions, its overweening aspirations; the terminology of aristocratic titles, reference to queens and duchesses and the posture of many homosexual people towards other people, the arrogance of the spoilt child, the characteristic of being homosexual became united with certain social attitudes that were anything but revolutionary.

Many homosexual 'marriages' took – and take – their cues from the institution that unites heterosexuals. I talked with one *ménage*, where the man said 'I think I have a duty to be true to my gender', and who referred to himself as henpecked; who came in from work to the cooking of his partner, exchanged chaste kisses, complained of the lack of salt or dryness of the meal, a perfect suburban model of marriage, with institutionalized roles of male and female, a perfectly assimilated couple, seemingly without any difficulty or self-consciousness. After dinner, he put the apron on and began to wash up, a double travesty of the man playing at being the woman, while his man-wife settled back to some domestic task like darning. Although many couples may assume these roles with irony, and a sense of self-distancing, yet, at the same time, there are no real alternatives open to them. There has to be an alternative if a real critique of the society is to be embodied in a life-style; and in this homosexuals are no less barren than some of the heterosexual marriages which they ape.

Simon and Terry, early fifties

They have lived together for twenty-seven years. Simon is fifty-three, Terry forty-nine. It isn't possible to determine the nature of their private relationship; but as soon as someone irrupts into their life, he or she becomes the recipient of conflicting laments and dissatisfactions; and throws into relief some of the absurdities, not only of the homosexual counterfeit, but of the original institution which has been so faithfully copied and so ironically deformed.

Simon and Terry lead a life of quite ordinary domesticity. They live on a new housing estate in a Midland city, an area in which the norms of family are very much in view everywhere. They have a mortgage; they enjoy gardening; they have two Borzoi dogs. Simon works as manager of a wine store, Terry is employed as a clerk by one of the local authority departments. Simon wears a grey pinstripe suit to work, of modern cut, wedge-heel shoes, a yellow and black sweater, large tie and floral shirts. Terry dresses more traditionally for work; but at home they both wear faded jeans and denim jackets, with studs and butterflies embroidered at the buttock pockets. They once inserted an advertisement in *Gay News* for mature friends interested in denim; a tenuous enough basis for friendship, one might have thought; but in fact, they met a couple who live in a neighbouring town, who almost broke up their relationship because of an infatuation on Simon's part; but they have remained friends, and go on holiday to the Continent or North Africa with them.

They are both slightly overweight, and act as vigilantes upon each other; and in the presence of other people, at least, take a perverse pleasure in noting signs of physical decay in each other; they will advert freely to gaps in the teeth, falling hair ('A white carpet in the bedroom, it's ridiculous, men of our age'); they are slightly at odds with the youthfulness of their dress style, and occasionally, when they are sitting down after dinner, for instance, a roll of fat edges like a wave that does not quite break over the top of their jeans, and the *justaucorps* shirts are distended at the buttons; so much so that the shirt tears slightly at the buttonhole. Simon is reputed to have a double chin; and this causes him to hold his head aloft so that Terry is denied the pleasure of being able to turn to him and say 'Look at his chins.' This gives him an air of constant hauteur; which in turn earns him the soubriquet of marchioness.

Because Terry is under fifty, he feels he can allow himself certain youthful indulgences which Simon's age denies him; he goes out alone more often than Simon; 'Cottaging,' says Simon contemptuously; although Terry says that he goes to see friends. 'You don't find friends in the places you go,' his friend retorts, 'you might see Phyllis.'; which is a joke of long standing to which Terry says 'Ha-ha' in a dismissive way. While he is out, Simon is restless and unhappy. 'I don't sleep till he gets back. Sometimes he brings trade; I'm not jealous, but you just don't know, you don't know who's watching, you don't know who they are; they might want money, they might start breaking the place up. I mean, you do hear some dreadful stories. I know one fellow, and he picked up this young man, and he came back the next day when he was out and stripped the house, literally, took nearly a thousand quids' worth of stuff, in broad daylight. Broke the window, opened the door, and took it all out in a van. Neighbours said "Oh, we thought you were moving . . ." And then some of them are on the make and they can be absolutely ruthless; there was that dreadful case where they tied him up in a chair and asphyxiated him with a gag, and committed all sorts of outrages on his body . . . They were taking out their own hang-ups on him, I suppose; but he died. They only got ten years. Vicious people.' 'Not in Leicester,' says Terry. 'It can happen anywhere.' 'Don't worry, you won't get involved.' 'I'm seriously thinking of buying a gun.'

Terry plays the role of irresponsible child/wife; Simon that of parent/guardian. Simon lies awake at night worrying. Simon deals with the money, pays the bills, Terry hands over his keep and contributions. But Terry is the source of light and laughter – such as it is – and Simon says he keeps me young, he's dreadfully irresponsible. He won't grow up, and then, with great satisfaction, 'I don't know what he'd do without me.'; and Terry says 'I'd have a bloody good time,'; but he doesn't mean it. Simon is eternally forgiving, but punishing; and when Terry has stayed out all night, Simon is inclined to be ill, and doesn't go in to work the next day; and Terry has to cajole and cherish him for a day or two, until Simon has got over his grief at Terry's infidelity; but when Simon finds somebody else – and he claims never to be actually on the lookout for sex, but if anything turns up . . . he is furtive, and never, never brings anyone into the home; this he says with the severity of a houseproud matron who will not allow animals indoors. It is a defence against the breakdown of their relationship; he is not prepared to jeopardize what he has with Terry; and this is the cause of his resentment against his friend, who doesn't seem to him to set a high enough value on their relationship, symbolized by bringing people into the house and by spending the night out sometimes. It has a quite symbolic meaning for Simon. Even if he goes out, he always gets home before morning; and when the phone rings for him he answers it in curt and almost dismissive terms; he says that he explains to his friends that he has 'a very difficult friend, who is madly jealous', which is far from the truth, but helps to keep the sense of distance between what he sees as his illicit amours and his stable relationship.

There is something mutually custodial in their relations; not simply a jealousy or vigilance about each other, but an act of discipline too: they fulfil for each other, the roles of family, kin; conscience, and control; a role which, on the estate can no longer be entrusted to community; the people move too frequently, their sights are set on ranch-style split-level homes in other towns; their preoccupation with mobility, lateral and upward, precludes any real vigilance on the lives of those around them; although Terry and Simon are on good terms with the neighbours, say hello to everybody, and anticipate the prejudice they sense by being decorous, pleasant and universally helpful. A propitiatory anxiety to please, they feel, keeps at bay the latent hostility, although they realize that it doesn't destroy it altogether. Occasionally ugly pieces of third-hand gossip makes them realize how precarious their acceptance is: Terry came home and burst into tears because someone had reported to him that they had been referred to as the Little Women of Low Acres (the name of the estate); when they pride themselves that they are free of the effeminate characteristics usually attributed to gay people. (But then so do most homosexual men; there is nearly always a tendency to refer to others in the general category in disparaging terms – 'cottage queens', 'tragedy queens', just 'old queens', in a dissociative way that appears to liberate the speaker from the category to which he refers.) They have been known as the Heavenly Twins, Castor and Bollocks; inventive butts of provincial wit. Simon confides that he feels he has to keep the marriage together. 'I have to be very patient, and it does take a lot of hard work. If it had been left to Terry, we'd have split up years ago; he does get infatuations for people sometimes, and of course in the early years I was terribly hurt by it. But now I feel fairly confident that he'll always come back to me, and that's the main thing. I don't pretend I like his unfaithfulness, but I've learned to put up with it. I'm much stronger than he is; he depends on me terribly. If anything happened to me, he'd go to pieces ... Of course, I've had my bits on the side, on the side, on the back, any position [laughs] I'm not fussy; but it would hurt him too much, and so that's why I don't flaunt it in the way that he does. I think in a way it's all he has: he has to prove he's younger and more attractive than I am; and I indulge him, really. I've had my chances but I wouldn't even mention them to him, because he'd find it unsettling ... I met an American – you'll never believe this – he came into the shop, and it wasn't very busy and we got talking, and well, I did go and have sex with him, and he wanted me to go back to the States with him ... I said no, naturally, although I can't say I wasn't tempted ... But I couldn't even tell Terry that; you won't say anything, will you? He regards me as a rock of Gibraltar, that's the way he needs to look at me, although it isn't much fun sometimes ...'

TERRY [I met him in a bar in the town; red leatherette stools, carpet, enormous fan of artificial flowers, ruched lamp-shades in muted red silk. Simon knew that I would meet him independently]: 'Of course I wouldn't leave him, but I have to assert my independence sometimes. I don't want to belong to him ... I think sometimes you think of all the opportunities you've missed; but I could do a lot worse. He's incredibly loyal; I couldn't have found anybody better, if I'd scoured the ends of the earth. Only possessiveness just makes me want to throw everything off and go wild. Which I have ample opportunity for. Not in this town. But I do go away a great deal. If Simon knew some of the things I did, he'd go green with fright. Not to mention envy. Because I know where I've got him. I'm that bit younger, and he thinks I'm more attractive than he is; do you think I am?; I don't personally, but it's not what you are, it's what you think you are that counts. I think faith can move mountains. If you think something hard enough, if you wish for it, I think you get it. I've always had more or less what I want all my life ... Well, there have been one or two exceptions; people as a matter of fact ... No, I think I wouldn't change myself or my life for the whole world ...'

A Happy Couple:
Len and William, late fifties

They live in a substantial terraced house in a North London suburb. It is set back slightly from the street by a small courtyard of crazy paving; small evergreens in tubs, a shiny red bituminous covering marks the garden path. An illuminated and chiming bell. A low-watt bulb shines behind the frosted glass panels of the front door, so that when Len opens the door, it is impossible to see anything other than an amorphous figure diffused through the irregular glass. Inside the house is warm, comfortable, cream-coloured, tepid, with many decorative items of *fantaisie*. In the lounge there is a colour television; a programme about curiosities of Northumbria is showing; there are deep damasked armchairs; Canaletto and a Pisarro print on the walls; green onyx table, lamps with white china animal groups at their base. We go into the back room, which is more functional, but still fairly ornate; a dresser with Capo di Monte figures, a bronze Roman charioteer, a china cockerel in bright colours, pictures – soulful dogs and cries of Old London; a silver-gilt candelabra. Some yellow freesias in a glass candlestick release a powerful and intermittent incense into the room. Two old dogs slumber on the hearthrug; a clock chimes daintily; a courtesan's bronze timepiece. Len comes into the back room, and William, who is more shy, joins us a little later. They are in their late fifties;

kindly, serious, generous. Len shows me a photograph of a Regency house called White Lodge – a long, low house with stuccoed pillars at the entrance, a fanlight early Gothicized, a canopy of wisteria. 'We bought this for just two thousand pounds, and when we sold it we got more than four times that amount, just five years later.' William comes in, and when they talk together one of them starts sentences which his friend finishes; and this somehow without interrupting: as though one of them initiated a thought and the other, sensing it, finishes it for him; the impression is of an extraordinary congruence of personality, a merging that reminded me a little of the fused characteristics of some of my old long-married aunts and uncles who had said the same things to each other almost every day for half a century, and where words are an arbitrary and almost insignificant outcrop of a profound flowing together of experience and character.

LEN: 'I think I love William as much now as I did when we were kids . . . We were both brought up in the slums of Deptford. We went to work on push-bikes; a lot of people did at that time, and I used to see him on his way to work. I think it was a case of love at first sight. It was for me anyway. We sort of got to know each other riding through Rotherhithe twice a day more or less at the same time. Will worked in the docks; he was a docker for thirty years. I did the same for a time, eleven years I did it, though not at the same wharf. Anyway, at the time I met him, I think he was expecting to get married. I don't think it occurred to him I'd got my eye on him.'

WILLIAM: 'I was going out with girls. Until Len rescued me.'

LEN: 'He sometimes sees the woman he might have married. She's dreadful. I say "Look what I saved you from." '

WILLIAM: 'I hadn't really accepted myself. I was twenty-three at the time, and Len was twenty-one.'

LEN: 'I arranged to meet him one night to go to the pictures or something.'

WILLIAM: 'And I never turned up.'

LEN: 'I chased him. I went to find him. And that was that. I wouldn't take no for an answer.'

WILLIAM: 'He thought he wanted me just for a pal, like, a mate.'

LEN: 'Oh no. I wanted more than that . . . I knew what I wanted right from the start. We couldn't have been better suited. Eventually he came to live with me at our house. Lodged with us.'

WILLIAM: 'I don't think my mother really accepted it, like yours did.'

JS: 'Didn't they mind? Did they know about your relationship?'

LEN: 'They must have. They didn't say anything, of course. Perhaps they didn't realize all the implications of it . . . I don't know, we were at the very bottom of the heap – my mother had been deserted by my father, Will's father was dead. My mother was deep in debt, she never went to the Assistance, the Guardians, only to moneylenders, and she had a tough time. They had other things to worry about than what was going on between us . . . When you're wondering where the next meal's coming from, you don't care about who sleeps with who.'

WILLIAM: 'I'm sure my family know. My nieces, they come in sometimes and say "What's she baked today?" Not in a nasty way. Everybody accepts us.'

LEN: 'We've been together for thirty-nine years. It's been wonderful. Nobody could have had a better partner. Whatever's happened – and we've had our tragedies – I've always been able to put my arms around him and say "Well we've got each other"; and that makes up for everything. We have our differences, of course. I've always been rather pushing and bold, but Will, he's so gentle, he's never said a word against anybody.'

WILLIAM: 'Well these last few years I have found a bit of temper. When I see somebody like Gormley [it was the time of the miners' strike] on television, you know . . . when I see what's happening to this country.'

LEN: 'Nobody has respect for authority any more. When I was young, you respected your boss, your parents, anybody who was a bit above you. But not now . . . You must remember, my mother was very Victorian and she had very strict morals. And I think I've got something of that in me . . . When you go to clubs these days, dances, you see boys dancing together with their hands on each other's buttocks; well, that kind of holding should only go on in private . . . You can dance quite well without holding each other there . . . There's no need for it . . . Things have gone too far. I can remember seeing Marlene Dietrich in *The Blue Angel* at the Trocadero, and she was really sexy and she was wearing more clothes than some of the girls you see in the streets. They think the less you wear, the more sexy it is. They're wrong, you know . . . I'm not a high Tory, but I'm a Conservative. William is a Liberal . . .

77

We're certainly not Socialists. I left school just before I was fourteen, and I was an office boy; I got ten bob a week. Of course that money you took straight home to your mother and she gave you your spending money. Even when I met William at twenty-one, I was still giving my money to Mother and getting half a crown a week... But it taught you to appreciate the value of things, which doesn't happen now... I remember saving up for a suit, and the pleasure in getting measured, waiting for it, trying it on, going out in the street in it for the first time... They know nothing of that today. But we knew how to enjoy ourselves. We used to go to the Running Horse, the Cannon Bar. They were known to be homosexual bars, but nobody interfered with you. We were discreet, you see. We used to go to the Trocadero, see two feature films for sixpence... But above all, we had our home. I think that is one of the chief bases for our life together. We've worked together for what we've got. We've done better than we could ever have dared to hope... Of course it's not easy. You have to have the will to work together. So many gay people expect Prince Charming to come along and they'll live happily ever after. You have to make the effort... Give and take... But I've had forty happy years; you hear people say gay people are unstable, they can't stick together. That's rubbish. Will and I have never even considered breaking up, and we haven't needed any marriage certificates to keep us together. We shall stay with each other for the rest of our lives now. And I couldn't want anything more... I don't want any more material goods – well, you know, you hear yourself saying "I want so-and-so," "We need this, that or the other"; and then you stop and think "No we don't, we don't really need it." We are hoping to sell this house and go and live in the country. That we would like... Anywhere where there's green fields and peace.

'I've always known which way my sexual preferences were... Whether William would have found out if it hadn't been for me, I don't know... The first homosexuals I ever saw must have been when I was a kid. There used to be some ex-army men, unemployed; they used to come round, four or five of them at a time, with a barrel organ, all dressed in women's clothes, and turn cartwheels and do the splits in the road, oh and then go round with a collecting tin... I didn't know at the time that they were homosexuals – they were dirty, their clothes were rags really... There was all horse dung in the road, and that never seemed to bother them... I was fascinated . . . I must have known about myself since I was twelve or thirteen . . . I know for a fact in the wharf where I worked there were five or six . . . You don't think of dockers as being gay, do you? But there must have been anyway, by the law of averages . . . We used to camp about with them, say "Hello Maud," you know, ordinary blokes like. We had some times.

'We were both called up in 1939. I did register as a conscientious objector. Although I don't have any religion, I think killing is morally wrong. It is for me anyway; although I couldn't justify it, the way I felt, to the Board. I went in the non-combatant corps. I couldn't imagine myself firing a gun at another human being . . . There was a famous playwright in the same corps, what was his name? . . . Christopher Fry . . . A lot of them in there were very intelligent, and we had some good discussions . . . I went to an officers' mess as a fatigues-wallah. When I got there, the bloke who was supposed to be the cook said "Do you know anything about cooking?" Well I did, because I do love cooking, and I'd had lots of practice. So I became the cook, and he did the fatigues, peeling potatoes and so on. Do you know, all the officers knew I was gay, and they all accepted it. I had a picture of William by my bed; and I wrote to him and he wrote to me every day . . . Of course, with the post being so erratic, I sometimes got six letters in a day and then none for a week . . . One day I was in the kitchen, and one of the batmen comes up behind me and puts his hand over my eyes, and says "Don't look, there's a surprise for you." And I said "What surprise?", and there in the doorway stood Will. I was overjoyed . . . They let us have the rest of the day to ourselves; so that shows how sympathetic they were to us, it proves they didn't have any prejudice. That was the longest time I've ever spent away from him. Three months . . .

'In the army I was unfaithful to him a couple of times . . . But it was done without love, there was no affection there. It was purely physical. We've often talked about it since; but I don't think I really betrayed him because there was no real feeling in it. Apart from that, I've never felt the need to go with anyone else . . . We've been in clubs, we've looked at people and said "What a nice chap," and I've perhaps caught somebody's eye and Will has said "You've made a conquest there." But as for that – nothing . . . Just don't let them tell you gay people can't be true to each other. It's funny, but I say sometimes "We're just like an old married couple."; which is silly, because I'm a man. I don't want to be anything else. But I'm retired now, I had to, on health grounds; so that means I stay at home and do the washing and baking; and I hang my washing out and say to the woman next door "Nice drying day." They talk to me as if I was a woman. And I do get a feeling of pride that my washing is perhaps whiter than hers . . . Isn't it funny? Will says I ought to write my life-story; only I'm not very good at putting my thoughts on paper . . . I seem to have quite a lot of time now . . . I had to retire: I have angina, blood pressure, and I'm more use to Will alive . . . We want to stay together as long as we can . . .

'We did sell up in London and bought a hotel in Cornwall. But we only kept it on for a few months, March till August. Twenty-seven bedrooms. We hadn't a clue about running a hotel, but we took it on and we found we were working eighteen hours a day. I had these pains in my chest, and they got worse, until in the end I had to go to the doctor, and he said quite simply "You'll have to give it up." I had to tell Will, so he agreed we should sell at once. We sold at a loss, but on that six months I had to pay a thousand pounds in tax, so you can tell what profits we made . . . But a thousand pounds in tax, isn't it dreadful?

'So we came back to London. Previously I'd been working for the council, in the Estates Department . . . I think if I could have had my choice I'd have trained as an Estates Manager. I went into the Department where I'd worked, and said "I suppose there's no chance of a job?" They said "Oh, but there is," and they made me Estates Manager. I must say, a lot of these university people who were working there, nice enough, but they don't have a clue when it comes to practical matters . . . But I had to give even that up because of blood pressure.

'I've had a contented life. I've had the best partner in the world. He's been everything to me.'

We drink tea from a chromium pot with a cosy; fluted china cups; silence; the gas-fire creaks where the metal expands and the heat has been turned higher. Cold March evening; the sodium lights dim the stars with a smudged orange glare and discolours the early almond blossom. Wind in the evergreens. They stand at the door, light from storm lantern in their face; still; Philemon and Baucis.

In many ways Will and Len found it easier to be connubial and faithful than most would today: for those homosexuals who were able to come to terms with and give expression to their sexuality in the twenties and thirties the only real model was the upwardly mobile and suburban; Len talks about his struggles, very much in the way that many people in suburbia talk about personal heroics in their attainments, even when these are attended by the most favourable social circumstances: for instance, Will and Len had no dependents; both being able-bodied and in full-time work, it would have been surprising if they hadn't managed to scrape a home together; but these are factors which few people take into account, when talking of their achievements and their social advancement. More than this: the model of fidelity in the aspiring respectable working class was very insistent: divorce in the working class is a comparatively recent phenomenon; and in a sense, having found each other, the fact that they remained together is perhaps less surprising than if it had happened within recent years. They took their social cues from the working-class (aspiring) rather than from the gay world, although they did encounter the world of clubs and pubs later. There is a much more widely diffused awareness of the norms and values of the gay world among young people who find themselves to be homosexual now: the promiscuity, the ready availability of partners, the expendability of individuals, the judgement of whether somebody is 'good sex' governing whether there is a second meeting, etc.; and this tends to militate against long-term stable relationships; the style of Simon and Terry seems to be more usual: an initial intense relationship which cools perhaps after two or three years, and then a separate existence, 'going our separate ways' as the euphemism is; sometimes acknowledging that this is the way they live, sometimes devising elaborate rites and avoidances, while going through the motions of extreme loyalty; this acts as a constant reaffirmation that the fundamental protective relationship is intact, and that all the rest is mere physiological necessity, a letting off of steam; it gives a decisive and meaningful background to the lives of people who sometimes feel threatened with the internal anarchy of endless promiscuity, all-engulfing desires, insatiability, boundless sexual appetite, unless they have some point of discipline, some concerned and mitigating influence on their tendency towards being anybody's, easy meat, an easy lay; from 'looking for sex all the time', as one man put it. 'I spend all my life wondering where I'm going to find it next; even if I'm in bed with somebody. I've got up and gone out, found three or four people in a single day.' This is a fear which appears to haunt a lot of gay people; and many feel the need for some – possibly simulated – stability in their lives. There are many embalmed relationships which serve just this function; they are never inspected because they don't bear inspection, but they act as a very real rampart against the fear of being completely at the mercy of appetites and desires that can become all-consuming, and as such become an elaborate self-buttressing process against chaos.

Charles and Tim, thirties

They live in a maisonette in West London. They have been together for nine years; their sexual relations are intermittent; 'occasional consort' as described in the V.D. clinic; but they have a very intense and close emotional relationship, and assume that they will live together for the rest of their lives. They value their relationship far too highly to put it at risk for mere sexual adventure; although the slight anxiety that a strong primary relationship with someone else could put their own at risk gives it a slight tension, an edge of jealousy, a hint of uncertainty which helps to keep their emotional rapport alive and dynamic.

CHARLES: 'I left home when I was quite young, and I've always shared a flat, so my parents were always used to the idea that I lived with blokes. And I did change about quite a bit, two or three months here, six months there; one place I only lasted a fortnight. It was a gay flat, and I'd slept with all three guys in the place within two weeks, and they decided I was a whore, so they kicked me out. [Laughs.] As a matter of fact, the first trouble I had with my parents was when I lived in a mixed flat in West Hampstead, and they were convinced that I was laying both the girls at the same time. I was probably at my most chaste at that time, anyway, so that was quite irritating. I was twenty-six when I met Tim; we had a very passionate affair – no – affair doesn't do it justice; for about a year we couldn't bear to be apart. There was such a powerful magnetic force between us; it was absolutely without ennui or tedium; I know that I'll never meet anyone again with whom I shall have that kind of irresistible need to be together . . . For the first time I felt kind of whole; and even when the first intensity began to wear off, it left such a residue of warmth, it has given me confidence and . . .

82

anyway, I'm sure that isn't interesting to anybody but ourselves, but I'm just trying to say how it was with us. We bought a flat, this maisonette, actually, within a few months of knowing each other. From my parents I'd been getting this why-don't-you-settle-down routine for ages, and it had been dying down a bit till I met Tim. And then it all started up again. Nothing was said, not in words; but I knew they sensed the situation; and if it had stayed that way, everything would have been all right . . . They know, you know they know sort of thing, you keep quiet about it and everybody's happy. I'd always had a good relationship with them; my father is diabetic, and has always been ill, ever since I can remember, and in a way I became a substitute for him as far as my mother was concerned, very early on . . .

'Anyway, they came up for a week to stay with me and Tim. They slept in the put-you-up in the living-room. Tim and I were both working, and at some point while we were out, she must have gone into the bedroom and seen the double bed. I can remember quite vividly, she was very quiet and subdued the whole evening; and when we were washing up – I guessed what was coming – she said "I suppose we've turned Tim out of his bed." And I said "What do you mean?" I knew what she meant, but I wanted to make her say it. And she said "Well, there's only one bed in the bedroom." I said "Yes." Not another word. They went the next day – they were going anyway.

'Then she started. She wrote to Tim to inform him that he'd corrupted her boy, and that I'd been an ordinary decent kid from Newcastle, where such things are not known, and that a combination of him and London had corrupted me. And she cast him in the role of unprincipled seducer, scarlet woman, in spite of the fact that he was two years younger than I was, and, if anything, I'd been the seducer . . . well that's a stupid idea anyway, it was quite mutual. And he wrote back to her and stated quite bluntly that if she forced me into a position where I had to make a choice between Tim and her, she might not actually be the object of that choice . . . So there was a long period of strained silence, and we didn't communicate for months and months. Then my father had a stroke, and she sent for me, and of course I went dashing home; tearful scenes. Actually it was set up as a deathbed reconciliation, but happily he recovered. Nothing was spoken, but it was kind of understood that everything was forgiven . . . As a matter of fact I resented that too, because I didn't need their magnanimous gestures any more than I cared for their comments on my sexual preferences; but I was quite tactful and managed to accept it with reasonable grace.

'When Father was better they wrote and asked if they could come and stay for a few days. Well. You have never seen such a transformation. They couldn't have been nicer to Tim, for a start. They treated him exactly like a daughter-in-law . . . She talked about food and household chores, and asked his advice and exchanged gossip, it was all girls together . . . It was as if she'd suddenly got hold of something to refer to, and she overplayed it actually . . . She was treating him just as she treated my brother's wife; except that with Tim she found she could be even more open, because she'd always felt a bit uneasy with my brother's wife. It was very funny. Everything he cooked she cooed over, you know, until that time she'd only cooked greens and roast and stew kind of thing; and she really relished the aubergines and ratatouille, and all the Mediterranean bit. "Rich but nice," she used to say; and you could see it extending her experience. She even started copying things he did. And then, after that, she wrote to Tim's parents, it was quite incredible. She went to Lancashire to see them. And they made friends. It's unbelievable, they go away on holiday together . . . I don't know what they say about us to each other, but they come to stay once or twice a year . . . She has her moments of regression from time to time; I catch her looking at me in a certain way, and you can read what's on her face so clearly that you can't take offence. She's too vulnerable . . .

'It was just that she didn't have any experience to fit it into . . . I think that all gay people should confront their parents with their real situation; they can see then that it isn't some ghastly and unmentionable perversion. I mean, I think Tim finds it mildly annoying to be a daughter-in-law. But what is really funny is that his parents treat me in exactly the same way: for them I'm the daughter-in-law . . . We are both daughters-in-law. They both attribute a female role to the one who's not their son, and that helps to mitigate the pain . . . It helps them to accept it. She once said "Why should it happen to me?" And I said "Nothing's happened to you. If anything I'm the one something happened to, and I'm not worried, so why should you be?" She said "I wanted you to give me grandchildren." I thought Yes, so you can gobble them up, like you tried to do with me.

'But they've accepted it in their way. They can relate to us, even though the way they do it is slightly absurd . . . We can collude with it because it doesn't seriously upset us, and it pleases them.'

*

As in all cultures, there is a shared pool of experience, which individuals sometimes claim as their own: stories recur, myths are propagated, variants on certain archetypal incidents are exchanged. Although much of this folklore may have had some basis in actual events, it is nearly always transposed into a position of total inaccessibility by the fact that it is reported at second or third hand. Sometimes it is an outcrop of fantasy or wish-fulfilment.

'This boy on Euston Station, a policeman comes up to him and says "Come with me." – and it was at the time when the police had those blue boxes where they could phone the station, they've gone now, they've all got two-way radios – and he took him into this box and fucked him. And he said to him "You'll be in trouble if you don't report here twice a week." So that way, the boy has to go back twice a week for a year.' That story has elements of sado-masochistic fantasy, as well as revenge against authority, a puncturing of one of the threats to gay people. There are many stories about policemen saying 'Come along with me' to homosexuals, and then, instead of the feared arrest, there is a wild time in the back of a police car, in the bushes, etc.

There is always in promiscuous encounters a certain risk of danger, fear, menace, and these sometimes furnish details of horror or absurdity that keeps alive a *frisson*. 'This boy met this leather guy and went back with him, and his room was in the basement, done out like a torture chamber, and he tied him in chains and kept him there for three days, and it was sound-proofed and he gave him nothing to eat, and the only way this guy could come was by hanging him upside down from the ceiling and beating him with a chain. At the end of it he had two broken fingers and a fractured skull. It damaged his brain; he's just a vegetable now.'

'This guy wanted me to strangle him; so I put my hands round his throat and he said "Squeeze tighter," and I did, and he said "Tighter," and I did, and then he lost consciousness. I panicked, and just rushed out of the flat. For weeks I was convinced that I'd killed him. Every night for six weeks I went back to the pub where I'd picked him up, and he didn't appear, and I thought "Oh my God." I watched for the papers and everything, but it wasn't

85

mentioned. And then one day, there he was in the pub. Imagine how relieved I was; although he has a permanent scar round his neck.'

There are stories about people having their heads cut off with a scimitar, people whose cock is severed and placed in their mouth; the various substitutes for a penis that people use in masturbation – milkbottles that shatter, etc. This folklore is the obverse of the extreme romanticism of all the fantasies about the idyll, the complete relationship. The mythology, scandal and folklore is perhaps heard at its most free in relaxed social gatherings between friends.

An evening in Windermere Avenue

A white-painted house in a suburban street in South-West London; traditional, luxurious, immaculate. White carpets, heavy Victorian furniture, velvet drapes; a cheval glass, marble pillared clocks, glass and china in cabinets. A cold February night. A gasmiser in a casket amplifies the central heating; slim corrugated radiators painted the same colour as the walls. Prints of inn yards, cries of Old London. Everything is cosy, tepid, inward-looking.

The sound of a car drawing up and the chiming bell is heard.

'There they are. I thought they were never going to get here.'

Simon owns the house; lives with Roddy, who is in the kitchen.

'I expect she's got her shooting pains or something; that's why they're late.'

'Hello, come on, don't let the cold air in.'

Brian and Alan are in their early thirties, perhaps a year or two older than Simon and Roddy. Roddy used to be Brian's lover; and he met Simon through him; the two households are quite close, and there was no rancour in the change-over of partners. There is an element of emulousness, but it is quite amicable, and doesn't seriously affect the supportiveness and gossipy camaraderie between the two couples; they are in fact fairly honest with each other, mildly camp, sending each other up.

ALAN: 'I've had a terrible day. I nearly rang you up, didn't I, Brian, to say we couldn't face it . . . I didn't get home from work till seven, and I had a splitting head.'

SIMON: 'I'll just let Roddy know you're here; you know what a state she gets into with all her sauces and savouries.'

BRIAN: 'Oh isn't it lovely and warm. The heater's gone in the car. Another twenty quid, I expect.'

Roddy comes out of the kitchen, a wooden spatula in hand. 'Hello loves.'

The bottle of Mateus Rosé is placed on the sideboard; the tissue paper detaches itself and floats to the floor.

There is a sound of a rather twittering osculation as they all kiss.

BRIAN: 'Oh what gorgeous shoes.'

R: 'I sprayed them with gold aerosol paint. They were peeling. I only bought them two months ago, and you've only got to scrape them and all the veneer comes off . . . I told Si, I said "I think I'll spray you as well, I'd like a gold boy-friend." '

S: 'Nothing wrong with my veneer.'

R: 'No, that's the trouble.'

S: 'Cheeky cow.'

R: 'Why have you had a terrible day then?'

A: 'Oh I don't know. I just felt I couldn't cope. It was just one of those days.'

B: 'Withdrawal symptoms. She always gets like that when somebody's withdrawn it.'

A: 'It bloody wasn't. I went out with two girls from work. We had dinner. I just felt ill. I think it might be the jaundice a bit.'

S: 'Oh no.'

A: 'Just a bit. I felt really sick.'

R: 'Pregnant.'

B: 'Not again. God what shall we use this time, slippery elms or gin.'

[Laughter]

A: 'No, I really didn't want to face anybody this morning . . . I've got some anti-depressants, but I'm sure they're not strong enough . . . Of course, I can remember when you could get purple hearts as easily as sweets, they're what I need. I went to my doctor one day and he said "You'll be selling them in the pub." I said "I most certainly would not, they're far too precious." But they'd stopped prescribing.'

S: 'What is it, the usual?'

A: 'Depression. I mean, it's nothing out of the ordinary. I think a lot of gays suffer from depression.'

S: 'It's because we're more sensitive.'

B: 'Well look what we have to go through.'

87

R: 'I think it's partly the play-acting we have to do. I mean, everybody thinks that gay people are camp and glittering on the surface, but underneath . . . I think being camp is just the gays' way of saying sod-off to the rest of society.'

B: 'If you're gay you get hurt more.'

S: 'Definitely.' He pours out glasses of medium sherry, and bitter lemon for himself.

B: 'You give your heart much more freely . . . When you're young anyway. I know I did. I couldn't understand that everybody wasn't the same . . . You get used to having everything trampled on.'

A: 'Still I've got it now, haven't I?'

B: 'What?'

A: 'Your heart. Gone a bit cold and leathery of course by now. Like your face, love.'

B: 'That's 'cos it's been in so many hands. You just happened to be holding it when the music stopped.'

A: 'Why aren't you drinking, Si?'

S: 'I'm off alcohol.'

A: 'Come on, what've you had?'

R: 'What hasn't he had?'

A: 'Are you .. ?'

R: 'He's had the clap.'

B: 'Oh, you poor thing.'

A: 'Where did you get it?'

R: 'Something he scraped off Battersea Bridge.'

A: 'Really? I didn't know Battersea Bridge – '

R: 'You don't know Simon. Anywhere . . . If he sees somebody on top of a 77 bus he's just as likely to drop his kecks there and then.'

S: 'I believe in seizing time by the foreskin.'

A: 'Don't you mind, Roddy?'

R: 'It'd be all the same if I did. I used to. I used to make terrible scenes.'

S: 'That's because you're such a terrible actress, love.' R goes into kitchen.

B: 'I don't think I'd be happy to be so open about it. I mean, Alan does have the odd one-night stand, and so do I, let's face it, but we don't talk about it. I'd never bring anybody home while Alan was there . . . Sometimes, when he goes home to Bradford

88

then I might go out occasionally, have a fling. Otherwise, I wouldn't dream of it. And when I'm away on a course or something, I know he has people in. But as long as we don't know, we don't mind . . . As long as it doesn't interfere with our life together. That's the most important thing, not to let anything come between us.'

R (coming back from the kitchen): 'The more who come between us the more we like it.' Mock shock; laughter.

B: 'But it's so boring, all those trips to the clinic, I've got better things to do with my time. I don't think it's worth it.'

S: 'Oh it's nothing. I'd rather have a dose of clap than a cold in the head any day. It's much less trouble.' To A: 'Where do you go when you go on the batter?'

A: 'I like the open air.'

S: 'Terrible risk.'

B: 'He's a fresh-air fiend.'

R: 'I met somebody who'd been picked up by the police in Hyde Park, and he was only sitting on a bench. They did a sort of round-up. Horrible. They advised him to plead guilty, because that makes things easier. A quick fine and it's forgotten. Only he wouldn't.'

S: 'I've been picked up by the police on more than one occasion.'

R: 'He's obsessed with uniforms.'

S: 'Well you work it out – if one in twenty is gay, and I think that's a very conservative estimate – there must be a certain number even among the most unpromising professions . . . I like firemen, police-men, soldiers, sailors especially, anything in uniform.'

A: 'What about traffic wardens?'

B: 'Or usherettes.' Laughter.

A: 'Out of it they're all the same.'

S: 'No it's not that. It's the uniform that turns you on.'

R: 'Like a blow torch.'

Laughter. Silence; as they drink.

A: 'So what else have you been doing?'

S: 'Isn't that enough?'

B: 'I think you must be insatiable.'

S: 'No, I'm not. I just want it all the time.'

A: 'I know somebody who went to have a prostate massage.'

R: 'Sounds fun.'

A: 'No, really.'

S: 'Prostrate?'

89

A: 'No, prostate. He was over-sexed, and apparently, he had quite a high position.'

R: 'Whoops.'

A: 'No, he was in the diplomatic service, I believe, and he used to go for this massage once a week, or once a month or something, because that helped to relieve the sex urge.'

R: 'How horrible.'

A: 'It's only like a masseur. I know lots of people who have masseurs. Freddy does. He has a Thai or a Vietnamese or something, very smooth, deft fingers . . .'

S (puzzled): 'Why did he have that done? I don't understand.'

A: 'Well, it was so he could keep himself in control. Apparently, he might have been a security risk otherwise. He wouldn't have been able to control himself. And he might have betrayed his country.'

S: 'I think I'd make a good diplomat.'

B: 'You'd make anybody who'd give you a second glance.'

R: 'Second: One's enough.'

S: 'No, I would. I'd love to be part of the corpse diplomatic.'

R: 'I must say' (ruminative) 'it would be nice not to think about sex all the time. If you could go somewhere like that, once a month, then forget it for a few weeks.'

B: 'Why?'

A: 'Have you gone off sex then?'

R: 'No, only sometimes it's not convenient. Like at work, for instance.'

B: 'You shouldn't do such a boring job.'

JS: 'Is being gay a full-time job, do you think?'

R: 'Well, I think you're aware of it all the time. I mean, wherever I go I'm half on the lookout. I think all gay people are . . . It's because we've been kept down for so long people have had to be so hole-and-corner about these things.'

S: 'Show me the hole, I'll find the corner.' Laughter.

B: 'Oh do be serious. I think what Roddy says is very important.'

R: 'Yes. I mean, I don't go out every night thinking I'm going to find Mr Right.'

S (tart): 'You're supposed to have done that seven years ago.'

R: 'You know what I mean. I think all gays are terrible romantics. We always dwell on the one that got away.'

B (sings): 'The night is bitter, the stars have lost their glitter, and all because of the man that got away.'

A: 'I know what you mean. You think of all the times you've exchanged a meaningful glance in the street, or you almost spoke to somebody in a pub . . .'

R: 'The worst thing I know is when you go into a cottage and it's full of awful old men brandishing their cocks at you like swords, and you come out feeling disgusted and as you're on your way out, the most beautiful boy goes in. You can't turn round and follow him in.'

S: 'Why not? I would.'

B: 'You'll finish up in the Sunday papers.'

A: 'Vice queen of Tooting Bec.'

S: 'I think gay people are more honest . . . That's why we're promiscuous. Most married straight people'd give their right . . . ball to be able to do what gay boys do.'

R: 'Are we going to eat tonight, or have Brian and Alan come to breakfast?'

S: 'Oo, she's so temperamental about the cuisine.'

R: 'Fucking hell. I did all the shopping and the cooking.'

S: 'All right, love.'

A: 'It smells really super. What have you been cooking?'

R: 'A Mediterranean stew.'

S: 'Tin of shrimps and an aubergine, that means.'

R: 'Fuck you.'

Everybody moves into the dining area. Victorian table, square, red wood; white damask cloth; silver gilt candelabra; a single rose in a crystal bowl; table napkins in white linen with ivory carved rings. Heavy imitation Georgian cutlery. Crystal goblet about eight inches high. A lamp which is a false oil-lamp surmounted by a shade in red satin, which casts a rosy glow over the table. The other lights are extinguished. A great green half-dissolved candle that glows from within and sheds a flickering sea-coloured light at the other end of the table. The rose colour is flattering, but the colour from the candle is pallid and corpse-like. The first course was prepared the previous evening: shrimp cocktail in a sauce, on a bed of lettuce with a half tomato on top, with a serrated border like a lotus flower, and served in a long-stemmed black glass meniscus. Liebfraumilch stands in a bucket on a trolley in crushed ice. Simon ostentatiously covers his glass with his hand to avoid wine; then relents and takes the teeniest drop, just to be friendly. There is an atmosphere of relaxation in the wholehearted enjoyment of the food; leisurely, timeless, a comfortable settling down to gossip. First of all the conversation is taken up about the delights of sex in the open air. Brian and Alan are rather fascinated by the idea, and ask precise instructions as to the places to go. Then the conversation turns to a discussion of the most unlikely places in which people have had sex.

A: 'On the beach at Bournemouth.'

B: 'In a railway carriage.'

S: 'How did you manage that?'

B: 'Well it was a non-corridor. Suburban.'

R: 'It must've been very quick.'

S: 'It's only about two minutes between stations.'

R: 'I don't believe it. You mean you made contact, and had sex, just like that?'

B: 'Yes; and we took our clothes off.'

R: 'Impossible.'

B: 'It was true. It was first stop Sevenoaks. And for some reason it was a very old train . . . It takes about twenty minutes to get to Sevenoaks.'

R: 'Wasn't it a bit public?'

B: 'How do you mean?'

R: 'Well, every time I go on those trains they're always stopping about five feet away from people's windows.'

B: 'I don't know. We were lying down.'

S: 'I had sex on the stairs leading down to Hampstead tube station.'

A: 'Go on.'

S: 'It's the deepest stairwell in the whole underground system. Nobody uses the stairs. You could hear them coming a mile off.'

A: 'I wouldn't have sex in a cottage.'

S: 'I met somebody who said he'd fucked somebody through a hole in a cubicle in Brockwell Park.'

B: 'How unpleasant.'

A: 'It's not very erotic.'

B: 'You wouldn't know what they looked like.'

S: 'Exciting though.'

R (to Alan): 'What was it like on the beach?'

A: 'Cold.'

S: 'Didn't you get sand in it?'

A: 'She was a sand-witch.' Laughter.

92

B: 'I once met somebody who wanted to have sex completely under water.'

R: 'Ugh.'

S: 'Did you do it?'

B: 'Of course not. I was afraid we might be drowned.'

R: 'You quite often find people who want to be strangled and that kind of thing.'

B: 'That can be very dangerous. I mean, if you go along with people's hang-ups . . . I know somebody who wanted to be killed. Literally. And this bloke said he didn't know what came over him, he just squeezed and squeezed . . . He said he thought he'd killed him . . . And when he next saw him, he still had the marks of his fingers round his throat.'

A: 'I think that kind of thing is dangerous. You never know what's inside yourself, do you? I think we all have it in us to be violent.'

R: 'I'm sure I haven't.'

A: 'No, I mean, if you were in that situation. Just for kicks, you can't predict what you might do.'

R: 'I wouldn't.'

A: 'How do you know?'

R: 'I know myself.'

A: 'You think you do.'

R: 'I do.'

S: 'Oh shut up, that's just stupid.'

R: 'It's not. I know what I know about myself.'

S: 'All Alan is saying is that some people, not you necessarily, if they were in a situation where somebody actually wanted to be murdered, they might do it.'

R: 'Well I wouldn't.'

S: 'No, but some people might.'

R: 'I suppose so.'

A: 'Well then. That's all I was saying.' Sulky silence. Knives strike the plates; conversation changes to mutual acquaintances.

B: 'Guess who I saw a couple of weeks ago.'

S: 'No.'

B: 'Well, you remember that pretty boy we had staying at our place, the one who told us he'd been thrown out by his parents? Kevin I think his name was.'

S: 'Mm.'

B: 'Well I saw him guess where. In the Gigolo. And the funny

D   93 thing was, he didn't see me. He was talking to this guy and telling him a very similar tale to what he told Alan.'

A: 'Some poor sucker.'

R: 'Blower.'

[Laughter.]

B: 'When he did see me, he looked straight through me. I've seen him once or twice in the last year. He pretends he doesn't recognize me.'

A: 'I think he's much older than he says.'

B: 'I think he must be over twenty . . . He told me he was fifteen.'

A: 'He was probably about nineteen then.'

B: 'A compulsive liar.'

A: 'But you believed him.'

B: 'Well . . . anybody would.'

S: 'With looks like that he could sell contraceptives in a convent.'

B: 'Well he had us fooled.'

A: 'He had *you* fooled. You picked him up.'

B: 'You believed him as well.'

A: 'Only because you told me he was genuine . . . I naturally assumed you'd vetted him.'

B: 'Good God, what was I expected to do, ask him for a certificate?'

A: 'He was a right little tramp. The most calculating little queen I've ever met. I never liked him.'

B: 'You liar, Alan.'

A: 'I beg your pardon? What did you say?'

B: 'That isn't true.'

A: 'It is . . .'

B: 'You went to bed with him.'

A: 'Only because he practically begged me to. That doesn't mean to say I liked him.'

S: 'Go on.'

A: 'I was fascinated by him. Ten minutes in bed cured that.'

B (pointedly ignoring him): 'Anyway, I wondered whether to go up to this guy he was talking to and tell him. But I thought well you can't really, can you? I mean, it looks as if you're doing something rather immoral.' Hoot of laughter from Alan. 'I don't mean society's morality (Superior)'.

R: 'I think you should have warned the guy.'

B: 'Well I did wonder. What do you think, Si?'

s: 'You never know. He might make out with somebody else and be okay.'

b: 'Well, I couldn't have been nicer to him.'

a: 'And nastier to me. You should've seen her. She was like a dog guarding a bone.'

r: 'Pubic.'

b: 'What?'

r: 'Pubic. Bone.'

b: 'What do you mean?'

a: 'God. You are ignorant about some things.'

b: 'No. Honestly. Tell me.'

s: 'It's what the blood flows through when you've got a hard on.'

b: 'It's not a bone though, is it?'

a: 'No, of course not.'

s: 'That reminds me. Delia was telling me this awful story about a lesbian girl who was having one made. A cock.'

b: 'Uh?'

s (enjoying everybody's attention. Slowly): 'She apparently had a small piece of bone taken out of her rib, and was having skin grafted on to it from various parts of the body.'

a: 'What was she called, Eve?'

s: 'No, really.'

b: 'How did they graft it on to her?'

s: 'She'd had the sex change operation. It was an experiment.'

a: 'It sounds horrible.'

b: 'Delia's fantasies.'

a: 'I think she's gay herself.'

s: 'I just think she's confused.'

r: 'She can be very good company.'

b: 'Fag-hag.'

r: 'No, she can be very amusing. I think she doesn't know which way she swings.'

a: 'How old is she?'

s: 'About twenty-five.'

a: 'Then it's time she did know . . . She was the one who asked me if I was circumcized at your party. Cheeky cow.'

r: 'Did you tell her?'

a: 'Did I fuck. A right dyke, I thought. Built like an all-in wrestler.'

s: 'She has boy-friends.'

A: 'Well I have girl-friends. But I don't use them as a cover. I like female company.'

B: 'That's why she spends so much time on her own.'

A (turning on him): 'Why are you being so unpleasant to me? I know why it is. It's because you've got an audience. He's always like this as soon as he's got somebody to perform to.'

(Silence.)

B: 'How are John and Trevor? I haven't seen them for ages.'

s: 'John's been terribly ill.'

B: 'No.'

s: 'Yes. He had jaundice, really badly. Hepatitis. He was in hospital for nearly a month.'

R: 'Do you know Trevor was out every night? He used to go straight from the hospital out on the troll.'

s: 'I think that's sick.'

A: 'Which hospital was he in? I wish I'd known. I would've gone to see him. Why didn't you let us know?'

s: 'Well we haven't seen you for so long.'

A: 'You've got our phone number. Poor John.'

B: 'I don't like Trevor very much.'

s: 'He can be very selfish.'

R: 'I think all gay people can be. I've met some really hard cases in my time . . . Do you remember Colin I used to live with? He was so unscrupulous. All those months, and I didn't realize he was taking me for a ride.'

s: 'Joy-ride though, wasn't it?'

R: 'It was no joy, believe you me . . . But you could tell, just from the way he made love. Well, you could call it love; he was more like a wolf attacking his prey . . . I knew one boy who had to have fourteen stitches in his arse because of Colin being so brutal with him.'

B: 'Impossible.'

R: 'It's not . . . You can get a fissure ever so easily.'

R: 'Oh how awful.'

R: 'I know it's true, because this boy was the reason why I split up with him. Tragic, really.'

B: 'Well I read somewhere that most cocks are the same size when erect. In fact, there isn't much difference, whatever the difference might be when they're limp.'

R: 'Well Colin's wasn't.'

A: 'Didn't know you were a size queen.'

R: 'I liked him for himself.'

A: 'I thought you said he was brutal.'

R: 'Yes, but at first, you just don't realize. Especially when you're younger. That's why I think as you get older your life gets better because you know your way around more.'

A: 'I don't agree with that. You can never replace your youth.'

B: 'Oh I'm a youth am I, very flattering.'

A: 'Don't push your luck.'

B: 'You couldn't replace me.'

A: 'Couldn't I?'

R: 'I was never happy when I was younger . . . I was terrible in bed for ages. I never used to realize why people never wanted to see me again. I didn't know what to do. I think that must've gone on for about three years. I got a real complex about it. When people talked about fucking, I thought they meant just jiggling about . . . I was really shocked.'

S: 'I think everybody has to find his own way round.'

R: 'Well it took me a long time. I wouldn't want anybody to go through what I did.'

S: 'I don't think they do now. It's all so much more in the open.'

B: 'Do you think so? I think there's an awful lot of people who never do find out about themselves. I think every gay person needs some guidance.'

A: 'I think there should be more gay education in schools.'

S: 'I think that will come in time. We weren't even told there was such a thing as sex let alone being gay . . . If you were queer when I was at school, you were expected to abstain or quietly put your head in the gas-oven.'

B: 'I think gay people have got a lot to teach the world.'

A: 'They always have done.'

B: 'Look at the gays in history. Shakespeare, Julius Caesar, Michelangelo, Somerset Maugham, look what they've given to our civilization.'

S: 'Well of course, you always find gay people in the arts and show business. That alone shows how much more artistic we are.' [Then follows a list of pop and movie stars who say they are gay or are said to be.] 'I met someone who'd been XX's lover for ten years [film actor]. He was the love of his life. Slashed his wrists when he left him. And I know that's true, because when I saw XX, I looked particularly and you could see the scars on his wrist in close-ups . . .'

s: 'I think people like that ought to come out, set an example to all those who are afraid. It would do so much good if somebody like YYY said "I'm gay and proud of it." '

R: 'I expect they're scared they'd lose all their straight audiences.'

The conversation fragments into discussion of movies, plays, records. Everybody loved *Cabaret*; and Simon puts on the LP of the sound-track; they didn't like *Last Tango in Paris*, but are unanimous on the value of butter. Follows a discussion of the use of various lubricants; agreed that spit is the best of all. Brian does an imitation of Helmut Berger imitating Marlene Dietrich, with a tubular metal kitchen chair. Then laughter, and after, the silence of satiation; the evening has reached a climax; an exchange of views on Moulinex *v.* Kenwood, the rival merits of Timex and Omega, clothes, shoes; the merits of shopping in fashionable areas or in untrendy Brixton or Peckham; holidays and the combination of plage and gayness. Then a few jokes. 'This Irishman went into a cottage, and saw a black man lying on the floor beside the trough where you piss, and he said to him "What are you doing?" and the black man said "Pissing," and he said "Why are you lying down," and he said "The doctor said I hadn't got to lift anything heavy." '

Departure about 11.30. Washing-up left till tomorrow. Brian and Alan do not speak in the car as they drop me off on the way home.

During the evening a Shirley Bassey record has been played; her appeal is discussed; they agree it is kitsch, but we love it. There is, in fact, apart from the heart-on-sleeve emotionalism, a message, which seems to address itself to gay people. It says 'My heart is broken, but I'll put on a happy face and the world will never know the hurt inside; I shall never find another love like this, but I'm going to laugh and sing and have myself a really good time, and then, who knows, maybe across a crowded room one day I'll start all over again, dust myself down, and when I find myself a new love that is impossible to find I'll die for it, I'll go to the ends of the earth, climb the highest mountain, there's never been a love like this mythic impossible love that I feel for you and if you should ever leave me I'd die, or alternatively start all over again, the first time I looked at you I just knew, I saw stars and you are my world, I've given you my heart and what have you done with it; but I have my pride, I'll start all over again', etc., etc.; and it resumes some of the contradictions in the constancy/transience duality, the permanency/

novelty, the yearning and the reality, the element of desire for the unattainable, as well as the self-dramatizing and the self-distancing, which is supposed to be the defence against the pain of being gay/human. They have records of many of these vigorous female figures – Dietrich, Garland, Lenya, Piaf; and Roddy says that perhaps they represent a public universal mother; but this is denied by the others, who agree that they are all too sexy for that.

Many gay people maintain a strong emotional relationship with one or more people, which underpins a constant search for an ideal companion, a perfect partner, a complete love-relationship. Those who find total emotional, sexual and social satisfaction in one other person are, I suspect, rather rare; or at least so securely embedded in their social environment that they are totally inaccessible. With most people there is a tension between the need for stability – as represented by someone whom they share a flat with, someone they can depend on/turn to, on whose shoulder they can cry, etc., and the belief that somewhere there must be someone who can answer to their needs. After all, it may well have happened once, in child-hood perhaps; and the rest of a lifetime may be spent in search of it, middle-aged and elderly waifs, inconsolably searching bars and clubs in remembrance of things past. Many people find it impossible to accept the absence of a total relationship, and so create it for themselves; distant perhaps in time and place, embalmed and placed beyond the reach of present reality. Someone who died, someone from whom one was separated by unavoidable circumstances, consigned to the past, sundered by tragedy, by an impossible choice between love and duty, by the machinations of a cruel and scheming friend . . . And in the meantime, casual and unfettered encounters are the norm for most gay people (i.e. those who enter the subculture; those who do not, lead quite different lives, and it is important to remember the distinction). This is generally referred to as 'promiscuity' by homosexual people as well as heterosexuals, but it has become a very emotional and pejorative word. It means, in this context, quite simply an encounter for sex with no obligations; although, in turn, it is often attended by a heavy sense of ritual, tacit assumptions, unspoken acceptance of a very clearly defined set of rules and observances.

Promiscuity is often a product of a leisured resourcelessness. The availability of sex can be its own determinant upon sexual desire. The elasticity of sexual supply and demand would perhaps bear some investigation. It seems to depend in a large measure upon the structure of the life of the individual. Many gay people are aware of this, and often involve themselves in an elaborate network of social activity which gives them a certain degree of shelter from the threat of expanding and all-engulfing exigencies of sex. Going to the opera, dinner engagements, evenings at the theatre, drinks with girl-friends, obligations to family, an often ritualized and self-conscious deference to 'mother', relationships with straight people and fami-lies. (It is surprising how many gay people deny that their principal social outlets are with other gay people.) All these things mean that there is always something interposing itself between being homo-sexual and the expression of that fact, which is often the pick-up, the casual acquaintance. It is probably this selfconscious process of structuring one's life that gives rise to some of the more baroque and fanciful eccentricities of gay life-style. I have always been struck by the interiors of many homosexual households (again the model for the consuming life-style might have been born in one of those elegant and gilded salons, among the *chaises-longues* and canter-buries, *escritoires, chiffonniers*; the pelts, brocades, carpets, *tapisseries*, drapes; decanters, crystal drinking vessels, goblets and glasses, china; paintings, *objets d'art, tabatières*, vases, clocks, marble and ormolu). There is a barrier, contrived almost, not against the acknowledgement that one is homosexual, but against a kind of existential dereliction which many gay people admit to being invaded by at times. It is an artefact, the life-style, and has to stand in the stead of what most heterosexuals derive from the day-to-day necessities of children, family, the network of orthodox social obliga-tions that bears them up and keeps them more free from fears and anxieties about lack of purpose. There is often that aridity to be found in the lives of homosexual couples that may be seen in certain childless marriages, or among those whose children have grown up and gone away. There are never quite enough relationships to prevent the boredom and sense of being functionless. Most families, after all, can rest at least for a time upon thoughts of children, and children's children; a specious hypothecated future, it may be, but it is denied to gay people. For gay people the future contains principally their own death; and this may well be important in the hedonism of the gay subculture (another feature in which the homosexual world has anticipated the philosophy of consumerism – the instantaneous gratification, the imperiousness of needs and wants, the perspectiveless moment). Not only this, but the fact that most homosexual people are not called upon to efface themselves for the sake of the next generation, means that they tend to remain with a concept of themselves as the children of their own parents. There is a tendency to retain characteristics of childhood – a difficulty in supporting frustration, a petulance against obstacles that thwart desires or prevent the acquisition of coveted things. It is, after all, far easier to be more self-indulgent than people with dependants. After an affair is over, if you're sad, you can always go and cheer yourself up with a trip down King's Road, a new pair of trousers, go and have a radical new hair-style, and you know you're not robbing a child of its strained prunes and apple dessert. And then, above all, there is the consolation and the hope of a night out, a new encounter; the excitement of renewal.

The conventions of promiscuity represent a reversal of the traditional patterns of sexual encounters. A more or less prolonged courtship has previously tended to precede sexual congress, except in the non-respectable working class. The whole idea of 'courting' – and even the word has a faintly archaic ring – mystified sexuality and deferred gratification. Its great disadvantage was that people grew up often in the greatest ignorance of physiology, psychology, interaction; and a perfect courtship often resulted in an unhappy marriage. I can remember all the working-class women in my childhood indicating that they didn't think much of it, that the sooner they did their bottom button up for good the better, and who had never been reached by any sexual experience in their lives. I remember sagacious, allusive references to things that could be safely uttered in the presence of children because of our supposed innocence, and which had the effect of kindling our infantile prurience. Perhaps it was because of the diminished importance which the uninstructed working class assigned to sex that caused them to over-develop the ceremonial of weddings. Because all marriages were the same, the weddings had to be unique and distinguished occasions. Certainly in the streets where we lived the rituals preceding marriage were cumbersome and tedious. It was not uncommon for a mother to stand on her doorstep and tell a man to stay away from her thirty-year-old daughter. Neighbours, relatives, work-mates kept a vigilant and repressive watch over those who showed signs of departing from the limited areas of admissible social intercourse. I remember being informed by my aunts that anybody who was out after 10.30 at night must be gambling or whore-hopping. The result was that the affective life of most people was filled with a very small number of individuals. Not many people had access to promiscuous encounters; and almost no women, except one or two prostitutes and girls who were subnormal. But this was a kind of freedom which few enjoyed – and it is doubtful whether even these known miscreants enjoyed it either, in view of the way they were ostracized by the rest of the community, and the scandalous reputation which made mothers tell their children to hold their breath and walk on the other side of the street whenever they passed by ('Never you mind why, just hold your breath and pray you don't catch anything.' 'Catch what?' 'Never you mind.'), and the occasional chalk marks that appeared on their door: 'Prossies' Corner' or 'Tarts for Sale'. And anyway, sexual experience gained in this way never developed further (most marriages didn't either); it was functional, a release mechanism. For most, courtship or a shotgun marriage was what they expected, both ritualized, inevitable and predetermined.

The immediacy and availability of unconditional sexual encounters (and again the homosexual convention has served as model to the hedonistic youth culture of heterosexuals and gays alike) allows of a quite different order of relationship. Because sexual partners are interchangeable – that is, there are always plenty more where any individual came from – sexual contact is made first, and from that contact a relationship may or may not develop. It is, in many ways, as rational and intelligent a means of human interaction as another, as valid as, say, arranged marriages or polygamy. But it sometimes has the unhappy consequence of leading individuals to the belief that there is always something better elsewhere, and at the first sign of conflict or ennui partners may be readily discarded and the search for someone new begins. There is nothing more ironic and sad than the personal columns of gay publications, where individuals of flawless beauty, intelligence and goodness advertise for their counterparts, and ask that similar people – categorized 'sincere', 'genuine', signal their whereabouts: 'no one-night stands', 'meaningful relationship', 'lasting friendship' are the phrases most in use, an aggressive laying down of conditions. And until such a relationship is found, it is put in a kind of emotional cold store, while there is a succession of casual encounters, and the constant hope that from a depersonalized and mechanistic release-process will emerge a profound and lasting relationship. It does happen, and quite often;

but the access to immediate sexuality means that many gay people go through an accelerated cycle of mutual knowledge, and the process of decay, boredom and rejection can occur within a very short time-span. Individuals are consumed, as any human artefact may be, and then the only problem is waste-disposal. And such is the efficiency of the sexual appraisal, the paralinguistic communication, that the meeting itself becomes ritualized, and the means of two individuals relating to each other is masked by the institutionalized behaviour. The publicly shared code obscures personal characteristics. To meet someone as a sexual partner can be as limiting and repressive as to meet them as a chairman or a headmaster might be. In the place of courtship deferring a proper encounter, the rules of immediate encounter get in the way of its development into anything else. There develops an insensitivity to others, a feeling that there's no point in making the effort, no need to bother. If it works, well and good, if not, *tant pis*. The experience of longing, search and fulfilment starts again. And many people who are no longer young rail against the inconstancy and fickleness of 'gay people', as though they themselves were exempt from the characteristics they deplore. It shows itself in statements such as 'I'll never fall in love again, I've been hurt too many times', 'I'm too sensitive to give myself ever again', 'I don't expect anything of other people now; gay people are so treacherous', 'There's so much bitchiness and insincerity in the gay world'. Sincerity is a key word in the gay lexicon; individuals who have known hundreds of people sexually are installed, inaccessibly, at the centre of their own experience, constantly injured parties, feeling themselves to be overflowing with an intense and exceptional capacity for love which can only be given to the right person – i.e. someone who values it at the same impossibly high level as the donor. It is a sort of narcissism, unassuageable and without remedy.

And people go on being consumed; faces merge into an indistinguishable blur; names, telephone numbers accrue, Christian names, which are exchanged as part of the ritual of the encounter. It is an act of politeness to take someone's phone number, because not to do so is an admission that the sex has not been enjoyable; the phone number is written on the edge of a cigarette packet which is thrown away as soon as the whole packet has been used. A sense of one's own inviolable core of goodness and love becomes increasingly detached from an exterior which endlessly repeats the acts of love, a kind of incantatory body-magic that will conjure forth the reality. The gay person remains, in many respects, a child. The idea of eternal childhood is important in the consumer-culture. The child/homosexual has engendered the child/straight consumer: out of his sterility another kind of sterility has been born. It is as though some antique fear of homosexuality has justified itself. The homosexual has a mythopoeic importance in the culture of consumption.

The succession of random sexual meetings is supported by the need to prove to oneself that one can still do it, hasn't lost one's touch. Many gay people tell how they lose interest once they know they have successfully aroused somebody's excitement in a club or bar. The ability to attract others has a central importance in one's self-regard; it is something that has to be perpetually renewed. It is as though every day that passes steals something tangible that has to be recovered; the child who needs repeated affirmation of the love of its parents by constantly testing it, goading it. There is often a disproportionate anxiety about the ageing process, a preoccupation with youthfulness, a fascination for youth/innocence. In this way, like so many others, the gay world has served as example to the whole culture. The homosexual, far from being outcast, can now be seen to have been a sort of prophet and pathfinder. He is the future incarnate, perpetually young, his needs and desires in a state of constant alertness. He is the prototype of consuming man, in face.

A disco in West London

A cleared space at the back of a pub, with a checkered floor; old cinema seats around the border in orange plush, worn away at the front with use. The amplifiers are so loud that even the patter of the disc jockey which punctuates the music is audible only as a friendly tone, a confidential voice at a microphone made incomprehensibly public. The whole room vibrates. The lighting is theatrical; changing reds and blues move across the space, slicing through the dark so that individuals dancing are struck by changing colours, with the effect of magical and instantaneous changes of racial or planetary origin; now a face is contused with purple light, now in a high fever, now gilded; and then, bizarre accelerated mortality, the decayed green of the grave. The people are young; or at least, youthful; dressed in a stylish mixture of manufactured nostalgia from the thirties and forties in a way those decades never were. The front lock of hair is bleached and cut in forties style; some people dance on huge shoes that seem to weigh them down, so that the movement of the arms are those of people drowning in the multicoloured liquid of the lights; cheekbones are painted high in peach and burgundy, with the rest of the face shading into white; nails are painted in purple so that they look as if they have dipped wildly into baskets of over-ripe grapes, plums, cherries; pieces of jewellery dazzle and explode as the spotlight catches them – a pair of metal hands reaching across a groin, a gilt spider biting at a throat, the tiny links of a chain that link identity bracelets – hundreds of mock fetters tethering nothing to nothing; a heart obliquely on a breast, as though it had been gouged and exposed; medallions, lockets, cameos; some beads twined round a dark throat red as scars; above all rings – antique seals, serpents, laurel wreaths, horseshoes, acanthus, Tudor roses, *fleur-de-lys*; trousers hang in silky folds, loose as skirts, buttocks moulded by the shiny material; insubstantial blouses, open at the throat, through which red buds of nipples are visible; gauze and cheesecloth, chiffon and muslin, smoky, insubstantial veils barely conceal the body; an occasional kerchief recalls a fisherman, a gold ear-ring a pirate, some spangled eyelids evoke stormy first-night galas; some clogs suggest sturdy peasant legs toiling patiently against the endless encroachment of the elements; some studs ornamenting the seams of a jacket talk of ancient frontiers yet to be conquered; coarse denim improvised lives pitted against nature; the wild pro-miscuity of style is matched by the warring scents that arise from the bodies in restless movement, like a medievel frieze of the damned; they dance as though to avoid an inescapable and ex-cruciating pain, buffeted by the black wind of passion; or perhaps like the sodomites on whom the burning flakes of fire never cease to fall. Here is the contrived bacchanal, the manufactured *Totentanz*, the permitted *sabbat*.

Our culture has created a new kind of human being. Released from bondage to class, social or racial identity, a pared-down creature, self-made out of a patchwork of freedoms of choice, released from history, without antecedents, freed from contingency and causation, whose sole function is consumption, whose con-sciousness of goods, services, sensations, experience goads into eternal action. We have been mutilated of all identity, so that a factitious and spurious replacement may be found among the heaps of glittering toys with which they deck out the bleeding stumps of our humanity; which only irritate the wound that has been inflicted upon us. We defy time, deny mortality, installed in an unquiet euphoric hedonism; ask nothing of the provenance of what we consume, demanding simply that it continue and increase. We are spoilt petulant children, whose desires must never be thwarted, who exist for fulfilment and happiness – who will grow into old age and death in a society that denies the existence of such things. The real amoralism of the culture is here: the wasting and squandering of the forces within, of which the concern with the wasting of the material resources of the planet is a hypocritical and despairing acknowledgement. Blind tropisms, incapable of asserting our will against the determining forces of a mechanistic profit-seeking economy. The liberation of people from the limitations of poverty, class allegiance, social identity has been simply to feed them to the machine from which it is intended they should have been snatched. Freed into an equal thraldom. The question of better doesn't arise. If the grandparents of the children dancing in their gay disco believed they were born to work and want, these young people believe they are born to be fulfilled. They are invited by the culture to be themselves, but the social context in which that self would exist has been taken from them. They have been placed in a vacuum, at a remove from obvious determinants; locked in unreason and lack of purpose, dutifully dancing into numbness and insentience. They are performing animals, dancing to an altered economic tune, but dancing nonetheless, a ghost-dance, with its doomed millennial belief that revelation and relief will come through the frenzy with which they fret at their body and senses.

And when the dance stops through exhaustion, there are the consolation prizes.

Greg and Nigel, mid-thirties

Greg is the son of a disabled railway worker in South Shields, and Nigel is the son of a laundry worker, an unsupported mother in Birmingham. Greg works as a maintenance engineer for the Electricity Board and Nigel works as a clerk in the head office of a building society in central London. Their individual incomes are not high; but together, given the fact that the only committed expenditure is to Nigel's mother – a few pounds a month – they are able to afford a high standard of living, though the mortgage payments are considerable and travel costs several pounds a week.

Of their relationship they say sometimes that they've got into a rut. They get home late, they're too tired to move, they don't go out in the week. On Saturday night they go their separate ways, but on Sunday there is nearly always a family dinner, reaffirming their solidarity after their wild oats of the previous night. Their lives, outwardly, are measured, regular and without excess.

They love their home; and much of their disposable income goes on rendering it more comfortable. They are avid scanners of catalogues, brochures and supplements, and gratefully take up all the offers of commodities that come through the door of their picture-window late-sixties luxury flat, as though these were suggestions for intimate and profoundly personal delights. Their needs are like an army of sleeping virgins, waiting to be roused to consciousness by the magic touch of the seers and visionaries in the employment of large corporations. Their lives have been rendered easy and leisured by every contrivance – infra-red cookers, barbecue stand and eye-level grill, a television elegantly dissimulated by a Chippendale cabinet, an electric fire casket to supplement the oil-fired central heating. There are lamps to throw light on every conceivable human activity – a TV lamp, a reading lamp, a standard lamp, a writing lamp, as well as an iron chandelier whose white plastic candles and simulated glass flame lend to their Norwegian pine table a suggestion of medieval barbaric splendour. Nigel is interested in guns – not as agents of mutilation, but as objects for collection, and against the flock wallpaper hang polished flintlocks and blunderbusses and duelling pistols. The walls are further decorated with the modestly functional artefacts of Mediterranean countries – an Arab blanket, a chased copper tray, some embroidery of a quotation from the Koran, Portuguese drinking jar, a Spanish dagger – not for plunging between the shoulder blades of hated rivals, but for opening documents, of which Greg and Nigel receive few, apart from demands for the rates, bills and holiday brochures. Their Triumph Herald is pampered and anthropomorphized. At Christmas they buy it presents of leopard-skin upholstery covers as a prophylactic against piles when they sit down on the cold leather, adjustable head-rests, a thermal plate for melting the ice on the back window, although the car is already well protected from the weather by a car-port in opaque plastic, more luxurious than the dwelling place of most people on this earth. Greg likes tinkering with his car, messing about in the house, fiddling with the electrical appliances, and pottering on the balcony, which is filled with conical upturned concrete tubs which disgorge fuchsias and clematis and geraniums, from which he spends much time chasing mildew and blight and aphids and eggs. Nigel, appropriately, loves cooking and talking about food, and they bring back from their holidays exotic recipes involving *lotte* and crayfish and crustaceans from warmer oceans than ours, and which they serve on occasional Sunday evenings to couples not unlike themselves. They are fond of restaurant meals, and sometimes go for an evening into central London, where they will sit for several hours in a place with an ambiance or an atmosphere – under the handkerchief-shaded lamps on French bistros or the chianti-bottles and plastic grapes of a Capri or Napoli, or the hushed and carpeted sacramental places of Indian refection. They expatiate over liqueurs, sublime distillations from off-the-map areas of Portugal, unknown to tourists, the aphrodisiac properties of which they can themselves vouch for.

They are very concerned about their health; and the cabinet in the bathroom is full of healing agents, creams and balms. They believe in remedies, specifics, potions and draughts contrived by a manufactured folk-lore – not the kind of things their own parents used to buy from the chemists for scalding urine or backache – but elixirs to ease ulcers and abate migraine, to mitigate nausea and retard the growth of cancerous cells. And they solemnly consume honey from clover grown in the shadow of a certain Alpine glacier, an infusion of lime-flowers or a paste of juniper berries smeared on charcoal biscuits, in the confident expectation that this will purify their blood, keep them regular, prolong life and enhance their enjoyment of it. They are profoundly concerned about their bodies. The health foods are matched by quantities of products that will help to make them more attractive to themselves and others. Much care and money are spent on wondrous products that wake up tired skin in the morning, shampoos that are manufactured from no less than eleven wayside herbs, conditioners that revivify and rejuvenate with their plunderings of nature; depredations upon the almost extinct polar ox to make distillations that will keep the ageing process at bay; crushed avocado and triturated poppy-seeds, lemon, honey, balsam and white nettle – a condensed and confectioned poetry as well as incalculable investment into research has gone into the products that will add lustre to limp hair, eliminate crows' feet from the corners of tired eyes, enable Nigel to slim painlessly. Whole industries have evolved around the search for the elixir of youth, baroque as a fairy tale, mysterious as an alchemist's kitchen, where electuaries of pounded chalcedony and moonwort have given way to miracle biscuits evolved by the world's most dedicated dieticians especially to keep Greg young and attractive, xenograft for Nigel's bald spot, vibrators to remove unwanted inches. On the shelves of the bathroom, fragrant dust in *art nouveau* tins, after-shave in flacons dainty and ceremonial as a lacrymal urn, liquids in silver cylinders that dust the air with the cone of their deodorizing particles.

Greg and Nigel are happy. If you ask them what this means, they modify it and say 'Well, we're not unhappy.' They will contrast the lives they lead with those less fortunate – handicapped or crippled – and sometimes with 'the bitchy queens who troll round Earls Court'. Then, a little later, they will modify the claim to happiness, and say that they're contented. They're realistic. They don't ask for the moon. As long as things go on getting better, as long as the unions toe the line, as long as law and order don't break down; as long as young people learn a bit of discipline. They have achieved all this – and they indicate the wine-rack with its twenty or thirty bottles of château-bottled wine, the leather three-piece suite, the water-softening apparatus and the Kenwood mixer – by their own efforts.

JS: 'But in a sense, gay people have an advantage, don't they, over people who have children to bring up, and families to keep?'

NIGEL: 'That's their choice. We've chosen to be gay. We shall have nobody to look after us in our old age, that's the price we pay.'

GREG: 'Neither will they, the way children treat their parents these days.'

JS: 'Do you think people choose to be gay then?'

NIGEL: 'Well not choose . . . But we could've spent our money, gone out and had a good time like these kids do; but we wanted a decent home, a bit of security, something behind us.'

GREG: 'You've got something behind you!' He pats him on the bum, and we laugh, and the conversation isn't really renewable.

The whole world has become a gay carnival; whenever those who are at home in the subculture meet, there will be ritualized exchanges about the merits of Acapulco over Copenhagen, San Francisco over Berlin. Certain cities are felt to be centres of gay concentration; trading centres, places of resort and pilgrimage. Even within the UK, some towns are felt to be gayer than others. London clearly has the advantage; and provincial towns are full of individuals plucking up courage for the move, dreaming of taking up their roots, starting a new life, yielding to the excitement, hesitating before the competitiveness of the London scene. 'Of course I shan't be here next time you come. I'm moving to London.'

Brighton and Bournemouth are felt to be significantly gay. Manchester is more so than Liverpool, Leeds more than Bradford, Nottingham rather than Leicester (perhaps it has to do with the traditional employment of places, lace and cigarettes being felt to be more frivolous and hedonistic than the more prosaic manufacture of boots and hosiery?). This may depend on long-term police attitudes, but sometimes the presence of a gay licensee or club-owner can give quite small places a disproportionate magnetism to the surrounding area. I can remember people who sat around in Northampton and Bedford on weary Saturday nights wishing they had access to a car so they could be transported to fabled places of delight and amusement in Walsall or Luton.

For many homosexual men, Amsterdam is felt to be one of the most accessible and desirable destinations. It is reported that, because it is frequently used as a weekend visiting place, there is a flight from Heathrow on Friday evenings known as the 'queens' flight'. Gay tourism, as a significant branch of that major industry, is an important constituent of the gay life-style: a restlessness and mobility that give rise to travellers' tales that have to do with half-glimpsed romances, interrupted rapture, vague, nostalgic romanticism, the elsewhere, the might-have-been.

Amsterdam

Windy streets, cold August of North Sea city; rolls of strato-cumulus lighted from underneath by the street-lamps. The unquiet movement of the streets comes from a meeting of homosexual and heterosexual, on the same contrived odyssey, the permitted quest. Individuals search for meaning, not in the spectacle of the sex-shops and brothels, but in their own sensory and physiological

apparatus, and the way it responds to the external stimuli. It is
not that Amsterdam differs significantly from London or Paris or
New York: they are all major centres of the new physical exploitation of capitalism – an exploitation of the human body that stands in
ironic and bitter contrast to the exploitation recorded during the industrial revolution. It has nothing to do with morality; it is the same
blind, mechanistic process. It is an economic necessity, in the
same way that it was economic necessity that stunted the limbs and
deformed the spines of our grandparents; and it imposes its compelling iron laws through the irresistible and haunting images of
flawlessness, fulfilment, sensation and beauty.

Here all the extremes of sexual deviancy and variation are
brought into the consciousness of everyone, simply to feed an endless
need for novelty, distraction. There is a tension between the promise
of limitless liberation which the spectacle offers, and the limitations
the human body is subject to. The search for fulfilment is aggressive
and intensely serious in the crowded night streets. There is a street
full of ululating women, lighted in their shop windows by a ghostly,
gaseous moonlight, a blue or red phosphorescence, and they open
their mouths and wail, and the uvula vibrates, so that a haunted and
unearthly sound echoes from the cavernous mouths and the tongue
flickers over discoloured lips. Groups of North African migrant
workers are swallowed in booths that promise performances of the
sex act on stage. Books tantalizing and inaccessibly wrapped in
cellophane are on sale everywhere, with titles like *Stud* and *Butch*,
pictorial essays on *The Boy*; stalls full of products called Madame
Orgasm-Creme, plastic cylinders which create a vacuum for artificial distension of the penis, unguents to sensitize or desensitize,
to lubricate, to facilitate, to heighten pleasure, to increase enjoyment, to achieve ecstasy: aphrodisiacs, mysterious decoctions from
the Orient, secrets from the Near East, the powdered bark of a takele
tree from within the sacred precinct of a Javanese temple, the
pounded root of a special liana known only to almost extinct tribes
of the Amazon Basin. For the homosexuals there is a whole literature, novels and romantic stories which combine extremes of physical
detail with romantic and exotic settings: 'They felt the sap rising in
their lithe young bodies, and in an instant they were entwined in
each other's arms, the full animality of their passion no longer able
to contain itself.' These books combine a 'natural' environment
with idealized relationships; there is nearly always a suggestion that

cities – ironically, the only places where such encounters are possible – corrupt and spoil the pure and spontaneous expression of the love which gay people can have for each other. They feed the mythology that the most sensitive people have always been gay anyway, and that gay love is superior to heterosexual relationships.

The daytime in Amsterdam is an unwelcome intrusion. It is always night that everyone is waiting for, and the diurnal occupations seem half-hearted and slightly impatient. And even then, when the dark comes down in the chill city, there is a reluctance to take advantage of it, a sense of savouring it, of postponing the moment of pleasure. It is not until late in the evening that the clubs get full, the gay parts of the Vondel Park are full of shadows, the wordless encounters in the baths where people are often not even aware of each other's nationality, the strobe lights are playing on the glass dance floors, the carrousel is in full movement. There is nothing in any of these phenomena that poses any threat to society. Nobody is pushing back frontiers: on the contrary, the process is a descent into dream, mysticism, nostalgia; individuals are locked within the limits of their own sensations as securely as if they were under the lock and key of stone cells. The people who have come to this city are welded together in the true supranational culture, united in a universal homogeneity of ways of being, life-style. With their crocodile handbags, *faux sabots* – which gives them the appearance of pawing the ground like genteel anthropomorphized horses, floral shirts, lace and muslin, denim and velvet, complexions orange-brown of a racial pigment unknown on this planet, they watch and form part of the parade and spectacle; the careful mannequin-like procession through the streets, the universal carnival; only occasionally a knot of veins in a hand is illuminated by an oblique shaft of light; beneath the crystalline sparkle of lacquer the hair appears thin and the skull is visible beneath the carefully arranged floss; a stomach ripples under some gauzy garment where the spaces between the buttons gape. Here is the real significance of all the rhetoric about the European idea: products of a culture of expanding consumption, spoilt children. Behind the tendentious vocabulary of the false internationalists, this is what they really mean by 'the breakdown of cultural barriers', 'the end of narrow nationalisms'. A far more profitable nationalism has been discovered – the nationalism of interest groups, well-defined markets: and here the homosexuals of Europe can gather, united in a somnambulistic total immersion in a new and magical holy water that will restore to them the identity they have lost.

International gay

It is perhaps significant that a society which has always considered it necessary to regulate the disordered desires of human beings, and to absorb in parasexual or non-sexual areas some of the capacity for sexual activity, has given way to an increasing belief that the principal aim of individuals is to maximize that capacity. That many individuals feel this to be an opening of the way to chaos may be simply the survival of an internalized repression and self-denial from the past, no more than a vestigial deference to the security of absolute and inflexible moral codes. Or it may be that the polymorphous and all-engulfing possibility of sex without limits is feared as a tyranny no less exacting than total self-denial, absolute monogamy. It may well be that sexual exigencies are perspectiveless, immediate and all-enveloping; judgement is in abeyance, discernment abrogated; certainly it is a more powerful agent for the absorption of people's energies than any of the diversions hitherto imagined: the experience of the body and the senses is at the core of the whole culture in which we live. It can stand individuals in the stead of all other beliefs and ideas; it can give a reason for living which suggests an opiate stronger than anything previously conceived; a means of social control rather than a path to anarchy. Once again, in this area, the homosexual has provided the model to the main stream of the society.

Because homosexuals have a higher disposable income than most other adults, it is not surprising that they should monitor their own needs and wants more closely than those with families (however reluctantly parents may make the sacrifices, which they constantly proclaim, for their children). 'I can't cope' is heard frequently, 'I can't bear it', 'I can't face it'; not only the permanent child supporting frustration badly, but with a tendency towards a kind of existential hypochondria, aggressing the world for a sympathy which most attached people expect as of right from wives, husbands, long-term emotional relationships. There is a tendency for gay people to discard relationships when the sex has worn away, and no one is forced to live with choices made long ago for legal or economic reasons; although there are often attempts made at a kind of indivisibility in the setting up of a home and living together, as a bulwark against the fragile and perpetually threatened stability.

Of course gay people are more mobile: they form a disproportionate number of those great migrations of tourism, at airports, hotels, holidays, cruises, excursions, stations. In a sense, the whole world has become a trolling ground, inexhaustible source of anecdote, competitive exchanges and folklore.

And the culture does have its own lore and mythology, its recurring fantasies, its defining edges, aspirations and ideals embodied in story and fable. Like any subculture it has a shared stock of stories and images, which individuals sometimes bring forth as their own. Perhaps the most common is the theme of the Great Romance. 'I met Emile when I was in Paris. I knew it was what I'd been looking for all my life. He was absolutely perfect. I don't mean his looks, although as a matter of fact he did happen to be very good-looking, the kind of boy people look twice at. But he was perfect for me. Fabulous sex. We had sex six or seven times a night for the first few months. I just thought "I'm not going home." I sent a telegram to the guy I was living with, "Not coming back. Tell them at work." Fortunately I had quite a bit of money with me. I'm not saying I had a premonition of what was going to happen, but for some reason I'd taken quite a bit of cash with me. I moved in with him near the Nation, and I managed to get a job with Berlitz, shocking pay, but we lived as cheaply as you can in Paris, that is in bed, and we used to eat rather rarely and the wonder is we didn't die of malnutrition . . . He was studying, only he seemed to have an awful lot of time free . . . I lived with him for six months . . . But it couldn't last . . . It was money, I think, that finally broke us up; or rather lack of it. We got on each other's nerves, because there was never enough money to go anywhere or do anything. Even if we went and sat in a café, we had to make sure it was a wet afternoon, and we could sit there for at least three hours; otherwise Emile thought it was a waste of money . . . I can't stand not having money . . . It really makes me unhappy, emotionally . . . We had rows. I think, in a lot of ways, we were too passionate. We burnt ourselves out . . . And then in the end, one day, I just knew it was over. I looked at him, and he said "Don't say it."; but I knew it was the end.

'When I left, I went from the Gare du Nord, tears streaming down my cheeks. I remember hating England as it came into view. I came closer to suicide, I think, then, than I've ever been before or since . . . I couldn't go back to Paris now. I wouldn't. It would make me too unhappy. As a matter of fact, I've made a vow not to. Too many old wounds. Which is a pity, because I love Paris and I have a lot of friends there.

'Of course, when I got home, I was in a terrible position. I really felt I'd woken out of a fabulous dream. It took me over a year to readjust. I stayed with some friends at first – my flatmate was furious when I walked out, naturally, I thought it was for ever, and I suppose I felt a bit uppity about it; and I didn't want to give him the satisfaction of saying "I knew you'd come crawling back." . . . Because at one time he and I had been lovers, but that had stopped way back . . . Anyway, I was on Social Security for about four months, and living in what was literally a garret in West Kensington. It was the most awful time of my life; but the other, oh, it was the most beautiful thing that ever happened to me, or ever will again. But at least, I can tell myself I have known love. I have known the meaning of passion and ecstasy; and that's something that all these bitchy tight-arsed little queens you see on the circuit these days will never know.'

Holiday romances are a commonplace of tourist-gay talk, peopled with phantoms, images of perfection glimpsed, the unattainable all but grasped, relationships barely consummated before being snatched away.

But even the romanticism is likely to be underpinned by an awareness of its random and arbitrary nature; even the chance encounter, the *coup de foudre*, is often carefully contrived; the grand passion is lived selfconsciously. Before going on a trip abroad, there is no sense in exploring the scene for yourself; heuristic knowledge is no good. You have to be armed with a foreknowledge of the places to go And so you consult your friends, who's been to Lebanon, who knows the scene in Turkey, who do you know in San Francisco, are there really brothels with boys in Thailand, what is the age of consent in Luxemburg, what are the penalties if you're caught in USSR, was Adrian really beaten up by the police behind the royal palace in Katmandu, where did Simon contract that penicillin-resistant strain of gonorrhoea?

Fortunately there are publications to set your mind at rest on most of these things, gay guides, which open up all the possibilities of romance, excitement and surprise without danger. The scene is set for adventure, love and sensation.

In these guides everything is rigorously subordinated to gayness: politics, morality, economics, religion are only important where they encroach upon the process of picking up people. Of one of the Latin-American dictatorships: 'Officially homosexuality is illegal, but it all happens, and nobody seems to bother very much.' On South Africa: 'Ask for details of what you can and cannot do under the racial laws. Be guided by the locals.' 'The Spanish police have, with Gestapo-like efficiency, been closing gay bars by the hundred, and have swept through the country leaving a trail of disaster. Behave with caution, and remember that especially in Spain, discretion is the better part of valour.' On Vietnam, this edition said: 'Due to the war we do not recommend Vietnam for a holiday. You may find that all the places listed are destroyed – and we do not plan to maintain a correspondent there just to find out.' Of Kenya: 'Homosexuality is completely illegal, and is persecuted ruthlessly. You have been warned. African jails are not the nicest places for a vacation.' In Italy: 'Everyone wants money for everything, especially sex ... Plenty of action in the cheaper places in the cinemas.' For outside cruising in Tel-Aviv, you are advised to try the yard behind the Synagogue Central, entrance from Ahad Ha'am Street or Har-Sinai-Lane. The massage salon of the Oberoi Grand Hotel in Calcutta is recommended. Of a place in Slough, scene of a recent brutal murder: 'Not recommended.' East Germany: 'All bars are state-owned, thus luxury, decor and atmosphere can rarely be found. There is an air of gloom and despair that contrasts sharply with West Germany.' Sahara Desert: 'El Aaiun. Get there by day trip from the Canary Islands to the Spanish Sahara. Arab proprietor and his sons are seductable – ask to be shown more stock upstairs.' 'Singapore is still worth a few days' stay. Many international air routes stopping at Singapore make it a convenient place to break a journey'; although the guide laments that 'the gay scene is a little less obvious than it used to be since the *New Nation* newspaper ran a series of four articles exposing homosexual life in Singapore. The effeminate types immediately left, and most of them are now living as whores in Paris, Amsterdam and other European centres.' London: 'Hampstead Heath: Big and beautiful. Can be wild at night.' Homosexual tourism, like any other, becomes an irrespon-

116

sible plundering of whole cultures and civilizations in its need to consume. There is a mythic restless movement of whole populations, in search of predetermined sublime moments; a vain and self-indulgent nomadism that rushes to different skies to find the love it feels cheated of in the home-place, which no longer lends identity and security, but is an arbitrary and interchangeable place of exiled sojourn.

Hampstead Heath

Darkness comes unevenly to the heath; where the birch and beech grow close, their branches exclude daylight quite early even in summer; and then in clearing it is suddenly bright daylight again, so that it is possible to walk in and out of day and night; and here and there in the low, damp places the sky is held in the puddles from recent rain – patches of silver against the dark earth which light the undergrowth from below. Before nightfall there are already people who walk in the darker spots, some with dogs, some alone, a few in pairs. The outline of shrubs and trees forms a jagged edge against a faintly starry sky; by ten o'clock the darkness at ground level is complete, although in the north-west a cool green can still be seen behind the deflated balloons of the great cumulo-numbus that have covered the sky for most of the afternoon. In the clearings people stand, aside from the pathways, in the long grass, perhaps leaning against trees; noiseless, as though risen with the mist from the damp ground, spectral, nearly all with at least some white clothing so that they can be seen against the dark. The dull, red circle of cigarettes glows more intensely as the smoke is inhaled, and the lower half of a face is illuminated with a momentary bloody glare. It is so quiet that the sound of the paper being consumed is audible. Here and there, where two people have established contact, a match is struck, and the wavering ellipse of its threatened flame illuminates the red cavity of hands that protect it, or sometimes the contour of the face of the other individual, which may be the real purpose of the light. The silence is made stronger by the movement of the trees in the drying wind; but the people – perhaps a hundred or more in the clearings, create a tense and watchful, ubiquitous presence. There are moments of complete stillness, and then everybody seems to move at once, figures on some chessboard, complicated changes of predetermined position, a ghostly dance dictated by some impenetrable ritual. People glide between the trees, down the uneven terraces where the tree roots claw the earth in vain; occasionally someone stumbles over a tree-root, a prosaic 'Damn'; then balance is regained and the noiseless progression continues; something antique and ritualistic in the wordless dark. And yet, as time passes, it is possible to get used to the night, to discern at least the outline of a face, the shape of a body, the tone of hair. It is like an allegory of love's blindness, an immersion in anonymity, darkness and silence. People walk their fantasies undisturbed like poodles in the long grass – something sedate, wilful and contrived. It is so important that the dream/fantasy/ideal should not be disturbed that other people must never present themselves as anything but shadowy and featureless respondents to deep, perhaps unanswerable, needs; the actual presence of others is too disturbing a reality except in the most physical way: a conjunction of fantasy and physical need that are exclusive, a fragmentation of individuals to such a degree that the imaginative and physical cannot in any sense come together. Sometimes a couple will disappear behind a tree, and a few minutes later emerge, separate, walk out into the sodium lights of the main road to catch the last bus or taxi. Occasionally a couple walk off together; they may reach the first pool of light shed by the lamp, scrutinize their partner, mutter some excuse and flee back into the undergrowth. Cupid and Psyche of Hampstead Pond. When people establish contact with each other, they sometimes accompany their meeting with a low murmur of imagery and articulations of the fantasy; sometimes infringing taboos about brothers and sisters, group sex, the size of cocks, racial fantasies; the instantaneous flaring up of perhaps weeks of repression in which something essential about the individual has been denied, and which asserts itself violently in a moment of feeling and sensuality.

It is unhelpful to talk in terms of individual morality; equally, it seems idle to argue whether the people who haunt the heath – or are haunted by it – are products of liberation or repression: it seems to be both. Some people are full of shame and disgust and cannot bear the risk of personal contact, while others may be so full of experience and so jaded with sensation that no actual individuals suffice for them; others simply seek an alternative perhaps to continuing relationships which have become tired through time and custom.

1. 'I only use Hampstead Heath for all the sex I want away from Ken. I go there perhaps once a week or ten days. I used to go more than that, but now fortunately we live much farther away and, anyway, I think you can die of exposure, if you see what I mean. But I don't go to pubs or clubs, I wouldn't go to pick people up in bars. I can get all I want there and it suits me.'

2. 'I feel very free in the open air. I know there is a danger from the police, but in a way that makes it just that bit more exciting . . . You never know who you might be having sex with; it could be anybody, you can let your imagination run away with you. I hate pubs. I find them pretentious, people stare at you and you stare at them and there's a whole language going on between you, while each one of you pretends it isn't really . . . But there's something about the heath that is honest and direct; you know you're only there for one purpose, and you can enjoy it without hang-ups.'

3. 'Well I don't want anybody to know who I am. I never tell anybody my real name. Not that they ask for it as a rule. But I always go in a roundabout way when I leave, so that nobody can follow me. Not that they ever do anyway . . . I've got this terrible fear that somebody is going to find out, because then my life would be ruined. It would. I've got a very responsible position . . . I live at home with my parents, it'd kill them if there was any scandal or anything . . . But I can't help myself . . . I only came across this place by mistake almost, when I was nineteen . . . I can't deny myself. I do of course, most of the time, but I find this does give me a sort of outlet . . . I can't say I enjoy it; but it's something you've got to do . . . Afterwards I always feel much better, because I can go home then and say "oh well, I'm free now for a couple of weeks" . . . And then – it's generally every two or three weeks, I can feel the need starting again, and for a few days until I pluck up courage to go, I feel really unhappy and miserable . . .'

Evening in the Royal Oak

A wet Thursday evening at the end of June; elongated reflections of sodium lights in the road, stationary traffic, lines of red lights repeated and smudged in the road surface; restaurants where couples look at each other over coaching lamps and glance through the gap in the goose-flesh misting of the windows; a bus draws to a standstill: people with sloping shoulders who expect nothing. The street is full of people, girls with painted-doll complexions and red berets stand on their platform shoes, and the rain seems to drip off them, impermeable as china figures. Two umbrellas touch as their owners pass, and they spin round to disengage themselves. 'I'm so sorry' and a scatter of silver beads cuts heavily through the drizzle. Breath condenses in the air; but some people still wear their arms bare, part vanity, part sympathetic magic to coax forth the warm nights associated with the summer solstice.

At a quarter to nine the pub is still empty. The bar is in the shape of an oval, so that it is possible to walk all round the same bar; and throughout the evening a steady progress of people occurs, as though the whole were revolving gently, like a carrousel that has almost stopped; and the same faces pass by from time to time. At the side of the pub the walls are lined with wooden settles, high and peni-tential, but with blue plastic cushions through which the foam rubber is showing. The settles are intended to add a 'period' atmo-sphere, but resemble nothing so much as pews; and indeed, certain individuals are seated in attitudes of meditation and detachment, perhaps following the observances of an obscure cult; reading fortunes in the sour amber depths of their beer, looking with hypnotized interest at the few ornaments on the wall – a hunting horn, a brass warming pan, a pyramidal arrangement of plastic palmy ferns and vague plastic malvaceae. At stools around the bar some people have already been drinking for quite a long time, and they exchange the kind of conversation that betrays a lack of interest in the person they are talking to, and an only marginal interest in the topic under discussion – a holiday in Corfu, cookery. One man is already quite drunk, and would willingly talk about himself, but this is always anticipated and headed off by whoever he addresses; and the latter return with a kind of bored aggression to the determinedly small talk. 'I'm the kind of person that everybody brings their troubles to; only I've got nobody who wants to listen to mine.' A sympathetic Tch, then 'I'd peeled completely and got brown again within three days. I thought, hello, this is it, because I was like a boiled lobster, but in three days I was just like mother's pride.'

On one of the settles a large woman in a red suit is entertaining two young men. 'So I said "I'm a designer," and he said "Oh, what do you design?" and I said "Oh you needn't worry, I shan't have any designs on you"; and the young men laugh appreciatively and throw back their heads as they laugh, partly as a pretext for taking in everyone in the room, and partly to display the plinth of their neck and their smile. One sits on either side of her, and she relaxes under their admiration, and holds forth at a higher volume than is strictly necessary in the depopulated pub. 'I think there is something so ill-contrived about the male genitalia; it's so clumsy and asymmetrical; aesthetically, you must admit its inferiority to the female.' One of the young men admits that he's never seen female genitalia. 'Well I shan't set out to remedy that for you, you'll have to make your own discovery. Of course I concede that men have a right to be attracted to each other; but all that paraphernalia, it's too absurd.'

Three young men with long hair look at them maliciously, and one of them leans forward and mutters something. They all laugh. They are talking about the possibility of a general election. Two announce that they will vote Liberal; the other is a Socialist. 'The Liberals have been very good on gay rights.' 'You wouldn't survive ten minutes in one of your left-wing régimes . . . Revolutionary societies are horribly puritanical.' They affirm their belief in 'the community thing'; this is where it's at, where it must start; and they agree that the Liberals have scooped this one from the outset. The Socialist says 'It's only an evasion, because they've nothing to offer at any other level.' 'That's the level that matters to people.' 'Yes, you wait till the economy collapses and go and ask them then about dustbins and cracked pavements.'

I sit on one of the settles. A man, handsome, fortyish, stylishly dressed in a brown suit, is at the other end of the settle. He says that he is a solicitor from a town in the North. He looks at his ale, says there's this, drugs or the occasional boy. He knows which he finds the least harmful. He has been in the same town for fifteen years. 'If anybody comes to me and says he's gay, I say "Then get out of here, go somewhere where you can be yourself." Life's too short not to enjoy it. It's not worth sacrificing yourself for anything . . . especially the narrow-mindedness of a place like B——. I know a consultant there who refused to let his kids do P.E. because the gym teacher was thought to be gay . . . You'll never break the prejudice and intolerance of places like that . . . People have just to get out; there's no sense in trying to reconcile things . . . Well you might eventually, but it'll take at least two generations. In fifty years perhaps . . . Everybody knows what you do in a place like that. I have a wife who is very understanding; but it wasn't always like that. It's taken time to achieve that kind of harmony . . . I wouldn't have a relationship with a bloke. Just sex. Men are too demanding emotionally. You have to break your life up into fragments, and just hope that the different sections dovetail in somewhere. I come to London one day every couple of weeks, and then wander home, late . . . No questions asked, home at dawn sometimes, with the birds singing . . . I've toyed with the idea of emigration, I've a young family . . . I've less money now than I had when I started fifteen years ago . . . Man isn't naturally monogamous . . . Life is too short to make a human sacrifice of yourself. At home I have to keep quiet. My word carries so much more weight if I'm in an impregnable position myself. It does carry weight, with the courts, for instance. People who get into trouble, you can help them so much more that way . . . But if they suspected you weren't beyond reproach, do you think it would be possible to work the things you can if you're to all intents and purposes unassailable? Of course not.'

He takes his leave; it is ten o'clock. In the last hour before closing time in the pubs, there is always an increase in tension, and they become much fuller. Most people find it a strain to spend the whole evening in a pub, if they are intending to meet someone casually. Even those who say they are not concerned about whether they pick anybody up or not, or who claim to be there simply for a friendly drink, are seldom unaware if there is somebody who shows an interest in them. People who have come into the pub with friends, but with the intention of meeting somebody if possible, detach themselves from their acquaintances and create around them a curious mixture of separateness and accessibility. Their stance says 'I am alone and invisible to everyone except anybody who may take an interest which I can return.' They take on a look of baleful concentration or somewhat unconvincing nonchalance, around the clusters of people who continue to talk in the central area; head lowered, beer-glass held in the fullest span of the hand, groin thrust forward slightly, thumb perhaps in the rim of the belt. Among those who remain talking together, conversations become increasingly distracted, as people look through transparent interlocutors, over shoulders, above heads, through lifted elbows, while trying to maintain a polite interest in what is being said. It is part of a convention: 'Don't let me keep you'; while from the safety of the group and under cover of an animation that is elsewhere, it is possible to stare, look, consider, evaluate in a way that would be impossible if you were standing alone.

A young man who evidently does not wish to take part in the ritual alignment sits down on the settle. He is fair-haired, in his mid-twenties. He is clearly depressed; his movements and sense of dejection show, a relaxed indifference that is absent everywhere else in the pub; the convention is at this time at its most obviously 'gay' in the old sense – animation, laughter, light-heartedness.

JS: 'This pub has a reputation for being a friendly place, doesn't it?'

YM: 'Does it? I've never found it so particularly.'

It is almost as though he resents being talked to. He is a student and the reason for his feeling of total extinction is that he has just finished a relationship – the first and deepest of his life so far. It lasted only three or four months; and this evening he had met the boy-friend with the intention of going out for a meal, but they agreed not to continue with the planned evening, because all they had done was start to reiterate the basic given factors in their relationship, which was in any case quite defunct. 'It was the way he did it. He just announced that it was finished out of the blue . . . Well I had guessed that things were going a bit wrong for a couple of weeks before that, but I hadn't expected anything as drastic as that . . . I still can't believe it . . . It just takes time, I suppose . . . But we had such good times together. I think the past six weeks have been as full of misery as the first months were full of happiness . . . He always said I was too passive – as a person I mean – he wanted me to dominate him; he'd been with someone who had influenced him very deeply, and this had left him with an idea of how relationships ought to be; and he always found fault with me because I wasn't the same; I couldn't live up to expectations that he'd derived from somebody else . . . I've always been shy. And I have a feeling of inferiority, and all the things that have happened to me have reinforced that feeling. I keep thinking, what is the matter with me, why aren't I good enough? . . .

'I'd like to become a priest; but I don't think I've any right to advise or help people, when I have these terrible insecurities myself . . . I identify very strongly with my Catholicism; that is part of my search for security; but that doesn't do away with the sense of personal inadequacy.'

One of the pub servers starts to collect up the mugs and glasses.

Slowly, the pub clears; people who were together originally rejoin each other on the way out; some, disappointed, turn on their heel and go, almost with a moue of petulance. Those who've picked up somebody go away towards the Tube station, protective, animated, possessive. The rain has by now stopped; the roads are still sticky and wet. Cars start up all round the pub. We wait in the Tube station. 'Now,' I say with a rather jolly insensitivity, 'you won't go home and cry into your pillow now, will you?' 'Yes,' he says tartly, 'probably.'

A gay party

Flat in South London, lower half of a late Victorian villa that has been carefully restored to its original state – finger-plates, varnished wallpaper, umbrella stands, dado and barometer on the wall; sentimental pictures which tell a story; square clock with painting of bluebirds half effaced on the dial, velvet peluche chairs, mahogany cabinets for books; the ensemble has a carefully re-wrought sense of style, much at odds with the rest of the street, where white paint and open bookshelves and picture windows show the invasion of trendies. Ecru lace at window, aspidistra, symmetrical crescent fronds drooping over the glazed pot with its smudgy medallion of the Esplanade at Scarborough. The curtains in dark blue velvet are tied back with a yellow cord with the fringed acorn of a tassel. Meticulous sense of period. Anthony is an eccentric and even affects Victorian turns of phrase. 'I trust you are well'; 'It is a melancholy fact that the dissemination of seditious ideas is one of the principal features of this lamentable age'; 'There has been no carnage throughout this sanguinary century to match the butchery of our mother tongue.' He apes a traditional gallantry – 'what an uncommonly becoming bonnet, shall we perhaps take due passi in the park if the heat of the sun is not injurious to your incomparable complexion?'; 'Would it not be improper to attend a representation of one of Mr Coward's plays unaccompanied.' A *dandysme* goes side by side with a *nostalgie de la boue*; he says that debauchery with the lower orders is his besetting strength. The party has been arranged for no other reason than that Anthony discovered – quite by chance, you understand – someone inadvertently brought home to him the fact that in a couple of weeks he would reach forty; it seemed a worthy reason for a party, as well as an excuse for discharging obligations to those people you don't actually want to spend an evening with – ex boy-friends, acquaintances who might prove professionally useful; a disagreeable and ill-assorted group, calculated to clash and quarrel with an elegant stridency. He is motivated as much by malice as by a desire for conviviality. And he is not disappointed. His friends are literary, theatrical, television. The first couple to arrive do so a little after 9.30, carrying a bottle wrapped in paper that bears the name of the vintner on the corner. How convenient, says Anthony, it saves people the disagreeable task of carrying heavy bottles of Veuve Clicquot across London. It performs the same function as Interflora – you can discharge duties with a minimum of bother. They have brought a bottle of Dry Martini. 'Norman used to be my affair,' Anthony says to me, explanatorily. 'Not, I hasten to add, of the heart.' Until Keith enticed him away. 'Do I look like an enticer?' Keith is a university lecturer, in his late thirties, traditionally dressed. 'Norman's a poet . . . I suppose that makes Keith a poet-taster.' Slight unease in these exchanges. The doorbell rings, and two girls, one rather fat with a hook nose, the other very slim and wearing a 1930s kimono-style tea gown. 'Oh, very Private Lives.' 'I wish I had, only Grace won't let me.' 'Ah, divine Grace.' 'Infernal, actually.' 'I've been rehearsing in a barn all day, I'm frozen.' 'What have you been rehearsing?' asks the poet. 'Her lines for tonight.' 'You want to try controlling yours, honey, you're getting quite octopoid.' 'What have you been rehearsing in a barn?' 'The second coming.' 'Only twice?' 'Christ,' she says, 'what do you do.' 'Out of bed I'm a poet.' 'What kind of poetry?' 'Obscure.' 'Is it good?' 'Of course not, I wouldn't be here now.' 'Where would you be then?' 'I should be feted.' 'You are.' 'To what?' 'Something worse than death,' says the university lecturer. 'You mean you're not here from choice?' 'Nobody is here from choice.' 'God,' says Anthony of Norman, 'to think he was my affair. I knew he would age terribly, that's why I got rid of him. He had no bone structure.' 'Well how delightful, we knew it would be a positive menstruation of insults.' 'You must be bored terribly to be like this all the time,' says the lecturer, who is not quite sure of the style. 'No,' says Anthony, 'I'm bored delightfully, thank you.' (Shrieks of laughter as he indicates his current boy-friend.) 'I like to see my friends occasionally, just to reassure myself that the ravages on their faces have kept pace with or even outstripped mine.' 'What about

E

the ravages in their heart?' 'Ne cherchez plus mon coeur, les bêtes l'ont mangé.' Anthony is supposed to be witty. It is one of the myths about him, and accordingly, whatever he says, his friends respond to with an exaggerated laughter. 'How's your novel?' 'Your novel what?' 'Are you still gathering material? How much have you got? Enough to make a pair of briefs?' 'Not to fit you.' 'How's your play?' 'Love or child's' etc. It is partly sparked off by the interaction, but in fact some of it is rehearsed, and many of the witticisms have been made before. At times it does flow with the sound of cleverly improvised dialogue, and if anybody asks a 'straight' question, anything earnest or serious, it is almost immediately mocked. 'Did you come by tube?' somebody asks the fat girl innocently, and she snaps 'Only Fallopian.' 'What sort of party do you prefer?' 'An innocent one.' They talk about the theatre, Anthony says the distinction is being increasingly blurred between the legitimate theatre and the operating theatre, both seem horribly strewn with entrails. Anthony abhors the slow descent into wordlessness that seems to have overtaken the English stage. It's only a question of time before we're confronted by two hours of total silence and asked to imagine our own dialogue. 'It's been done.' 'What about *Acte sans Paroles*?' 'The only acts *sans paroles* I like are sexual ones,' says Anthony. 'Oh really? Norman keeps up an incessant stream of chatter,' says the lecturer. 'Not chatter, it is a carefully studied erotic talk.' Follows a discussion as to whether there is any such thing. Anthony and Grace maintain that the body has its own language and that words are an intrusion into love-making.

By this time more people have arrived, and it is not possible to follow more than one conversation at a time. Anthony delivers a number of epigrams, at which the predictable rapture is always forthcoming. Of one young man present he says 'Keith puts the youth in youthanasia.'; then 'Passion should not be spent, it should be squandered.' But he is very tense; and it becomes clear that beneath the joking hostility towards the university lecturer there is a real animosity; he resents him. At one point he asks Norman what he sees in him, and Norman says he sees stability, and Anthony says you might as well get infatuated with Ben Nevis.

Grace, asked about the condition of gay women, says I can't answer for all of them, but mine is pretty good, why? Much of the conversation is a competitive percussion of words and meanings, a terrifying evasion of contact, except that as people drink more, obvious pairings off occur, and couples become involved in serious and intimate conversation; and these become far less witty, which is reserved of course for public consumption, which only those who have no partner, or who fail to get off with anybody, persist with. Anthony and Grace are involved briefly in a discussion about the best word to use for one's current affair; this word is dismissed as too commercial; lover is felt to be too effusive and too often mendacious, boy-friend too coy, consort too regal and pretentious, and they finally fix on 'fucker' as the most honest and accurate designation. But all the time Anthony is watching Norman, who stays with Frank. Later, Anthony notices that he is in conversation with Roy, the young man who is living with him at the moment. And this proves too much. He breaks off his conversation with Grace and asks them what they are talking about. 'You, of course,' says Norman, 'what else would we have in common?' 'Oh, and what are you saying about me?' 'We were comparing notes.' 'You sound like budgerigars.' Anthony says Frank will be jealous. Norman shrugs. Anthony says 'I think you could have chosen someone a little more inspiring. After all, it reflects rather adversely on me. I think one should at least be allowed the concession of nominating one's successor, a kind of heir-apparent.' 'Frank is very sweet.' 'Sweet,' snorts Anthony. 'That's what they all say when they can't think of a single redeeming feature.' 'He's sincere; he means what he says.' 'He can afford to, he seems to be practically devoid of the power of speech.'

Grace is quite drunk. She is telling stories about her personal life. 'So she said "I'm a Sapphic, you know," and I said "Is that a sign of the Zodiac, or are you trying to tell me you're gay?" I said "My dear girl, why do you strike these absurd postures?" She said "I've been repressed." I said "You're practically obliterated, one can hardly see where you've been." '

Anthony is kissing Norman, not with passion, but with a kind of triumphant proprietary assertiveness. Frank orders Norman to come home. Silence, except from the other room, where laughter and the sound of glasses continue. Norman hesitates a moment, and then meekly follows Frank. Anthony breaks down and cries; with mortification, one feels, rather than passion; a feeling that is reinforced by the fact that it all occurs quite openly. He cries inconsolably for about five minutes, and submits to the cajoling sympathy of his friends; and then abruptly, he stops. Grace ironizes 'Well, love, at least it clears the air.' Anthony snaps that the air couldn't be more vitiated if it tried. Then he says 'I'm tired, I'm emotionally exhausted, I want to go to bed, only I can't, because there are people fornicating on it.' Grace says why don't you come home with me, and she calls a taxi and they leave the party to take its course.

Godfrey Levin, thirty-one

Manager of an agricultural hardware store in a small country town. House on a new estate in a town some twenty miles away from where he works. Sunday afternoon in March, misty, silent, trees hung with immobile crystals from a condensing fog; grass just beginning to grow after the winter; dazzling stars of coltsfoot in sheltered places under the hedges. The estate is built aside from the cold livid stone centre of the town. The estate is new; ready-grown shrubs and trees, willows and conifers lend it the aspect of Madurodam; the streets are full of children on tricycles and choppers, all dressed in warm, bright clothes.

Godfrey lives in a bungalow at the back of the estate. The interior is warm and sheltered; everything is furnished in dark chocolate, oatmeal and fawn; a glass table, tubular steel-framed sofa, hi-fi, TV, units for books, a drinks cabinet, storage heater; a painting of the selection of a pope from among an assembly of cardinals, a pop painting of a dark-haired idealized Latin male with a lock of hair falling over his forehead and pouting lips; a *beau ténébreux*.

GODFREY: 'I've been here for six months. In fact, I came here purposely to get away from London. I like it, only sometimes it's very lonely . . . Everything is aimed at the family, it makes you feel terribly odd in a way. I do know of two gay girls in the town, there must be a gay guy somewhere, if I knew where to find him; you know, just a friend, someone to talk to from time to time. Friends do come up from London sometimes. They did in the beginning, especially, but as time goes by they don't seem to want to make the effort so much . . . I go to London every few weekends.

'But you have to create your own life in a place. I don't want being gay to dominate me too much. I go Scottish dancing, I belong to the local dramatic society. I'm trying to get them to do something a bit more controversial, they'd do *The Hollow* and *Quiet Weekend* for ever otherwise . . . I felt I had to get out of London.

I was working in a court there, and a lot of the cases that came up, they were men who'd been arrested on the tow-path by the river, and I felt it came too close for comfort. I was sure I would see somebody I knew one day. And of course I did. One day, there was a man in court who I'd tried to pick up a few weeks previously. I remembered his face; he was rather attractive, and there he was, in the court. I didn't know where to put myself, I don't know whether he recognized me or not. It was a strange feeling. I knew a lot of the police: I couldn't walk down the street without meeting somebody I knew, and they were always very friendly. Obviously they had no idea I led this double life. So that's really why I came away. I did become very promiscuous, I used to go in cottages and along the tow-path. I was lucky not to have been in trouble.

'I suppose I was what is known as a late developer. It amazes me now, how naïve I was. I must have been twenty-six before I realized I was gay. When I look back, it seems impossible. I had a very puritanical upbringing. My parents were Catholic; I still am. But my mother, she's rather neurotic, not too intelligent and very moralistic. All my masturbatory fantasies have always been male, but I always assumed that was simply because all the experience I'd ever had of sex had been with boys in the lavatories at school, and I sort of assumed that as soon as I got some heterosexual experience all that would change. I've got one brother, and he's gay as well. My parents know about him, but I don't think it would serve any purpose for them to know about me as well. I didn't tell him about myself until quite recently . . . We were in Sydney, Australia, and we went out one night, and I said to him "I'm the same way, I'm the same as you" . . .

'I was born in Worcester, and I left school when I was fifteen. I think my education came later; from being interested in the theatre and music and so on. I went into an estate agent's office for the first five years, and then into the magistrate's court . . . It took me ten years after leaving school before I could bring myself to leave home . . . I know when I did leave my mother felt unhappy. "What do you want to go for, when you've got a good home here?" It just couldn't enter her mind that you need to go away to find yourself . . . It was sad, because I had this woman friend in Worcester, and I was quite close to her; my mother was jealous. She just couldn't understand that I should stay talking to her till the early hours of the morning. It was a very narrow town. I suppose it must be hard for my mother to think that neither my brother nor myself has produced any children, when everybody else in the street is married and settled and has given their parents some grandchildren.

'I think it was the strictness of my upbringing which prevented me from realizing my true sexuality. I had girl friends. I used to kiss them and there was heavy petting and all that, and I enjoyed it, but I never thought it particularly exciting. I could always contain myself. It never disturbed me. I remember now – God I must have been stupid – I used to look at boys in the street, but I used to rationalize it by thinking "Oh, I wish I looked like that" or "I wish I had a suit like that or a shirt like that." I didn't realize my interest was sexual. When I worked at the estate agent's, I used to have to go to the bank sometimes, and I always timed it so I went past the Borough Treasurer's office when the young men were coming out of work, so that I could look at one boy in particular; but I justified it by thinking that I admired his looks.

'It was funny, how slow I was in waking up. I did go to live in London eventually. I could justify it because I'd gone as far as I could go in my job, and it seemed a natural thing to do. I lived in a room in a house, and I got friendly with the people there. The land-lord was a Guyanan, and I remember one night I shared a bed with him, because he'd got some friends staying with him, and I woke up in the night and found him playing with me. And I enjoyed it. Nothing was said afterwards, no mention was made of what had happened. And about that time, I used to belong to a drama group, and there was this boy who I was producing in a play, and he used to come round to my place, officially for coaching and extra rehearsal, and I became aware of a very strong attachment to him. He was actually on probation to the court where I worked. Nothing happened, of course, but that was the point at which I had to admit to myself what the situation was. I was absolutely shaken . . . I can't tell you . . . In fact I confessed to my woman friend at home, and she advised me to go to a psychiatrist, which I did. She was shocked, I think, although she accepts me now, and our friendship survived. The psychiatrist did help me to accept myself, and I went to some gay friends I had and told them, and said "What shall I do?" I'd been out with girls; I'd slept with one girl in particular at my flat, done everything but fuck her. It's odd, I stopped short of that and thought I was being very moral. I thought it was sinful to indulge in sex before marriage; and so I thought I was being very virtuous by not going the whole way. I was such a prig. I was rather snobbish and self-satisfied, in fact. But when I realized, I said "What shall I do?" They said "You must go out and pick somebody up off the street." Well, I can't tell you how that shattered me. I hadn't the faintest idea of how to pick people up. I didn't know where to start, what to do, anything . . . I felt absolutely desolate. I knew nothing about how to carry on, what to do, what to say . . .

'In the end I did, of course. But that period of initiation was the worst period of my life. And then, when I'd had some experience, I thought I'd better leave the court job, because of all these people coming up in court. It seemed such a hypocrisy. So I joined the merchant navy, and went round the world a couple of times. And I camped it up there like mad, and got to know my way around. There are a lot of men, not necessarily gay, but who will play around simply because there's no women around, so that's where I really learned to find myself . . .

'Then when I came out, I worked in a shop, and as a salesman, and I had a good time. I've never really had any long relationship; the longest I've ever been with one person is perhaps three months . . . I would like a friend . . . I used to wander around in Worcester, sit by the river, go for long walks,thinking "If only I had a friend . . . Everything would be all right . . ." I think it can be very destructive, to be promiscuous all the time. So I decided to get away from London, because I was very lonely there, and there are all the temptations. At first, in London, I used to go round the West End. Once I got robbed of a fiver, and that was rather horrible. So I decided to come to the country. It gives your life a discipline. I'm on the church council . . . I felt the need to give my life some form; so I got this house. I don't know the neighbours very well. I want to keep myself to myself, lead my own life. I'm still a Catholic, but I don't have a very strong sense of sin about being gay. I go to Confession. I find it hard to believe that what I do is particularly awful. I'm not madly promiscuous. No chance here. Which is what I want. Only sometimes you get low and feel lonely . . . There is a danger of getting set in your ways.'

Sometimes the acknowledgement that one is gay is a long and tortuous process; the process of socialization smothers it like a pall; and sometimes a life can be spent in fighting one's way out of the upbringing, discovering something vital about the self; there seems to be a correlation so vague that no generalizations are possible: the conjunction of authoritarian and absolute principles of parents with a certain pliability of the child leads to a more effective stifling of the needs of the individual – if that means anything. And the process of disengagement from the embrace of the parental values can be long and painful; and then, at some point, when the process seems near completion, a new fear can arise, the threat of that all-engulfing promiscuity which caused Godfrey to place himself on a new family-oriented estate in a small country town, in order to place himself in the custody of the community, which can result in depression and isolation. Godfrey described for me his feelings up to the point when he tried to liberate himself by picking somebody up for the first time.

'I had been wandering around all day and I was fed up. In the morning I walked up and down King's Road, Chelsea, and when I couldn't stand it any longer I gave up and went into a picture house. The film was good and the cinema was dark, and I was able to forget, for a while, anyway, the purpose of today. When I came out of my temporary refuge it was still daylight. I had been crying in the cinema, and I noticed as I passed a darkened shop window that my face was pale and drawn. Would I have the nerve to go through with what I had set out to do? At that moment I doubted it. It had all seemed so easy when I was thinking about it last night, but now . . .

'I walked on, passing through an old churchyard where children were playing in the closing rays of the evening sun. I remember being struck with the poetry of the scene when I was in the middle of a large and almost deserted playing area. It seemed to emphasize my isolation, and to a background of children's voices I stood and gazed in wonder at a beautiful oak tree, the leaves of which were already turning brown with the change of season.

'When I reached the station no one seemed interested. I hung around for a while and then went in search of somewhere to eat, resolving to return afterwards with renewed energy. It was dark when I came back to the station, and a long-haired old man, who was sitting on the pavement playing a guitar, had caused a large crowd to gather. I stood and waited, not knowing who or what was going to happen. Nothing did. People came and went, passing me by without so much as a glance. I wanted to scream out, but I couldn't. It started to grow cold, and I decided that something was wrong somewhere: either I had come to the wrong place, or there was something I should be doing and wasn't. I caught a train home.

'A few stations before the end of the line I got out of the smoke-filled compartment and waited on a gloomy and deserted station. By now it was very cold and quite dark, and I remember thinking that summer was decidedly over. I hadn't been there more than five minutes when I saw him. He was standing some way away from me in the shadows. I moved away; he followed. He passed by me, his eyes never for one moment leaving mine. I began to tremble inwardly. I walked round to the other side of a hoarding. Out of the corner of my eye I could see that he had followed me halfway round. I looked at him, tracing his countenance for some sign; but there was nothing. I was finding the strain intolerable. I was willing him to give me some sign. If only I could be sure . . . He continued to look at me very hard, and then suddenly moved off in the direction of a public toilet at the end of the platform. My whole being sensed that he wanted me to follow, but I couldn't. I remained rooted to the spot, and I was beginning to lose my nerve, but I couldn't allow myself to give up yet. I was still shaking when he came out. He stood about twenty feet away from me and continued looking at me over his shoulder. "For pity's sake speak to me," I thought, "before my nerve snaps." Then I heard my train approaching. I began to panic, because the seconds were passing quickly and in a moment the platform would be covered with teeming people and it would be too late. I looked at him again and nodded my head very slowly. It was almost imperceptible, but I was sure he was nodding back, but very gently. The train came into the station, the doors opened. Without looking at him I got in, and he followed. He sat next to me and the train moved off. Throughout the journey we never spoke or looked at each other. I began to have doubts: perhaps I had been mistaken. I couldn't think of anything to say and he seemed to be looking away from me. I wondered what on earth I would do when it was time to get off the train. The train arrived at the terminus and everybody got out. We were the last to leave. He walked alongside me down the platform, and all I could do was to mutter a garbled "Where?"; but he did not seem to hear. He said he was sorry not to have spoken on the train, but someone he knew had been sitting opposite him. In the booking hall for a second we separated, not knowing which way to go, and then I think he said very quietly "This way." Anyway, I followed him, and when we were walking along a darkened alleyway by the side of the station, he told me his name and asked me mine. By this time I was openly shivering and my teeth were quietly chattering. At the end of the alleyway we turned into a road where his car was parked. I got in, but I was so nervous that I have no recollection of the car or the journey, except that it seemed endless and that conversation was stilted.

At last he pulled up outside a block of flats and we went up in a lift. When we were outside his flat, a neighbour came out. He spoke to her but I could not even look in her direction. Finally, the safety of his flat was reached, and the door was locked. The first hurdle was over . . .'

Karl, twenty-nine

'When I first came to London, I thought how exciting it all was: now I think it's pathetic, I think central London is the tattiest part of the whole city, Leicester Square with the ghastly Odeon and the bits of Gothic and the slabby glass offices and those pathetic trees and the pigeon shit; I think it's unbelievable, queues of tourists shuffling through Piccadilly Circus as though they were filing past the bier of a dead dictator; it's funerary sleepwalking . . .

'But when I lived in Bolton . . . I think I understand something about the appeal of metropolitan areas: everybody at home you could more or less pigeon-hole, you knew what they did, the people waiting for the bus to go home, the few drop-outs, everybody's life was an open book; but in London everybody seemed full of mystery, detached from any boring background, they were all beautiful and exotic, there seemed to be an indefinable potential bond between you and everybody who passed by in the street: at home, you knew what relationships were possible, they were very limited, and most of them, if you were gay, just weren't on. But there was a kind of invisible cord that made London a place of unlimited possibilities. All an illusion, I expect, but it gave an impression of freedom that I yearned for . . . I knew quite early on that I was attracted to people of my own sex, but that didn't really disturb me, I've always felt that life was full of strangeness and novelty, so I took it as a matter of course, and I enjoyed some mildly hopeless love affairs while I was at school . . . It was university that was the strongest discipline on me. I fell in love with a boy who was very pleasant, but who had absolutely no feeling for me whatsoever. I made a dramatic confession one day to him, and he said "Oh well, I understand, but I can't do anything about it." I made the mistake of sharing a flat with him; he thought he was being magnanimous, but it just became a focus for my anxiety and emotion; in the end he got married. I was best man at his wedding, as a matter of fact. But I knew I had to get out of Bolton, I couldn't have gone back there from the day I went to university; and unfortunately when I was at Manchester, it was before all the gay lib and gaysocs; and I think as a homosexual I was pretty isolated.

'I came to London in 1969, when I was twenty-four; it took me three years after leaving Manchester to get to London. A circuitous route, I came via Birmingham, where I had my first job in the Housing Department, where I went as a graduate trainee, although to this day I shall never know what I was being trained for. But I had my sights firmly set on living in London: it became an ambition, an obsession. I rather imagined I was going to take it by storm; I used to write. I got through a novel, and I could see myself being feted and welcomed with open arms. In the end I took a rough job in a big hotel in the kitchens, utterly squalid, and I got a bed-sitter in Finsbury Park. It was an utter disaster in every way. Not only had I cut myself off from my so-called professional career, but I was literally adrift; I had friends in London, but they were people who lived in fairly orthodox flats, and had jobs in merchant banking or were studying law or in teaching; I knew a guy who was on a BBC training scheme; but they all seemed uninteresting, compared with what I knew I had to do: and that was find out what the gay scene was all about. Well, put like that, it all sounds very simple and straightforward. It wasn't though.

'I had this room; I paid about £7 for it, in a big grey-brick house which had about twenty rooms let off in single or double units. There was one couple with a baby, they were so sad, they'd actually taken the house just as a couple and they had to hide the fact they had a kid. The landlord lived a few doors away, and they were always furtive whenever they took the baby out for fear of being seen. She was called Joanne, and she used to talk to me sometimes when I was there in the daytime, because I did shift work at the hotel. But a lot of the others I never did see, and I was there about ten months altogether. At work there were some catering students from time to time, they were quite nice, and a few devotees of the *ancien*

135

régime who'd been there for ever, professional servants, and I used to enjoy talking to them. But apart from that I had no contacts; I'd severed all the others so that I could go out and about and start to realize some of this incredible potential that I'd always felt when I'd been on a day trip and got to catch the last train home and always imagined fabulous encounters if I hadn't got my return ticket in my pocket and only two quid in cash . . .

'I was fairly systematic about it. I went to the gay bars; and at first I didn't pick people up . . . I felt I was savouring it a bit, then it occurred to me after I'd been to the Coleherne for about the sixth time, that nobody had actually spoken to me, and I wanted them to, very much. I started talking to people, and got the brush-off a few times; I ought to have realized that the approach – which was kind of Northern friendly, you know where you adopt a com-radely assumption that people (a) want to talk to you and (b) have a similar approach to life. They didn't, and I wondered what was wrong with me. I started going to cottages a lot, because I felt very hurt by the apparent rejection of me by the people in the Coleherne, and the Salisbury, which I'd always found a bit glamorous: mainly because of the décor, I soon realized, and not because of the clientele . . . I suddenly felt a tremendous insistence of sex needs. I had to get it, and this became a completely full-time thought. When I was at work I couldn't wait to get out, so that I could go trolling. I used to be impatient for the evening to come, and I'd go round Piccadilly Circus loo, Leicester Square, all the central ones; this hideous spectacle of all these men standing at stalls rhythmically sort of masturbating and looking furtively to see who was on their left and right. Sometimes I followed people out; and then went after them, oh for half an hour and then said Hello; and quite often they froze or just turned away, and I felt like saying Hell, you stood in that lavatory, it was quite obvious what you were looking for; and now, all bland and uncomprehending . . . It became a tremendous spur to action, just getting people . . . I would literally go from bed to bed, three or four separate operations in a day. I did the parks, the cottages, the open air, the tow-path, the commons, all the known trolling grounds, and a lot that weren't, the tube, bus-stops, shops; it became a point of honour to make every-body who was gay, as well as a lot who weren't, who claimed not to be, who had to rush off to meet their wives . . . It lasted for several months, through a whole summer, in fact. I went round in a state of exhaustion, I fell into bed at three or four o'clock, then I got up and went to work, and straight after work, off to Trafalgar Square, Piccadilly, then out to Earls Court or Hampstead or Shepherds Bush. At times I used to be scared myself, I could see my whole life going on in this way, for ever; I had no interest in anything at all. I couldn't read, I couldn't go to the theatre, I didn't want to know anybody who wasn't a sexual contact. My life became unbelievably restricted, but at the same time intense . . . I shall never forget that summer, I wore through a pair of tennis shoes in about three weeks. I was propelled by a strange sense of urgency. I didn't eat properly, my throat was often parched, my limbs ached, I remember thinking as I walked the streets "This is me, look what you're doing." I had a sort of split feeling about it, a me and not-me; it was, I suppose, the shock of discovering that I had the capacity for just as much sensuality as anybody else. I wasn't ashamed exactly, just fascinated. Moral feeling didn't enter into it at all. I was literally on a sort of voyage of discovery, and I felt I had to push it to the limits; I'd no sooner picked somebody up than I wanted him out of the way ready for the next; and sometimes, if people showed a tendency to persist, I made excuses to get away, to be rid of them . . . I even gave wrong telephone numbers to people so they couldn't find me again.

'It stopped in the end; I met Stephen – in a cottage, so if anybody ever says to me how can you do such things, I just say I happened to meet the best person I've ever known in one of those sordid places, so what . . . And, I don't know. I spent an evening and a night talking to him, which was unusual, I'd got to the stage where I parted with a minimum of functional detail; but somehow, I suppose I'd really worked out of me this strange intensity that had been driving me on, and I remember looking at him as he talked, and thinking "He's as nice as anybody, he'll do." Whether it was some search for stability that had been the cause of my wanderings I honestly don't know . . . But I stopped completely. There's a limit to the amount you can do with people's bodies. Perhaps it was *that* I had to learn . . . I didn't exactly settle down with him, but we did live together for three years . . . I wasn't monogamously faithful or anything, but as long as he was there . . . it formed a backdrop to my life. And although I've had bouts of promiscuity since then, they've never been quite so single-minded.

'I've thought about it a lot since. It was a way of laying the ghosts of my repressive puritanical upbringing. It was a purge of that petty bourgeois morality that I'd been brought up with. I don't know, in some ways it was exciting. I'm pleased to have been through it, although at the time it was hardly pleasurable. It was an addiction. I've talked to most of my close friends, and it doesn't seem to be at all unique. There has to be a period of total abandon before you can accept yourself; and I'm sure a lot of the really unhappy people are those who are afraid to go through it, or too immature ever to emerge the other side.'

It is sometimes a long and damaging process, the search for identity as a homosexual. Such a possibility is never envisaged by the official agencies of socialization, with the result that many people make desperate attempts to conform to a heterosexual model, which does violence to the individual and makes him feel isolated, abnormal and ashamed. The effects of this experience can last a lifetime. When the psychological discomforts of individuals was felt not to be a concern of society, people like Bill Wexford went unnoticed, silent, subdued, their extinguished sexuality disturbed by an intermittent and troubling nightmare. The function of people like him lay elsewhere: it was to be totally dispensable labour, servicing the machinery of capitalism, and their feelings and needs were not considered to be of any importance at all. It is sad for them to realize that the discipline of factory and work-place for which they were formed robbed them of fulfilment in every conceivable way. And if there is now an apparent concern for the well-being of similar individuals – as evidenced in the great growth industries of education and welfare – it is half a century too late for Bill Wexford, and is not because capitalism at some point discovered a conscience, but simply because more sophisticated labour is required, and because the essence of consumerism is a deep concern about the body and the fulfilment of all its marketable needs and desires. It is hard for people who grew up to believe that their sexual needs were some kind of ugly deviancy, to see those needs no longer considered shameful; it makes a bitter nonsense of their self-control and self-discipline.

But even more bitter is the way in which the liberation from this kind of bondage is threatened by the exploitative power behind the new tolerance – a tolerance that is derived from the profit to be got out of it and which is a false congruence between the exigencies of capitalism and the needs of the individual; if liberation means nothing more than the freedom to be rootless, desocialized individuals who are nothing but stomata, appetites, desires created by an economic system for the sterility of gain, then how does it represent any advance on the cruelty of total repression?

Colin, thirty-three

'I can't begin to explain the sense of desolation that occurs at times. It's as though one's whole life was drained of substance, and everything else that one is is obliterated from one's mind . . . The one central fact of existence is the fact that you are homosexual, in isolation from everything else that you know about your life: you may be clever, you may have lots of friends, you may have a preference for one kind of food over another, you may enjoy the theatre, or making money or dancing or gardening; but at times it is as though you are quite incapable of relating it to any other part of yourself . . . My identity is dispersed in a lot of places, deposited in the custody of many people. But it evaporates at times, and is simply lost in the central given fact of my orientation, which takes on a suddenly exaggerated and overwhelming importance. Exaggerated, because at other times it's almost absent, except in a kind of detached and theoretical way. By that I mean that you are nearly always aware of the attractiveness of other people, you register things, a face, hands, eyes, hair, without any real excitement, almost in a camera-like way; and yet, somehow, all these rather pleasant details accumulate and . . . become food for insatiable fantasies later on . . . When this feeling of utter helplessness descends I know there is no alternative to going out and picking up somebody. At such times, I can't tell you how bleak it is, how inimical the world seems. It isn't the urgency of sex; I think that is an only secondary component of the mood – in my case anyway. There is just this sense of being annihilated. I look at my books or I turn on the television, and it all seems totally alien. I ring some people up. Perhaps that may keep it away for an hour or two, but you know it's waiting to seize you the moment you stop to think . . . Then the decision is taken; it's not that you make a decision: it imposes itself. A bath, talcum powder, after-shave, an astringent lotion on my cheeks because that makes them feel taut and all butch; then a T-shirt, leather jacket, boots.

'I think part of the depression I feel before going out is the realization that I have to assume a false existence, borrow an identity from the things I wear, my manner of being towards the world. I cease to be myself. It is a kind of make-believe – dressing up . . . If I started talking to anybody I met about the things that really interest me, I'd get short shrift. I think that must be why gay people talk about sex so much: that is the only thing that's common to us all. I know that sounds obvious. Sometimes you manage to transcend the role thing, and there can be a real encounter between people. But by that time, I find, the sex almost invariably deteriorates . . . But the actual experience of going out, starting up a conversation with somebody, going home with them, the body needs its own sense of release, and then afterwards, next morning, whenever, you start to feel your own self – what you recognize to be yourself – starting to flood back into you. You think "Oh I've got that dinner engagement, I've got this appointment, I must remember to do that at work", and then you wonder why all these threads that link you with your daily ongoing existence were absent the night before when you felt utterly detached from your own life and its accumulated experience . . . I don't know whether other people have the same experiences, or if that's something peculiar to me . . . I don't think I've ever spoken about it before . . . Isn't that odd? . . . It's strange, how many things you take for granted in your life and you never give words to them . . . It seems to me quite an interesting phenomenon now that I've talked about it; but when it's happening, all I feel is a despairing acquiescence in the inevitable cycle of going out looking for sex, going on the troll. That's an interesting expression too. It has a rather brutally evocative power. A lot of gay slang is like that: it has a directness; perhaps that's why it is so good for one – sobering; it suddenly draws you up, when you think everything is well-ordered and neatly packaged in your life, there's this sudden feeling of everything being overthrown, chaos is come again . . . It must be very good for one, only I don't think I'm very good at coping with it . . .

'I don't want you to think that what I'm saying is a result of self-disgust which homosexuals are supposed to feel for themselves. Far from it. I've no sense of shame or anything like that. Only . . . I wish my life were more integrated. I don't know whether that is a result of being homosexual or whether it's a result of social pressure. I'm not sure that it would ever be possible to find out – human beings don't exist outside of society – even the outcasts form their own quasi-society. I know that with most of the people I meet I'm laconic to the point of mutism . . . I never tell people what my job is, I never mention my family or friends; occasionally we might talk about a movie or a play, sometimes listen to other people's life stories. Sometimes, actually almost invariably as a result of really good sex, somebody will conceive an almost violent passion for you. And then it's endless phone calls and when can I see you, I must see you . . . and then, because it's easier than going out and finding somebody new, you go to bed with him a second time, and then it's undying devotion and the whole works, and the more you try to disentangle yourself, the more intense the misconceived passion becomes. Then it's I can't live without you, I've slashed my wrists once you know; then in a fortnight you're forgotten. I say this, not because I am aloof and simply the object of these curious distempers, but because I've had the same experience myself, several times. And then, afterwards, when one realizes that the feelings generated inside you are not reciprocated, you're left with a residual feeling of self-amazement, and you feel a sort of shame when you meet him again. You either simulate a continuation of the feeling, in order to appear to have an inner consistency you don't, or you avoid; or else you pretend that the *inamorato* is worthless, beneath contempt; it was a momentary aberration . . . And that's another thing. I'm always being treated – usually when I'm in bed and at my least interested – to accounts of a really sublime passion, embodied as a rule in a single individual, and well insulated from daily reality – a sailor I met in Piraeus, a fabulous boy who worshipped me, John who tried to kill himself three times for me, a man who left his wife and children on my account . . . It surprises me that gay people manage to keep their illusions in mint condition, while at the same time professing a great cynicism about human affairs. An odd contradiction. The thing I wonder all the time, is there the same phenomenon in heterosexual society? I merely wonder, because I'm not sufficiently interested to do the research to find out.

'My relations with others? Strained, I would say . . . I find it very difficult to live with people. I have done, three times. All a disaster. I think I developed my own way of coping with being gay at a time when it was a deeply shaming experience. I discovered I was homosexual at Oxford; previously I knew only the concept on one hand and my own inclinations on the other. It wasn't until I was nineteen that the two came together, somewhat explosively . . . That was the trendy nineteen-fifties, the golden age of oppression. I learnt to be secretive, furtive, guilt-ridden, and to break my life into fragments – actually that isn't true, it was in fragments from the start and I never got round to constituting it into a coherent entity. The only consolation I had was a literary education, the equipment to analyse exhaustively. It isn't much use. I simply understand myself completely, which is just about the most fulgurating disaster anyone can be subjected to.'

Theo David, forty-eight

'I shall be forty-eight in September; I've been married twenty-six years. I've a boy twenty-three and a girl seventeen. My wife is utterly dependent on me. Last year we celebrated our silver wedding, and we had a hundred and fifty people there. And among them there wasn't one person who knew that my sexual preferences – peculiar that, one talks of preferences, as though it were a matter of choosing something in a shop display, my sexual needs . . . I sometimes review my life, as I did on that occasion, and I find it very difficult to imagine how it all came about.

'You must remember, I was young during the war, and although my family was certainly not poor – my father was a country doctor – I was very much influenced by the moral values of the time. I went to a minor public school, had to be pinched and scraped for, you know the rhetoric, I'm sure; and thence to Cambridge.' We discover we were at the same college, and discuss our relative experience. 'I was happy; it was a marvellous experience. And I was lucky, because a colleague of my father's had a daughter who went up to Girton at the same time; and we did have quite incredibly idyllic times; I can remember tying a punt up in the bullrushes and lying in a meadow of leggy buttercups and being infantile. No it wasn't infantile, it was light-hearted. And through Elizabeth I met Ursula. She was vivacious and small, with dark hair and green eyes, and I was utterly captivated; to the point of being unable to speak to her for months and months. She was one of a group of girls, and I always addressed my remarks to others, but all the time I was observing her reaction. And then through Elizabeth I learnt that she was interested in me; . . . It was all so predictable. But for two years I was in love with her. And feeling as I did, I was able to work; we worked together in silence for hours, just exchanging smiles; I can't describe to you how closed and profound our own world seemed to be. She was a historian and could be rather witty; and we slept together, which at that time was really felt to be the equivalent of an engagement in a droll sort of way. And there was all the stealth of hiding her in my room; and my bedmaker, who was a tolerant and understanding soul, wise beyond her generation or standing, used to cover up for me; and she used to indulge us and look at us with a fond understanding; I wrote to her until she died . . .

'Ursula and I got married as soon as I came down from Cambridge. And we had a flat in Camden Town, rather unfashionable and a little bit of an affected continuation of Cambridge, I suppose. And we were happy together. It didn't have the same vibrancy of the early stage; but I was working, and she taught part-time in a poor school – we had a slight element of social commitment, not exaggeratedly so. My father had voted Labour in 1945 and this had shocked my mother, and both Ursula and I felt that we were inclined to a liberal radical view, and this helped us enormously. And then Gavin was born, and I became deeply enmeshed in professional and domestic life; and I worked in a practice in Leeds and then in Worcester. And during this time, the processes that overtake you unawares . . . My parents died, and being an only child, I inherited some money. Not a lot, but we lived comfortably, and in my relationship with Ursula – it's funny, I always called her Ursula, although it's rather a mouthful – we became comfortable, and then, I'm sorry to say, completely mechanical, and then indifferent. This is over a long period, you must remember. You can pass a long time in review and say "That happened," but by such small degrees that you probably couldn't trace the subtle changes. And for many years up to the age of forty I suppose I was restless. I felt I wanted to move, to leave medicine, change my style of living, go away. She used to mock it rather and call it middle-aged wanderlust.

'I never had another woman. I suppose the intensity of what I felt for her had set a tone for my life that I expected to be maintained. And I suppose I've never recovered from the "every fair from fair sometimes declines"; and I resented the decline of our happiness; and who is there to blame for one's resentment but the person who

143

appears to be the source of the happiness, and then the source of its extinction? I wasn't very kind to her.

'And throughout my thirties I was aware of an interest in young men. No more than a fleeting and immediately suppressed fascination. As Gavin grew up and brought his friends to the house, they became gradually more interesting as they grew older. And I used sometimes to linger when I was clearly an embarrassment to my son; and I suppose I was not without a certain interest for some of his friends, being rather un-parental, and certainly as amusing and capable of conversation as any of the young things who came to the house. And of course, there was one young man in particular; he seemed to seek me out, to ask me questions; he was hoping to go to Cambridge, and I was able to advise him; and I found myself becoming increasingly disturbed and distracted, and in fact one day I simply woke up and said to myself "I'm in love with him." And that was hell.

'Of all the things that I'd doubted – and I've been a fairly sceptical person – my sexuality was the only thing that hadn't occurred to me. Of course, I at once put myself at a great remove from all contact with the boy. I could not deal with such a situation. But it's something I'm constantly aware of; wherever I go; even professionally. I'm living a nightmare at the moment.

'I can find all sorts of rationalization. I did love Ursula so passionately, I know that I could never achieve such another relationship with a woman; and whether the disappointment at that caused me to turn to males. I'm seldom attracted by women these days . . . How to account for it? Why should it have lain dormant all these years? Was it always there, was I in the first place attracted to a quality of androgyny in my wife in the first place? No . . . It's been a time-bomb. I feel ashamed and embittered. I don't want to make a nonsense of my past life by putting an end to my relationship with my wife, but I don't see how I'm to get through the next twenty years or so without some means of self-expression . . .'

Michael, thirty-two

Lives in East London, in a half-derelict shop that he has turned into an antique shop, an unpromising, uncommercial enterprise; a few objects for sale in the sparsely filled window, a phonograph, a

Chippendale chair, some dried grasses in a glazed Victorian pot.

'I don't enjoy being gay. I find it inconvenient and unrewarding. I'm not happy and I find it impossible to have any relationship beyond that of affection with people. To cuddle people is as much as I want to do, but, not surprisingly, most people get cross when they find this is the limit of your ability to express what you feel for them. I would have liked to have a normal life, whatever that means. I know a few married couples who are happy; not many, but a few. I don't know of any homosexual relationships that have lasted . . . They all seem so . . . unequal. One brings in the money and the other brings in the sex, so to speak.

'I think I had my sexual development crushed by my parents. Although they were always quarrelling, I think in fact, she colluded with him to destroy both me and my sister. I was brought up in an atmosphere of extreme violence . . . I can remember Sunday tea, there was celery in the celery jar, the winkles neatly laid out in a dish and a pin for getting them out; then all of a sudden my father would seize hold of the tablecloth and the whole lot would go flying in the air. Then everybody just fled, like holidaymakers in a storm.

'I still resent my parents and what they did to me. My father's dead now, so I know that resentment is even more futile than it was when he was alive. But I can't deny it; it's still there, choking, suffocating. My mother too. I find that I resent her just as much as I always did; more in fact. Now she's taken refuge in old age, like an asylum. I feel sorry for her as an old lady, but not because she's my mother.

'It's funny, they filled me with the idea of how clever I was, right from the start, and then proceeded to deny me any way of expressing it. I was never allowed to do the things which my intelligence craved. I was not allowed to play the piano, or to study music; we couldn't afford this, there wasn't enough room in the house for that; all untrue . . . I'm not quite sure whether I was really the son of my father or not. That might explain a great deal. Doesn't help me, but it might explain. There was something strange about the circumstances of my birth; my survival is perhaps the strangest . . . My mother was on the verge of a nervous breakdown – whatever that means – and she's stayed there ever since . . . They always are, mothers, perched on the edge of a nervous breakdown like houses on the side of a cliff . . . And he had left home at the time. And at my father's funeral his brother was at her side, I don't know if it was true or not . . . But in any case, I shall never know now. It seems strange that my father may still be living when I think of him as in his grave. And that is precisely as I do think of him; without any feeling; but in his grave.

'I know that the effect of whatever drama it was they were playing on me, my father left me with a desire to murder in place of sex. And that is unacceptable. The only way I can achieve satisfaction is through extreme cruelty. It's very unfortunate. It means that one always wants to destroy the object of one's love. That's why I say that cuddling is as far as I can go. Why should I be glad about that? Why should I be glad to be gay?

'I left school when I was sixteen, simply to get away from the situation at home. I went to London; I got a job in a hospital laboratory. I had no idea that I was homosexual at the time. All I knew was that I was pursued by these images of my childhood. I always have been. I still have nightmares every night about my father and what he did to me. I've never been able to sleep, because I've always dreaded sleep . . . I've always put off going to sleep to the latest possible moment, because of what I knew I'd find there. It was the one place where he could always find me; where I wasn't in control; where I reverted to being the child I've never ceased to be.

'The people where I first worked were very good to me. I had a relationship with a girl, and we tried to make it together, unsuccessfully. And it was funny, at the same time I had a friend who had a big American car and he used to take me out to working men's clubs and pubs and he gave me cigarettes and tried to get me drunk, which wasn't difficult in those days. Still isn't . . . And I used to give these cigarettes to my girl-friend, and she said "Do you think he is Good for You?" And I didn't know what on earth she meant. I think I was the last person to know about being gay. Everybody else seemed to have been aware of it for ages. I feel they might have had the charity to inform me, if it was all so obvious . . .

'Eventually I did break down . . . I just got home one night and I sat and cried for about six hours. And I thought "That can't be right," and I went to bed, and the next morning when I got up I felt I didn't want to talk to anybody. I went to work and spoke to nobody all morning. And then somebody eventually spoke to me and I burst into tears again. So I got sort of taken to the doctor, and she was very brusque and said "Well what are you here for?" And I just started crying again. She became very kind and solicitous then, and

146

said "You'd better see a psychiatrist." So I duly did, and he said "I think you'd better come into hospital." I couldn't see why, only I was aware that something was drastically wrong, so I did as he said. I stayed there fourteen months. June 18th 1960. It was three o'clock. I remember it very well indeed. It was a very leisurely existence, but I had the misfortune to fall in love with Hugh, who was in one of the wards upstairs. A very nasty piece of work he was. He was very beautiful, and knew it; and he boasted that two people had already committed suicide on his account. I don't know what his score must be by now, probably quite impressive, but I'm thankful not to be among their number. He used to take delight in making people fall in love with him. To no purpose but some strange gratification of his own . . . Anyway, it worked with me. I met a lot of good people there, and we all shared a house for a time when I came out; although that was very fragile and given the composition of the household, not destined to last.

'I came back to London, and lived in a basement in Queen Anne Street. And then I got very depressed, and that's when I tried to do away with myself. It wasn't that I was actually on my own, I've always had lots of friends. Harry and Jane who lived in the house were very kind. One Saturday night they'd gone to a party and I took an overdose of Nembutal. Actually, I'd been getting drugs with great abandon that I'd started in the hospital; it was the golden age when drug addiction used to be called chemotherapy. I had a very ancient doctor, who I used to go and visit almost every day, and he had a surgery at the top of a huge house, a tiny room with a gas fire and full of cats, and he used to say "What can I do for you?", infinitely obliging, like an eager shop assistant, and I said "I want some Nembutal and some amphetamines." Like a shopping list it was, and he was literally so ancient that I practically guided his shaking hand across the paper as he wrote the prescription. And he always gave me what I wanted. The customer was always right. It was all before the time when anybody realized what these things could do to you. I used them like sweets, literally. I discovered it was nice to get a feeling of being drunk, cheaply and without bloating one's belly with beer, and I was taking thirty or forty a day. Even the man at the chemist's said "Didn't you have some of these yesterday?", and I said "Yes," and he said "Well, what have you done with them?" and I said I'd lost them or the cat had eaten them or something . . .

'At this time life seemed as though it would carry on like that indefinitely. I was still hopelessly in love with Hugh, I was on National Assistance, there really didn't seem to be anything to live for. There still doesn't, but it no longer seems such a catastrophic issue. I was taking so many of these drugs, so naturally I didn't eat, and I don't think I was very clean, and so this Saturday night I'd got a great store of Nembutal stored up, so I put *Lucia di Lammermoor* on the record player and took the lot. In fact, if I hadn't been so used to taking the things, the dose I took would certainly have been lethal . . .

'Anyway, Harry and Jane came back from the party early because it was boring, and they got me into the Middlesex just as I was losing consciousness. I think I was out for about four days; and the next thing I remember was my parents turning up and I heard my father asking the nurse "Will he live?" and she said "If he lives through the night he'll have a chance." And so, being a prudent and thrifty man, my father went home on his day return. Anyway, I appear to have lived, after a fashion, although I fear I may have actually damaged my brain somewhat. I feel less alert and creative than I did before that happened . . . The next thing I remember was the chaplain – who seemed to be dressed in a brown sack with a cord tied round the middle – accompanied me to the police station, because at that time suicide was considered a criminal offence. What kind of a society is it, you may wonder, that is so unbearable that people who try to leave it by the shortest route are regarded as criminal? Anyway, I think the police were quite nice about it; and I was put on a train for some reason to my aunt's in Southampton. And I hadn't been in her house for more than half an hour when they came and drove me off to the local loony bin and slapped a twenty-eight-day order on me. It was horrible. I was in there six weeks, and none of the family came anywhere near me. It was degrading. When I went into the hospital I was asked, rather perfunctorily, "You're homosexual, aren't you?" and I'd never had it put to me quite like that before, and they said "Will you be able to contain yourself in a ward full of men?" . . . Well, if you had seen the poor wrecks of humanity who peopled that ward, their manhood was precisely what they had been robbed of. I was quite interested that an institution that claimed to have some thin connection with mental health should have been so crude and degrading. It was worse than a prison or the army. The lavatories were very low, no wooden seats, no doors . . . It was the most disagreeable experience of the many many very disagreeable experiences in my life . . .

'I remember when I was let out, I ran down the hill, and I got a bus and just disappeared. I went to stay with somebody I knew in Birmingham, because I wanted to hide. And when I eventually rang up my aunt, she said "We've been worried sick about you." But I was literally scared that they could just shove me back inside, so for ages I wouldn't let them know where I was.

'I've had a better relationship with my cats than I've had with my family. At least the cats haven't tried to destroy me. I think the question of being homosexual isn't a question of being happy or unhappy about it; you can't separate it from the other strands of your life. It's just part of a complete situation. It's like a preference in food or a taste for nineteenth-century opera, you accept the conventions. It's always there, but it doesn't necessarily come to the surface all the time. I can see no reason to conceal it – I can see no reason to conceal anything, except for strategic reasons occasionally, one's date of birth. I don't want to go round and proclaim my gayness. I see no reason why it shouldn't appear as you get to know people, gradually, just as your other characteristics might. If I've been unhappy, it's not *because* of being homosexual; that's all too simple. I'm afraid the whole process of interaction and relationships with other people is much more complicated than the idea of liberation allows. I can't reverse what my father did to me, nor can I dispel the residue that relationship bequeathed. I don't believe in instant conversions to liberation any more than I believe in other mystical instantaneous processes.'

Bri Corbett, forty-three

Small, balding. Has lived in a South London suburb that has declined over the past forty years, so that it is now an area primarily of transients and immigrants. He lives with his mother and father, who are both now in their mid-seventies. 'It's not a very nice area. I'd like to have a place of my own, where I could have friends in, have coffee evenings and so on . . . But if I take anybody home, it's not long before one of them puts their head round the door and asks if we want a cup of coffee. And my bedroom's so small, it would make them suspicious if I took anybody there . . . I feel a responsibility towards my parents; they brought me up, and now they rely on me utterly. I don't think they'd understand, if anything happened it'd kill them. That's why I don't run any risks, cottages and so on . . . I don't pick up many people now. I go to Morocco twice a year and I save it all up for then. I like boys, you see, younger people, and there's no way of getting to know them here . . . I mean, you can go to swimming baths and that, but it is dangerous . . . As soon as I get to Tangier I go down to the beach and there's always a boy, you know he'll stick to you till the day you go, and make you feel you're the only one. You say "I'll be in such a bar at such a time," and he'll be there. You ask to meet him at night, eleven o'clock, twelve o'clock. He always turns up. Of course you have to pay; you expect to pay. But it's worth it. Once you've got a boy, the others'll leave you alone, they won't bother you. I sometimes wonder if I might bring one back to London, although you can't keep them if you do that – they go off with a girl and get married. I know people who've been terribly disappointed doing that. But they do know the art of making you feel good . . . Although last time, near the end of my stay, I was sitting with him in a restaurant, and he had his eye on this American sitting a few tables away. He was already making arrangements for when I'd gone . . . It's frustrating, but it's worth waiting the six months for . . . I'm due for my next trip in five weeks' time.

'I have got friends, gay friends, people to go out with. Not for sex though. It's a bit of a handicap, liking boys . . . I do two jobs, one nine to five, then an evening job, to be able to pay for my holidays . . . I did have a friend once . . . seven years it lasted. When I was about twenty, I went to help with a fretwork class in Bermondsey, and of course, the inevitable happened. This boy was about twelve then; but I used to take him out, cinema, holidays. It was wonderful. I had his parents' blessing, of course. I suppose that was the nearest I ever came to being in love, but it wasn't satisfactory . . . He never loved me like I loved him. He was grateful to me. I used to buy things for him, I bought him his first pair of long trousers. In the end he got a girl-friend . . . We went on holiday together, and he said to me "Bri, it can't go on, we shan't be able to see so much of each other." I knew it had to happen, but it hurts. I think we agreed to meet now and again . . . When we got back, one night we went to the pictures, and I always used to get on the bus and go as far as the Bricklayers' Arms, then I had to get off to get the last bus back home. And as I was getting up to go, he said "I can't see you any more." And I never saw him again from that day. That was fifteen years ago. Since then I haven't had any very close friendship.

'I don't know why I'm like I am. I don't think it gets you anywhere, wondering about it . . . My mother's always been the boss . . . In fact, my Dad can hardly read or write. He was a coalman when he used to work, but of course he retired a long time ago . . . He had a horse and cart, as a matter of fact . . . I think I've always known I was this way . . . Even when I was ten, I used to go into the park, and I met a bloke there and I used to sit under the arbour sort of thing, and put my hand in his pocket and play with him . . . I used to go every Saturday . . . Then it got so that I went two or three times a week. I knew I liked it. I think there's a lot of rubbish talked about children being seduced . . . I mean, it could damage them if it was done against their will, but that wasn't the case with me at all. I used to enjoy it . . . I remember one day I was walking down Brixton Hill with him, and I saw my father's horse and cart. I said to him "Here's my Dad." He stops his cart and says "Where do you think you're going?" I said "This man's taking me to the pictures." He says "Oh no he's not. Get home to your mother, you." I think the chap just bolted. I never saw him again.

'I'm not happy and I'm not unhappy. I do the washing and the shopping and cleaning for my parents. They depend on me. I'm all they've got. I had a brother who died not long ago. I've got a sister living in the Midlands, but she's not really interested. I don't complain. I'm only doing what I have to do. My mother has been in and out of hospital. Perhaps my turn will come . . . Of course the street has gone downhill . . . I'm not prejudiced, but my parents are. We quite often have arguments about it, but they're too old to change . . . I've never voted in my life. Nor have my parents. If I did I'd vote Conservative.'

Mr Beattie, fifties

A schoolteacher. Whitish hair, traditional schoolmaster style of dress – grey-ribbed jersey, sportscoat with pens in top pocket, black elastic-sided shoes, brown trousers. Lives with relatives in an orthodox suburban area. 'My life is completely binary. I've always accepted the need for duality, just as one is dual inside the family and outside. When I want sex, I simply stay in London after school and visit the cottages. I go to the obscure ones or ones in public libraries; that way you get to know some of the people who visit regularly, and you can make acquaintances quite easily. I've never lived with anyone, the question has never arisen. I don't think you can in my profession. Well you can if you're young, in the inner London areas, but not beyond that. I come from a teaching family. I didn't have any difficulty in accepting myself. I went in the army, and that is where I found myself, and discovered what I really wanted. I enjoy going to the cottages, because you never know who you're going to meet there . . . I was in the Middle East during the war, and I think I was there long enough to let the fatalism of Islam affect me. Today, tomorrow perhaps . . . I lead a quite separate life as a homosexual from my professional life. They simply don't meet. I become another person. Of course, one has to be careful at work, in the presence of young people. But I'm completely in control of that. I think cottages are the principal places where homosexuals can meet.'

Jocelyn, forty-one

He is an actor, well known on stage and television. 'I can see now where I went wrong. I allowed my homosexuality to get the better of me, in a strange kind of way. So I had to prove myself in other areas, I had to over-compensate, I think the term is. I felt dissatisfied with myself, and this acted as a constant impetus to action. I was always having to prove something. I didn't know at the time that I was trying to make good some deficiency – it wasn't really a deficiency at all, it was part of me . . . I remember all through the years I was at Central School, and when I started acting, I kept thinking "It'll be all right when I achieve that or do this," and then with each achievement you have to go a bit further . . . You haven't really expiated whatever it was you imagined you were. When I was in [he mentions the play in which he was first enthusiastically noticed], I remember reading the notices, and I felt really happy. But by the end of a few days it meant nothing . . . No, that isn't true. There was an afterglow, it buoyed you up for a while, but then it left you feeling somehow that you hadn't succeeded. So it began all over again, a cry for recognition. But what I really wanted all the time was a proper relationship with somebody. I had sex, that was never a problem, but it was rather unimaginative. I took it as my due that girls liked me, everything seemed to be in order. They used to say of me "Oh, he can get any woman he wants," and that was no lie, because really I don't think I wanted any of them in the true sense. I knew people who were queers or homos as they were so picturesquely called, but I think my rather puritanical upbringing caused me not to associate myself with them in any way. I used to look at boys rather a lot, but I was able to rationalize that as jealousy. I never thought I was anything to write home about, physically. In fact I was frequently told so by girls who used to get infuriated by my relative coolness to them. And I thought "Oh they're just feeling resentful because of my irresistible hold over them." I did have the most inflated and banal self-images. I used to think of myself as a heartbreaker, a proud and aloof *grand seigneur*. God, how powerful that is. I'm sure there must be people who go through life without having that shattered.

'Anyway, by the time you realize what has happened to you, it's too late. When I was really well known, I had these dreadful morbid outbursts of temper. Temperament. You see, there's always some ready-made answer for everything, especially in the theatre. But my success – again there's a load of old corn ready in the wings – was sour. Pagliacci, it's all there, waiting to deceive you, there's an image, a cliché, a ready-made answer, waiting to ensnare you. You drown in a sea of clichés . . . But sooner or later the real you may assert itself – that's another cliché, but it happens to be true in my case. And it did. But it needed me to fall in love with a man twenty years younger than myself . . . Of course, you dash off to a shrink, and you start to find out how little you know about yourself. That's cliché number 150. You'd think that actors would be in the forefront of self-knowledge. They're not, you know. It all depends on instinct, because once you've actually got to know something about yourself, it has repercussions all through other bits of you . . . I'm not saying that if I'd found myself when I was young I wouldn't have been an actor. But I might have been a less good one. So I don't wail about it. I try to ironize, but that isn't easy, because, after all, you've only got one life, and it's a dreadful bore to float through it and not to find yourself . . . But perhaps it needed time. When I was twenty-five, perhaps the whole process would have been disastrous for me ... Perhaps a lack of self-knowledge is most people's defence against the pain of it all? Self-knowledge, which most people have thrust upon them as an act of violence in their relationships with each other, makes you unhappy? ... I don't know. I merely wonder. I speculate before you.'

JS: 'Do you think it's probably necessary for some people to remain in ignorance about themselves?'

J: 'If you mean that if we all stopped and looked at ourselves, we'd probably leap into the sea *en bloc*, yes.'

It may be that repression, while it remained a bitter infliction on most people, remained for some a haven in the past; and the kind of pressures towards declaring oneself, accounting for oneself if one fails to announce that one is gay, are increasing. Liberation may be an act of violence which some personalities find insupportable because of the way in which they have been damaged. I met one man who sobbed with desolation every time he reached orgasm, and for that reason would not go to bed with anyone. He found the experience too shattering; but those of whom he asked counsel laughed with scorn and said that their only trouble was it didn't happen often enough, and he should consider himself lucky to have the chance to reach orgasm so often.

The principal acknowledged outlets for homosexual people are commercial organizations, the services of bars, clubs and pubs; the gay scene is strictly private enterprise, and the values which prevail there are, not surprisingly, those that characterize the whole mainstream of the culture: the marketability of the individual, youth, fashion, style, the self-presentation of people who exercise their consumers' freedoms like pets on leashes. It is in this benevolent atmosphere that most homosexuals learn to be themselves. The liberationists who react against these limited and licensed freedoms represent only a small minority of gay people. The homosexual subculture has already become institutionalized in ways that render it harmless; it is a token of the tolerance of a self-congratulatory liberalism. That is to say it is as exploitative and repressive as the ignorance and superstition which it has replaced. Whether individuals remain unrealized and self-hating, prisoners of residual moral values that have nothing to do with the culture of hedonism and consumption; or whether they obediently carry out the demands of that society, pursuing the search for a self supposedly free of all social determinants, and which they are invited to construct from the carefully packaged artefacts furnished by mass consumption: both are in an equally exploitative relationship to that society.

A gay relationship: Oliver and Richard

OLIVER: 'I'm twenty-two now, and there's no doubt that my homosexuality has been the most important influence in my life over the past two years. From puberty till around nineteen those inclinations were mostly either re-channelled, ignored or suppressed. Now and then it would break through the walls I had built around it, and I actually felt that to be sexually aroused by another male was the *right* way to be. This occurred in the form of frenetic mutual masturbation in the school lavatories. Their function was officially, among the bots, a safe place to smoke; so cigarettes were always carried with us as a precaution against discovery by our own schoolfriends. The blatantly crude animal release in a dingy cubicle smelling of stale tobacco, urine and Harpic led to such immense feelings of guilt and fear of discovery that I made great efforts to conform to the preferences of my heterosexual counterparts. I practised my own aversion therapy, by forcing myself to think of naked girls in various erotic positions while I masturbated. Unfortunately, in the background of this orgiastic vision, there was always a naked man.

'The other part of the therapy was a self-enforced duty to have girl-friends. The relationships were either platonic – looks exchanged, hands held – and these might last two or three months; or they were abrupt physical encounters where I demonstrated, at least to myself, complete sexual incompetence. But the idea that I was "queer" or "pansy" seemed so ridiculous that I discounted it completely. I regarded *those* people as fantastic and unreal, as the word "fairy" implies. The limp-wristed, camp theatre associated with poufs could hardly be applied to the urgent and often brutal masturbation indulged in in the stone-walled cubicles of the outside lavatories.

'My last and desperate attempt to conform to a hetero image occurred in the back row of a cinema showing *Klute*. There was Jane

Fonda discussing her sexual hang-ups with her psychiatrist on the screen, and there was I, with one hand inextricably wedged between a tight-clinging elastic bra and a limp sweaty breast, while the other was hooked under a knee-length skirt enmeshed between garters, tights and what seemed innumerable layers of undies. I was also trying to retrieve my tongue, which I feared had slipped somewhere into the depths of her trachea, as we performed what may have seemed to her a passionate French kiss. It occurred to me "What am I doing entangled with an inanimate lump, which I find positively unpleasant, when this would be regarded as the ultimate pleasure by any of my friends?"

'I finally accepted that I could not possibly belong to the breed to which I once believed my own organs gave me automatic membership; but the concept that there might be millions of others like me still seemed, from my experience, quite absurd.

'So I took my A levels, and left the school, from whose culture I had taken my cues for so long. I had freedom to seek out my own identity, but at the same time I was frightened and isolated at the thought of floating aimlessly in a new, alien and supposedly real world. Hanging on to the only security I knew, I kept in close touch with my ex-schoolfriends, and even went to France on holiday with one of them. Travelling around that country, my personal uncertainties grew, until the craving for some sort of physical and emotional release could not be suppressed. Why should they be, now I was free in the outside world? On arrival in Paris, the young American girl in the room opposite ours warned us "You know that bar down the street?" We nodded, having stopped there for a drink *en route*. "You keep clear of that, it's where all the faggots go." "Oh!" I nodded, with a derisive laugh. "Thanks for the tip." I realized that the pub was probably the only logical place for me to go to.

'One night my friend was tired, and went to bed early. I announced I was going out and would see him in the morning. By 8.30 I was seated in the bar, trying inconspicuously to make a small sherry at four francs last an hour. There was a group of French and Italians at one end of the bar, gaudily dressed, lounging arm in arm on the red velvet-padded sofa. They were shouting and laughing drunkenly.

' "My God, I'm not one of them, am I?" Even in this strange environment, my own residual logic thankfully dismissed the

156

thought. I then noticed another French man in tight yellow pants and a flowery yellow shirt, who was looking at me with casual deflected glances. Thinking "It's now or never," I stared clumsily and directly back at him. To my surprise, he turned, looked in any direction but mine, and walked straight out. Naïvely, I couldn't decide whether that was a subtle invitation or a blunt rejection. Anyway, I followed him. Under the awnings of a grey Montparnasse street the man in yellow stopped to buy a magazine, and I stared at him so intently that my own daring frightened even myself. The man walked and I still followed him (a little more discreetly this time), and he returned to the bar. I then decided that I had been unquestionably rejected. I bought some dreadful untipped cigarettes from a battered machine on the street corner, hoping to use them as a conversation piece with someone else in the bar. On returning, I found it smoky and full. I sat down on the first convenient edge of a bench I could find and hurriedly tore open my packet of cigarettes.

' "Have you got a light please?" I ventured swiftly to the dark figure on my left. August in Paris gave me at least a fifty per cent chance that he would be English or American. "What are you smoking?" came the response in a deep, friendly voice that was unmistakably English. "Oh, some rubbish. That's all I could get at this time of night," I said quickly. The man began to probe me gently with questions about what I was doing in Paris, where I came from, etc. He perhaps thought that I was a student traveller who had strayed accidentally into the pub. Beneath the warming influence of the sympathy I could sense, I began to unfold. I began to vocalize every scrap of evidence I had to support my affirmation that I thought I might be gay. At every interval the man would give just the right prompt for the next feeling or incident finally to be released from the depths of my memory. As each thought and fear was made explicit, I felt chain after chain clamped around me snap effortlessly. Being so bound up in myself, I unquestioningly put total faith in the man asking questions, for I was barely conscious of him, the pub, the atmosphere, even the city or the country I was in: the only country was myself, and I was able to explore it for the first time.

'Finally, he said soft and clear: "Can I go to bed with you?" And I was thrown off the platform he had become for my own hang-ups, and began to regard him as a personality in his own right. In my uncertainty, I mumbled, "If you like." It was late and the pub was closing. We went out into the light constant drizzle of a mild Paris night. Wearing only a T-shirt and jeans, the man put his short grey jacket around my shoulders, and said ironically "Never mind, you'll be all right." I warmed quickly to a parental warmth and security where I could be totally honest; and we walked quickly through the wet streets that threw back blurred reflections of the lamps above. Soon after entering the simple functional room, he put his arms round me and smiled. I looked up at him, smiling. He seemed to be in charge. Nervous and exhausted, my remaining inhibitions floated away, and I melted into the warm paternal embrace. He hugged and kissed me, running his fingers through my hair; and I knew at last that this was the only way for me to be.'

RICHARD: 'I met Oliver in Paris last summer. The evening I met him was one of those prematurely dark evenings in August that do more than hint at autumn, and yet everything was geared to a summer that was absent; metal chairs on the pavements in front of the cafés, folded striped umbrellas like toadstools, chestnut trees with leaves brown and withered at the edges. I'd been in Paris for nearly a month, and I was very bored; I'd been with friends but they had gone South, and I had spent a week on my own. I knew some of the gay places, but I wasn't particularly looking for sex, I was kind of interested in just being alone, and wondering why isolation didn't particularly depress me as it ought to have done. On that evening I ate an expensive omelette in one of the few restaurants near where I was staying that still seemed to be open. I went to the bar in a spirit of complete negation; I didn't expect anything; but I hadn't been sitting down for many minutes when I was aware of a young man asking me for a light. I didn't display any particular interest, except that he seemed rather hunched and tense; and when I lit his cigarette he was trembling slightly. It was very touching in a way, because his whole life-situation was immediately obvious. I spoke to him in a kind of gentle and caressing way, and I received the whole story of his life – his public school, well-to-do background, the restrictions and inhibitions, the struggle to acknowledge his real self, the timidity and anxiety, lack of confidence; he didn't immediately indicate that he thought he was gay – he suggested it in a roundabout way, by saying that he had great sympathy with minorities and so on. I asked him if he would go to bed with me, and he said "If you like" in a sort of nonchalant way that said "I'm abrogating all responsibility for what happens to

158

me now." He was very trembling and afraid, and, in fact, I felt more like a surrogate parent than a lover; which was what I was for him. We spent a long time together; and later on he looked at me, as though for the first time, and he looked at me and said "You must be a heck of a lot older than I am." I said that was undoubtedly so, but I was aware of a kind of revulsion that had taken place inside him against his admission of being gay. I think that look he gave me was one of the reasons why I defended myself against becoming too involved with him. As it was raining when he went, at about three o'clock, I walked with him, and lent him a coat, which he said he would return the next day, because he was leaving for Aix the day afterwards. I saw him once after that in Paris; when he returned the coat, politely, like a dinner-guest who had borrowed an umbrella. I gave him my phone number at home, and told him to contact me when he got home. I didn't imagine for a moment that he would. He sent me a postcard, saying thanks for making Paris such a nice place to be. He did phone when he got back to London; and we met in that September and October in Green Park, in between lectures, and we sat in the striped deckchairs, just touching, under a veiled sun which wasn't really warm enough for deckchairs at all. It was very idyllic; and we talked a great deal. But all the time I was aware of a feeling "Here is a young man who is more than ten years younger than you, you can't get involved, he needs you only as a temporary reference point for himself, and then he'll be off, launched on to the gay scene with you performing the ceremony with a bottle of champagne." And so, although I found him very attractive and appealing, and I felt protective and paternal, I defended myself against any other deeper emotions. And that was a mistake; because he proved to be capable of a degree of affection and loyalty which I would not have thought him capable of. And in a sense I hastened to precipitate the end of a relationship that could possibly have been one of the best things in my life. That may sound melodramatic. I don't use it as a sort of emotional escape hatch. I think that I underestimated his constancy, and in some deep way disappointed him also. I still see him regularly, and the affection is still there, and I had an effect on him far greater than I anticipated. It is sometimes not easy to predict the course of a relationship, although you may be familiar with a pattern that has emerged in your own life. You learn to expect certain things, a kind of cycle of mutual excitement, involvement, then withdrawal and finally boredom. None of my relationships with other people have ever ended in stormy "I never want to see you again" resentment and recrimination. They always perish from inanition; they seem to want stimulus; and always they end in a kind of resigned melancholy. I think I must be very defective in passion; perhaps I'm merely over-defended against my own emotions. Whatever the answer, Oliver remains one of the most delightful and unexpected people who have ever been wafted into my life through the chance meetings of a promiscuous gay existence.'

Mark Moynihan, twenty-four

His manner towards others is arrogant, disdainful and cavalier. He is aware of this, but says he cannot help it; he knows that he is called a little queen; but fundamentally, he says, he is lonely; and he attacks almost every new person he meets in the design of wresting from them something he calls a 'lasting relationship'. He is boastful and vain in social situations, moistening his lips before turning on his dazzling smile, and dropping carefully rehearsed anecdotes about famous people he knows: what he said to Bette Davis, how he was received by Noël Coward before he died, what observation he made to Mick Jagger; which invites the response quite often 'Well what the hell are you sitting here for?' He has been a dresser in a theatre, an assistant stage manager, and has worked in super-markets and shops. He talks authoritatively about who in show business is gay and who isn't. 'Oh definitely, my dear, camp as a row of tents, camping his drawers off, a raging pouf.' He talks about the bad language and unprofessional behaviour of this star, and is always hinting that he could tell you a lot about this artist and knows a thing or two about that one, but is enjoined to secrecy. He is essentially in the know, and cannot bear to be contradicted in conversation, whether he is talking about the temperamental vagaries of Shirley Bassey or the politics of Spain or Victorian morality, to which he claims privileged access.

'I'm an artist. I can't be told what to do. It's my mother's fault, really. She made me think I was superior to all the other kids. I was going to do great things. She used to tell me I was going to leave my mark on the world. She told me that when I was far too young to understand what she was on about. I was told I was better than everybody else; not as good as, but better.' He was always better dressed, better spoken. She was related to 'somebody important' on her side of the family; but had been disowned after she was divorced by her husband. 'It would have embarrassed the government of the time,' was all he would say about it. Mark was brought up aware of breeding and manners and standards that had to be maintained, despite straitened circumstances. He was not particularly clever, and when he went to school, his sense of superiority ought to have taken its first knock. She couldn't afford to send him to prep school, but she did buy him extra tuition and lessons in music. He was mocked by his peers, much tormented at the South London comprehensive, and had a great deal of time off school, through vague, unspecified ill health: a pervasive neurasthenic malady; being highly strung – which affliction later developed into an artistic temperament. He withdrew from those of his own age group, and through adolescence had no friends. He had a cousin at Repton, and sometimes in the holidays he went to his cousin's, whose parents had a farm in Oxfordshire. His mother always affected a countrywoman's style. 'My people have been on the land for generations,' she would say, striding across Wandsworth Common with her flat shoes and her switch to keep away the other dogs from Nero, a basset hound, and her silk scarf with horses in a gold ring at her throat. With Mark, Mrs Moynihan was all indulgence. 'He can turn me round his little finger'; 'That smile will break some hearts'. 'Of course, he takes after the Dearsleys: they've always been extremely good-looking.' She kept up her imitation of the life style of the landed classes in a long, depressing street in Balham, in a rented flat which she filled with oval photographs in leather frames of pictures of her father and grandfather, impressive men with beards; she had eliminated her husband from her life, and had reverted to being the child of her parents again. Mark was told from his earliest years that men were bad, unreliable and untrustworthy; that his father had been a wicked man, who had taken advantage of her, promised the earth and then abandoned her. It was an irony that she protected him from the influence of men, and men became the object of his sexual attraction.

Mark's reaction was to profess a lofty contempt for everybody; and when he began work – having left school at sixteen with two O levels and three CSEs, he began in an insurance office, and alienated his colleagues by his obvious rejection of the work and all those who worked there. He developed no close friendships. Nobody was good enough for him. But at the same time he became aware of the need for a complete love relationship. He looked round at the young men in the office, and found them very attractive; but their conversation, their lack of intelligence, their vulgarity appalled him; and especially the way in which they referred to women. He'd always been taught that women were superior; he was confirmed in his belief in the unworthiness of men; but was disturbed by the discrepancy between their unworthiness and the way in which he was attracted to them. After almost a year he left the insurance office, after a spectacular quarrel 'in which I told them what I thought of them. They won't forget me in a hurry.' He went to work in a department store in the West End, much against his mother's wishes. There were angry exchanges between them. 'I didn't want my boy to be a shop assistant, bowing and scraping to people who treat you like dirt; I was on the verge of a breakdown.' In fact, Mark thought of himself as an artist, which was the only way he could reconcile his aspirations with the thwarting of them by everybody else. His mother at last felt she could accept 'his artistic side', and finished by colluding with him in this concept of himself; as it seemed the surest way of tethering him to her. She ransacked her memory for one of the Dearsleys who had been an actress. He paid for tuition at a small private drama school in North London (having been rejected by the better-known ones), but left after a few months because of the distribution of parts in a play, in which he was given a part which seemed to be at odds with the way he saw himself. He was not a character actor, but a *jeune premier*, and refused to play the part of an old man. *Firs in the Cherry Orchard*. 'It was ridiculous, I don't know if you know the play. It was a silly play anyway, and this old man was about ninety. I told them, I said "You can keep your part and your two-bit school." She was a hag; these schools ought to be investigated, anybody, it seems, can set themselves up. She was no expert, she didn't know talent if she saw it. If Laurence Olivier had gone in she'd have said "We might find you a walking-on part, dear." '

Mark's first experience of sex was when he was twenty-one. He fell into conversation with a distinguished-looking man he met in Kensington Gardens one summer afternoon. This man had written plays, and claimed to have been quite well known in the theatre in the rather sterile period after the Second World War. He became a protector to Mark; and his mother approved, because he was already in his sixties, and he conformed perfectly to her idea of a gentleman. They went out together a great deal; and this flattered and delighted her. 'Of course, one doesn't call into question the motives of a gentleman. I think he wanted to help young people, and I think Mark was for him the son he never had.'

Mark visited him in his South Kensington flat twice a week, 'to listen to music and talk about my future'. Through his friend he got jobs as ASM, dresser, general assistant and in the box office of various West End theatres. The rather thin income from this inter- mittent employment was supplemented by his patron's generosity. He died in 1968, when Mark was twenty-seven. 'The only real relationship I ever had. And it lasted six years. He died of a heart attack, and I was the one who found him. I knew something had happened. I sensed it, as I got off the tube. I believe that Harold was trying to tell me; his spirit was warning me that I'd find his body . . . I didn't realize exactly what he was trying to say, but I had like tight bands round my forehead, and I was vaguely dis- turbed. When I got to the flat, I let myself in – I always had a key, he used to say "I could trust you with my life itself" . . . I let myself in and there was no one there, and I went by instinct straight to the bedroom . . . And I had been given strength, perhaps by his spirit, because I wasn't at all surprised. I coped marvellously . . . But that funeral. I never want to go to another one as long as I live. I've told Mother I shan't go to hers, when it happens . . . She understands. There were quite a lot of celebrities turned up – it's funny how when you're dead all your friends remember you. I suppose it's because they know you can't ask anything of them when you're safely tucked up underground – people who'd been in his plays and so on; and all of a sudden flocks of people appeared, relatives, people who claimed to be relatives, people I'd never heard of; he'd never men- tioned them. I doubt whether Harold had either. They looked daggers at me, I could feel their eyes piercing me in the ribs, and I just cried and cried at the funeral, and of course, they must have known. Anyway, he didn't leave me as much money as they thought . . . I suppose I'd already had my share. Fortunately he only left me a few hundred pounds, because if it had been any more, I'm sure they would have contested the will and God knows what.'

Through Harold, Mark made many contacts in the theatre; and with his death he was able to branch out socially. 'While he was alive

163

he was furiously jealous; and I didn't mind, because he'd been everything to me. He used to say "I don't mind when I've gone, but while I'm still alive I can't bear you to be with other people." ' Mark made other relationships, but has always had to be wooed and courted, and was incapable of approaching others. None of his relationships has lasted as the one with Harold did; Harold was the only person who showed him the total acceptance he needed, and on his terms; very much the relationship he'd had with his mother.

His arrogance remains. He is intolerant. He says he is on the far right of the Conservative Party. He is punctilious and condescending with most people.

JS: 'But you can be so nice if you want to.'

MARK: 'Why should I? What are other people to me? The only ones who mean anything to me are both dead.'

JS: 'You have a respect for propriety though, for formal politeness.'

MARK: 'Courtesy is something else. I think there's no excuse for bad manners.'

JS: 'And you like tradition?'

MARK: 'Those traditions which are good; yes. I think we're in danger of forgetting those things which make us English, our common sense and good nature and spirit of co-operation. I hate the lack of discipline, the boys I was at school with, I still wake up in the night in a cold sweat about it, can you wonder if industry is on the verge of collapse and nobody seems to care? I expect they're all shop-stewards now.'

JS: 'You were one of them don't forget.'

MARK: 'I was not. I am an artist.'

JS: 'Why do you ask for special treatment for yourself, and yet condemn everybody else in that sweeping way?'

MARK: 'I was different. My background . . . everything . . . I was a victim of circumstances, my mother's awful marriage . . .'

JS: 'Aren't we all victims of circumstances?'

MARK: 'I find working-class people greedy and insensitive and selfish.'

JS: 'Do you have sympathy with other minorities?'

MARK: 'What do you mean by minorities? You're assuming that I think of myself as a homosexual. Well I don't. I'm a gentleman. If that's a minority – and I dare say it is – then yes, I do. But not all this homosexual agitation by scruffy students. That is repulsive. I'm a gentleman who happens to prefer members of his own sex. I don't like all these pigeonholes.'

Some gay people undoubtedly borrow an identity from conformism and traditionalism, who invoke authoritarian values, eternal truths, just as there are those on the left who do the same thing; perhaps it serves as a bulwark against chaos and isolation, a barrier to the incomprehensibility and violence of their own emotions.

Cedric, twenty

Tall, elegant youth, brown hair, slim, wearing short black leather jacket, clogs, blue jeans. He comes from Mansfield in Nottinghamshire, and had just arrived in London when I met him. Father is a haulage contractor, unsympathetic to deviancy. His mother knows about his sexual orientation, and is far more accepting; only there is no outlet for gay people in small industrial towns. He feels he must get back to London, 'So that I can be myself'; he did live in the London suburbs with his grandmother for a time when he was seventeen, and that was far less inhibiting than living at home. He spent nine months in San Francisco, and lived with various individuals who were kind and hospitable; but he had to come home at last, because his parents indicated to him that if he didn't do so their door would be closed against him for ever. He hadn't particularly enjoyed being at school; he was ill for a term, and that precipitated leaving early.

I met him a few times while he was in the process of moving back to London. He went to Brook Street Bureau and got a job in a travel centre; he got a flat-mate through *Time Out*, radical change in his life achieved within a few days. He had been living at home on Social Security for a few months, and this had finally exasperated his parents, who, in the end, were content to let him go. He wanted to work in travel, in which he has always been interested. He has a rather ill-defined personality. When we talked together, it was as if he were being confronted for the first time with *ideas* about the gay world, about society, about relationships; and he considered each new suggestion before answering; as though it were a great novelty to talk in this way. He is 'looking for a relationship'; not in a frenzied or desperate way; but in a rather desultory state of preparedness and expectancy; a bit like sitting at home waiting for the taxi that will take you to the station for a pleasant journey. This may give way over time to a slight petulance if it fails to appear. In the meantime there is the world of discos, clubs, fleeting relationships, exciting sex, but nothing like a serious relationship. Cedric has known since early adolescence that he was gay. It did not surprise him; neither was he shocked or ashamed. He knew about such things, and was aware that it was a perfectly reasonable way of living. It seems that by identifying his gayness early, other areas of his personality have remained undeveloped.

There is no doubt that CHE, Gay Liberation Front, the 1967 Act, have diffused a much greater awareness of homosexuality than ever before. This means that increasing numbers of young people are able to recognize their homosexuality, and often to accept it at a far earlier age than occurred widely in the past. This is felt by homosexual people to be a good thing; and, given the anxiety, repression and misery which has attended the process of self-recognition of so many people, this is perhaps so. But being gay, and becoming aware of being gay, may become a strong determinant on all future development; indeed, the only determinant, pervasive, exclusive and all-enveloping. In this way, it is possible that many other potential areas of discovery may remain hidden, other talents smothered, and the whole evolution of the gay life-style subserves one permanent truth established at the centre of the individual consciousness: I am gay. It becomes an expanding awareness, opening out like a great tree in the shadow of which nothing else can survive; which spreads a sometimes sterile shadow; all other points of identity can be subordinated to it: economic, social, occupational, intellectual. Among gay people some of the most frequent comments are 'I don't believe in politics', 'I've got no time for politicians', 'I can't be doing with trade unions'; in which they doubtless faithfully echo convictions widely held among heterosexuals; but somehow, having cleared the ground of the dead wood, more room is created for the expanding minutiae of being gay. Gay people are among the first to become de-ideologized, pared down, so that the process of restructuring through artefacts may begin; they are surrounded by a kind of social deodorant, a mystical search for the self, the relationship. The highly politicized GLF represents a small number but creates some ill will among many homosexuals, despite the fact that the publicity they achieve rebounds to the advantage of the whole gay community. (Itself an interesting concept, and widely used: the gay community implies a place; the politics of gayness borrow the rhetoric of nationalism, of oppressed and colonized nations; the professional gays are like ambassadors to the country of the straight. One has the impression that it is another country, an ironic conferring of identity, the identity that has been erased from the place of origin: the identity of arrival rather than departure; the end of the journey.)

To find identity in homosexuality is a substitute for identities that would have derived more directly from a clearly defined locus in the class structure, to which gayness would have been subordinated in the consciousness of the individual. It is idle to assess whether one is 'better' than the other; it is certainly true that by finding identity in homosexuality, a major obstacle is removed to freedom in one area; but the fact is that it has to become a so pervasive identity obscuring much else that is valuable and worthwhile – and after all being gay doesn't objectively release you from a position in the socio-economic scale. On the other hand, that group of gay activists who assimilate themselves to other oppressed groups – blacks, women, mental patients, prisoners, the working class – are imbued with a roman-ticism which endows them with a sense of kinship with the revolu-tion, and which ignores the fact that gays – like blacks and women – are distributed throughout the socio-economic scale, and it is doubtful whether privileged homosexuals will be tempted to desert their positions (and the pressures for the embourgeoisement of gays are even greater than for that of almost any other group, ironically by their release from the family/procreative role) in the name of homosexual liberation, let alone whether they will be open to sugges-tions of consanguinity with blacks or prisoners or mental patients. It is a kind of sentimental wishful thinking to talk about white male capitalist oppression, when that oppression already offers the model of Consuming Man as an alternative to universal brotherhood in revolution; and many gay people will be among the first defectors.

Victor, twenty-one

He is of medium height, small boned, with fair straight hair which hangs in a fringe over his eyes, which are large and rust-brown. His skin is slightly pitted, and an occasional pimple or inflamed spot is only imperfectly concealed by a flesh-coloured ointment sold on the grounds that it obscures all skin blemishes. When he has spots he becomes very concerned, and will not go out, if he can help it, for several days. He works in a boutique in South London – a shop of limited items of display – an elegant suede jacket on a basketwork model, three or four pairs of trousers in check and denim fanning out to where a pair of high-heeled parti-coloured shoes stand at right angles. A metal grille covers the window, and the background for the display is a papier-mâché palm tree with coconuts on a velvet floor. Victor is pleased with his efforts. He came from Birmingham two years ago, after hesitating 'for ages before taking the plunge'. He is vague about his background; he speaks of his father with contempt and of his mother with pity. He claims to be fond of a sister who lives in Coventry.

He is very concerned about his appearance. He dresses well and unobtrusively, but always in clothes that follow the contours of his body: matelot sweaters with square necklines that set off the sculpted plinth of his neck, dark-coloured vests that show off the polished shaft of bone of his shoulder, flared trousers that mould the rippling concavity of his buttocks as he walks. He wears platform shoes, because he would like to be slightly taller than he is; but, as he observes, so does everybody else so that leaves him at square one. He dresses in beige, browns, dull red (his lips are quite full, and although he doesn't use make-up, he knows that by biting them, they become suffused with a rich carmine colour). He is fastidious about his hands, and varnishes his nails with clear polish. He tends to wear belts, large clumsy appliances with big buckles that rest on his hips like some medieval object of punishing constraint. He is afraid of sounding effeminate, and he is careful to enunciate each word, detaching each one from the next and releasing them with thought and calculation as one might homing pigeons, because he is intensely selfconscious and aware of the effect he will create on others. He enjoys talking about the people he almost picked up, the frightful old queens who had the audacity to think they might make out with him, the bold and the arrogant who dare to think he's easy meat. He says he is very selective about who he goes to bed with. He takes good care not to be so remote that he gets a reputation for being a prick-teaser, but says he prefers a 'meaningful relationship to one-night stands'.

Victor exists in a social dimension that seems to be abstracted from any recognizable social locus; and he refuses to allow himself to be identified with any social group: he doesn't believe in society, only individuals. He worked in shops in Birmingham when he left school at fifteen, and from time to time he had jobs as a night telephonist. When he first came to London he was installed in a love-nest in West London, where everything was provided, but he became a *hausfrau*, wasn't allowed out on his own, and in order to amuse himself, learned to cook and knit and even do macramé, read fashion magazines and designed window displays. That lasted for almost a year. 'I was a prisoner, literally. I'd go for days without talking to a soul except Lorenz. I don't even know to this day whether Lorenz was his real name. When he was away, he used to ring every five minutes, just to make sure I was there. I got so that I didn't even dare to go out to do any shopping. The thing was, when I first got to London, I didn't know anybody. I'd only arrived a few days before, got myself into a bed-sit in of all places Tufnell Park, when I got picked up by Lorenz. It was quite casual, he cruised me in this Porsche when I was just going home from a really dismal night in Earls Court; and he whisked me off to all kinds of places, parts of London I didn't even know existed. It all seemed incredibly exciting at the time. I remember thinking, this can't really be happening to little old me. And he was ever so kind. He bought me clothes, and he used to take me out with his friends, you know, dinner parties, and I was thought to be . . . rather present-able actually, although I'm not so sure he'd think so now . . . We went to the opera sometimes, and to first nights occasionally . . . I must admit, I do adore first nights, even now . . . He had a marvel-lous dress sense, and he used to guide me on what to wear, because I think I must have been horribly provincial at the time . . . He taught me how to move with ease among people. I think I could go anywhere now, but if you'd seen me at eighteen or nineteen, well I was gauche as all get out . . . Lorenz went abroad a lot. He took me to Portugal once, and then we had a memorable two weeks in New York . . . But I wasn't allowed any life of my own. I was utterly without friends . . . I even rang the Samaritans once, but they were worse than useless, they didn't seem to understand . . . Anyway, I couldn't tell them the address where I was . . . In the end he saw less and less of me, and then told me I had to go. As though I was dismissed. Your services are no longer required. I said "Even domestic servants expect written notice." It was a terrible humiliation. I felt like some cheese-counter assistant . . . By that time I just loathed the sight of him. I did. I felt murderous. But I thought to myself "My God, you're not going to cast me off just like that." So I threatened I'd kill myself, and I got hysterical. I started off just to give him a scare like, embarrass him, only it sort of got out of control, and I really did get worked up into a dreadful state . . . It worked. He gave me a cheque for £500 . . . I don't want you to think I did it for the money. I didn't. Nothing was farther from my mind. But I thought "Oo it's an ill wind, isn't it, that blows nobody any good" . . . I took it, of course, and went to find a flat as far away from him as I possibly could . . . Well, I could have gone further. I went to Chiswick . . . That's one reason why I don't enter into anything with just anybody . . . And I never accept lifts . . . I've walked home right across London before now without a penny in my pocket, and when cars have stopped and this number's looked out and said "Can I give you a lift?" I say "Why, am I sagging terribly?" Or something that's a put-down . . . I'm very careful about who I talk to . . . I've got friends now anyway, and I prefer to go to clubs or discos, in a group . . . I share a flat with an ex-affair, and I know it sounds really awful, but I always get Tom to vet people for me. I take them home to him; he says "It's like bringing them home to Mummy," but I do let myself be guided by him . . . And if he says "No, Victor," that's enough. I accept his word, even if I want to, madly, you know. Because I respect Tom . . . He is the only person I've been really in love with. He was one of the first people I met after my experience with Lorenz, and he was so sweet to me . . . I still do love him a little bit . . . But I don't have anybody at the moment who I'm passionate about, and I think that's what everybody needs, to give life some spice . . . I told you I was very careful about who I get involved with, and I think the real reason for that is not just because of Lorenz, but because I am a very passionate person, and I could so easily go overboard if I did let myself go. I have to hold myself back, up to a point . . . But when I do give myself, I do it completely . . . Of course that means you're likely to get hurt, because you can't give yourself to people without it rebounding on you sometimes . . . Love is my life, I think. I wouldn't be a person without love . . . I expect one day I shall meet someone I can settle down with . . . That's what I'd really like . . . I go out to clubs a fair bit. I adore dancing. From Thursday to

Sunday, if I get home before three o'clock in the morning I ask myself What's gone wrong . . . Although I'm proud of making the window look nice, I'm not really interested in work, selling clothes, putting your hand up all those people's inside leg as though it was an inanimate object. Money doesn't mean a great deal to me either, although I like the things it can buy. I like clothes, I adore good restaurants, I like to enjoy myself. Life's too short to do anything else . . . What I'd really like to do is dance professionally . . . But it's too late now. I've had no training. I did think of modelling, I know somebody who models clothes, but honestly, it's such a cut-throat world, I don't think I'd last ten minutes . . . I wouldn't mind theatre design . . . You see I left school when I was fifteen. I suppose it shows, doesn't it? Can you tell? I bet you think "What a silly little queen" . . . No honestly . . .

'I don't want to talk about my parents . . . I don't see them. They took no interest in me when I was young, so why should I show the slightest interest in them now? I don't go home. I didn't go home last Christmas, I spent it in Devon at a gay hotel. It was gorgeous . . . I don't care what they think of me. I've made myself what I am, without any help from them . . . And I don't think I've done too badly . . . Do you? I expect you think what a callous hard-hearted bitch I am. But I'm just honest, I just say what most other people think.'

Victor has been desocialized. He has no interest in social or political issues. 'I don't know how to vote.' It is a little like asking fish in an aquarium to talk about the concept of water-tanks. He regards any such questions with a quizzical disdain. 'I don't know why people want to fill their heads with all that sort of rubbish.' He wants to know what is the good of analysing things, and believes in just letting things happen. The fact that this may well be followed by pain, misunderstanding and rejection means that you just pick yourself up, paint on a new smile and start all over again. Despite his claim to selectivity, on the several occasions on which I met Victor, he was always with somebody new, whom he introduced with a fervent and tenderly protective enthusiasm. Victor can contemplate an infinite stretch of different and new relationships in a sequence of future time undisturbed by social institutions – marriage, school, uninterrupted by childhood, the exigencies of family; and the only spectre – that of growing old – can be deferred indefinitely. Everything conspires to maintain Victor in a state of prolonged adolescence; and on this count, consumerist values have caught gay people in a conjunction of two of its most self-conscious and self-indulgent categories: the young and the gay – two of the most inexhaustible markets of all. As gay people relate their past experience, the succession of lovers, the long sequence of one-night stands, the individuals they recall – or whose names they can't remember, but who gave them a fabulous time – there accumulates a sense of growing waste product, human detritus, the accompaniment, unrecycled waste of consumption. It is a legitimate cannibalism, and human beings become another product, undifferentiated almost from the glittering prizes of artefacts which are the objects of desire.

Mike, eighteen

His greatest fear is of growing old; too old, that is, for his calling of professional *poussin*. For the past three years he has haunted the playland, crystal room, public lavatory milieux of central London, has been picked up by men who have offered him safety for a night, a few days, a week; once he stayed with a pick-up for almost two months, which seemed to him an eternity of safety and security. Rows of machines with winking lights, the sound of detonation of air rifles, a whirring and jangling of music, a minor avalanche of money and tokens; in a hexagonal booth in the centre of the arcade sits a man with thin hair, eating a sandwich of processed cheese and giving out piles of pennies and two-penny pieces, as 50p and pound notes are handed through the aperture beneath the glass cage in which he sits. Occasionally he is dislodged from his perch by the insistence of somebody who declares that the machine isn't working, and has swallowed money without yielding its promised reward, and he unlocks the front panel with a bunch of keys that hangs from his belt, revealing a complexity of oily intestines inside the machine, and sets it right; or, if he discovers that it is working properly, he tells the kids to piss off. A policeman and a policewoman walk through the arcade. A few people leave; others, whose interest had been elsewhere, suddenly concentrate on the machinery with a rapt intensity. The policeman and woman interrogate two black kids who look about thirteen. The arcade is full: the poor, people sheltering from the cold, kids, people with assignations, hustlers, a few delighted Latin tourists oblivious of the cues being exchanged by the other visitors to the house of amusement.

'Most of the geezers who come here only want chickens. I've always looked older than I am. I've been told I look twenty-five. I used to like that, only with this game you can't go on much after you're twenty. I like my life. There's nothing wrong with it. I come here three nights a week. I don't always come here, I move about a bit, you don't have to stick to one place too much. I've got some mates I can crash with if I don't have anywhere else to go. Four mates of mine, we've got a room; only there's never more than two of us in it at a time . . . We don't use it to take anybody back to, not unless you've got to; if it's a tourist, or somebody you know you can make a bomb out of, then you might. Take 'em round a few alleys, up some back doubles so they don't remember where they've been. They're too scared most the time. If we go back there, we share it out, anything we make. Otherwise, you're on your own. I go to hotels a fair bit. You get to know what hotels have got somebody on the door to sort out them who don't belong there, know what I mean? . . . But there's more than one way into most places. I've got mates in some hotels, you can slip them a few quid now and again, and they'll let you in. So you ask the geezer where he's staying at, and if it's one where you don't know anybody, you say "Nothing," and if it's one where you got a mate, you say "Oo no, dicey, it's guarded like fucking Pentonville." And so you up the price, and say "Well we'll try." You have to be careful you don't scare them off, but you say "I've got a mate who might help," and then you get in easy as a knife through butter; then you say "I'm taking a risk," and they get all grateful.

'You don't know some of the places I've been in . . . Not only the bogs, I don't use them now, too risky; phone box, what you can do in a phone box, two people, it's fantastic, people walking past outside, I'm chuckling to meself, ain't I . . . Doorways, trees, get into the park after dark, bushes, building sites, stairways down the Tube . . . But I like going with people best. Some know how to be nice. Some don't. Some sort of blame you for being poufs, when they're the poufs like . . . I think some of the people I get to know, I think they're somebody big, high up like . . .

'I've been living in London three years. Well, I was born in London, only it was like right out, a long way . . . I was brought up in a home. I did live with me mother for a few years, I was eight or nine, and she had a bloke. And he fancied me. Yeh, he did. Well, I never gave him a chance, only I know he did, he was always waving his tool about in front of me . . . But she moved on, and they chucked me out and I went to live in this home. Well, it was different homes. They were all right. Only they lived behind doors marked Private, and they had their own family. They did their job . . . There was about half a dozen of us, but I stayed there the longest. They had a lot of people, helpers like. Some of them was all right. I left school my old lady said I could move back and live with her. She thought I was going to tip up me wage packet. Well, I went back for a bit, and I got a job, in the parks. Cutting grass, wheeling a fucking great trolley about, full of shit and wood and stuff. That was all right, in the summer. I got brown. Only I used to notice the men who used to go to the toilet there, and I got sort of interested . . . And one day, I followed this bloke in, and he took me in a cubicle . . . I liked it . . . They might tell you they don't but they're fucking liars . . . He was old . . . So I started thinking. And I thought I could get near where it was all going on like . . . So that's what happened. I went home and I packed the job in and I said to the old lady "I'm going to fuck off," and she said "What about me?" And I said "You can do what you done before," and she said she'd put me in a borstal. I said you can't now . . . She couldn't anyway. I never told her where I was going. I did send her a card once. A bloke I met said I ought to let her know where I was, so she didn't send the fuzz looking for me. Missing like. I am missing, and that's the way I'm going to keep it. So I did send her a card. I think he was scared for himself, cause he hoofed me out after that . . . But she wouldn't send the old Bill after me, she's got too much trouble herself.'

JS: 'What are you going to do then, when it's all finished and you can't carry on?'

MIKE: 'Dunno. Find somebody to look after me . . . find me a job . . . I do get looked after, only it's different people. I'd like to settle down . . . [Grins] For a few days . . . No, in the end I might . . . I might get married, find a nice house somewhere.'

JS: 'Do you like girls?'

MIKE: 'Yeh, course I do . . . [Grins] Not for sex, though . . . A lot of the boys make out all they want is some nice little chick who's gonna love them and all that. Not me . . . I'm not scared of the future . . . Only I don't want to get old . . . Cause when you're too old you're finished . . . Something'll turn up before then. I'll find somebody to stick with.'

Philip, twenty-four

A bed-sitting room in North London in a villa, Edwardian, with white woodwork, tessellated court before the house; stained-glass windows; a house of long, dark passages thrusting out into a neglected and overgrown garden; heavy heads of dark peonies, rain causing the red folds to decay prematurely. A windy night in May, when the wind shakes the husks from the new foliage and the leaves sweep the air for the first time since last summer; and the almost forgotten sound of wind in the trees already seems to foreshadow the autumn again.

The room is painted grey-blue; high, with a french window. A crucifix over the bed – which consists of two single beds irregularly placed together and covered with one large, striped bedspread. On the dressing table – 1940s utility – there is a reproduction of an ikon; a fan-heater and a glass lamp with a red bulb are the only concessions to comfort and decoration. The narrow kitchen has been formed from a corner of the former salon: contains an old cooker, a white sink, a deal kitchen table and two bamboo-style chairs.

'Gay Lib meant a great deal to me when I was younger. In adolescence I was badly repressed. I realize in retrospect that I had a very strong and probably incestuous relationship with my mother; and she died when I was twelve. I don't know whether my sense of rage at the bereavement has pursued me since. I don't have long-term relationships with people. I've been in love, or thought I was, for perhaps three months at a time, but then, you know, you get on each other's nerves . . . When I first came to London I was very promiscuous. I think it's perhaps something all gays have to go through. A kind of catharsis. It's very easy to become insensitive to other people, and the technique of picking people up and discarding them without any sense of pain to oneself can have a very de-humanizing effect.

'Over the past few months I've been withdrawing, I suppose, from the gay scene. I've decided that I'm going to be a priest, and I'm going to a college in the North. I did visit a college which is very

175

radical and very gay, and I know if I went there I'd have a fantastic time, but I don't think that is my answer. I expect you've come across the baroque fancy-dress Anglo-Catholic phenomenon, I know it well, but I don't share its attitudes. I think what is needed is a kind of asceticism; it is so easy to give in to the selfishness and self-indulgence of material well-being. It needs a new St Benedict, you know, "Come out of the cities." Basically, I'm thoroughly optimistic. I don't think one should be too much of a Cassandra, although I think what one says is interesting.

'I come from Sheffield, from a working-class family. My father was on the railways. I think they've accepted me now, although it was probably difficult for them in the beginning. It was difficult for myself. I went to a really awful school, and then transferred to a Comprehensive when I was thirteen. And from there I went to university to read History. I think it's quite difficult to get beyond political discussion with people in Gay Lib; quite often they'll refuse even to discuss things like what makes some people gay and not others, people who've been subjected to almost identical experience. They just say "There it is, you're dealing with a situation, not trying to attribute causes." In my own case I think there was a deep involvement with my mother, but I'm sure the same isn't true of many of the people I know. And anyway, the connection that is commonly made there may be false. There may be other factors; it's impossible to know. The people in Gay Lib won't go into generalizations, and I think they're probably right. If they are fighting for gay rights, they simply state their position. It can be a sterile and circular argument that doesn't help anybody.

'I think repression is a very real phenomenon. Not necessarily in that people can't admit to being gay, although of course that is still very much there. But it's something internal, it's the opinion you have of yourself. I wouldn't say, by and large, that gay people are brutally treated by society, but there is always the danger that you may internalize society's views and you become the agent of your own repression, leading a double life or hating yourself or denying your sexuality. I think you've got to be constantly aware of what's happening to you. I mean, there's no point in society going to the bother of quelling you, when individuals so obligingly do it themselves.'

JS: 'It seems to me that the danger is "out of the closets into the boutiques."'

PHILIP: 'I agree with you when you say the invitation to self-indulgence is also a form of oppression, it can be a very effective way of dealing with homosexuality, better by far than the shame-oppression mechanism, because it's more efficient.'

JS: 'Is promiscuity to be reconciled with being a priest?'

PHILIP: 'I've thought about this one for a long time, and I'm forced to the conclusion, reluctantly, that it isn't. For me, anyway. I can't answer for other people. Some of my friends in Gay Lib find it a bit strange, I know.'

The enthusiasm of Gay Lib is often evangelical in tone; passionate, intense, impatient and sometimes intolerant. The doctrine is sexual freedom, personal liberation and fulfilment; the rhetoric is nationalistic – like an oppressed or colonized people, which is precisely what gay people have been. The uninitiated are looked on with a mildly irritated pity. It is there for everybody, if people will only look for it. It is a state of grace; and is accompanied by some elaborate and heavily disguised moral imperatives. Liberation is identifying and expressing sexual need; a sort of metabolistic detective work, a diligent experimentation, an unremitting auscultation of the body and its needs, in order to leave no stone unturned to find out if there are not areas not yet opened up to fulfilment. Fulfilment is a kind of ultimate goal; but like absolute and transcendent states, it tends to be elusive. The elimination of 'hang-ups', the discovery of an uninhibited and untrammelled self is its goal; as though the self were a treasure to be found at the end of a fairy-tale, sex being the mediator to the state of beatitude implied by the concept of the fulfilled person. It is aware of something which it calls repression, oppression, puritanism, sometimes capitalism; but relies heavily on negations in order to define the development and growth of a gay consciousness. It is like some profane divine comedy; quest, pilgrimage: all the imagery of transcendent mystical experience are brought to bear upon the body and its capacity for sensation and experience; a medieval pilgrimage, or its nineteenth-century equivalent, a voyage through the senses – Baudelaire, Rimbaud, Huysmans. It marks the spread of another formerly aristocratic privilege, popularized and turned into a mass movement.

By over-reacting against the romantic rituals of courtship and monogamy and the stifling limitations of straight society, it is in itself a profoundly romantic view of human life. Even at its most absurd – like the people who systematically visit cottages in order to rid themselves of their irrational fears of the police, or in order to exorcize their own self-disgust – it is deeply determined by the society in which it exists, and to which it cleaves as an indivisible caricature; and its absolutes and imperatives are as imprisoning as the society of which they are an outcrop; and which threatens so effortlessly to re-colonize the areas which gay lib has liberated. It is rather like those newly emancipated nation-states, which tumultuously assert their liberation from colonialism, only to find themselves tethered to their oppressors by links other than brute force.

Eric, twenty-eight

'I think I'm fairly well-balanced about being gay. I wouldn't say it was quite effortless coming to terms with it, but the fact is I accept it and feel at home in my skin. I don't need to con myself or other people. If they don't like it, they can do the other thing. I'm not interested in people who judge you without even knowing you as a person, who see you as a sex role. Because, let's face it, I'm a person first. I mean by that that my sex isn't the most important factor in the majority of people I meet. Worse luck. No, I don't mean that. I'm quite serious. I meet more people than I go to bed with. Therefore my role towards them isn't primarily sexual. There is I suppose an element of sex in most relationships, however casual. I work in the Social Security Offices in B., on the counter. I don't exactly ask people to go to bed with me through the grille, see what I mean? I've been to bed with one guy I met at work. They don't take the piss out of me at work, if it amuses them to when I'm not there, that's up to them. But on the whole they've been very nice; and they're not the most enlightened people on earth. They're all right, I go to dinner with them, and if they say bring a girl I say it's a boy, actually, and nobody's ever cancelled the invitation. There is one boy there I fancy like mad, and he knows it, and we have a kind of running joke about it. He makes out he's flirting with me. Well, he is. He knows he's not going to have sex with me, and I know he's not going to. So we have a laugh . . . As a matter of fact, there might be something there, deep down, but I shan't be the one to discover it. I can let him send me up, because I know that it's not done in a spirit of malice . . . I go to discos. I like Catacombs, I go to the Champion. I like Hampstead Heath, Wimbledon Common, Ham Common. I'm not ashamed to go trolling, I don't regard it as an admission of defeat. I like the open air. I like the uncomplicated thing about sex that has no consequences. Unless it's crabs or clap – and they're no problem . . . I don't want you to think I'm blasé, I'm not. I just enjoy myself. I have my ups and downs. I'm a bit neurotic over some things, spiders for instance, but I don't come across many of those, and I don't go to bed with them . . . so . . . I don't like prejudice . . . I feel like one of those ads on the tube, Cherry Mulholland likes . . . I like Arab boys, café au lait, thirties movies . . . I refuse utterly to admit that I have any problems to do with being gay. It's the best thing in my life. It gives me more pleasure and enjoyment than anything else, I'm quite relaxed about it. I'm not obsessed, I just think about sex all the time. [Laughs] I suppose somewhere I feel it would be nice to have a permanent relationship, but then I'd have to give up all the other things, like sometimes you meet somebody and you have an absolutely crazy time for three or four days, you spend all the time in bed, you don't know whether it's day or night, you eat in the early hours, drink, smoke . . . I wouldn't give up that for all the tea in China. Or even all the hash.' [Laughs]

Andrew, twenty-six

'I think liberation is something inside oneself. If you can get rid of the self-loathing, the putting yourself down that comes from accepting what Big Daddy says you ought to think about yourself. You have to get rid of all the hang-ups that society wills on you. I get sex as much as I can, and I'm not particularly bothered about how I get it . . . I go cottaging because there's nothing to be ashamed of and because I think you ought to get rid of your fears about the police. Sex in a cottage can be enjoyable . . . I had a very difficult time when I was younger. My father died when I was six, and I was brought up by this very traditional lower middle-class woman who happened to be my mother. I have no feeling for her at all, she was just a very boring and totally insignificant individual who society had for some reason put in charge of my upbringing. Anyway, I knew I was gay from the age of about ten or eleven, and

I was about thirteen when I had my first experience, which was with somebody of my own age, and after that there was no stopping me. I lived near a park, and I got to learn the best times for being picked up; three-thirty in the afternoon, about twenty minutes after the pubs closed I was there. I used to place myself strategically near where I could see the entrance to the lavatories, and take a school-book and pretend to be engrossed in Mears and Carter or whatever it was. And then whenever I saw anyone interesting going in, I used to follow . . . Of course, some of the blokes were a bit put out, seeing this kid of thirteen or fourteen flashing around, but most of them managed to overcome their prejudices . . . Then, when I was fifteen, I discovered a boy in the same class at school, and we fell fantastically in love. That was the most completely overwhelming experience I've ever had. He was a working-class boy, and that's when I started realizing that all the bits of trite morality that this woman used to ram down me were just bits of trite morality . . . Anyway, same old story, we used to write to each other in the holidays, because I went with her to a caravan near Bognor and Graham wrote to me and she intercepted it; and being fifteen, it wasn't in the most moderately couched terms. She was fantastic; I can remember every detail, all white-faced and tense and what is this filth, and where had she gone wrong, and I told her that we were in love – I was probably priggish about it, and then she cried and went on about being ill and getting a cure. And she got the first train back to London and dressed up and went to see his parents and showed them the letter, and they took us both to our doctors! Mine was really a sod, although apparently, I discovered later, Graham's had told him not to worry and cooled it with his parents. But mine shook his head and went all grave and ponderous and said We must see if we can get treatment for him, and they sent me to a psychiatrist, I suppose, quite a nice man, who wasn't quite so unsympathetic as the GP. I sat in front of his desk, and he asked me with great interest what we did together, and I told him, all rather casually, and he said to my mother to get me among female company. I said No thanks, I've had nothing but female company since I was born, and really it would last me a lifetime. So she tried asking girls to the house, and I carried on with Graham as before, even long after we'd stopped caring, because I suppose it was forbidden . . . So in a sense I was lucky, I had liberation thrust upon me. I realized that I had to survive and I wasn't going to let her stop it. I suppose it's because I had a difficult time that I'm so liberationist in outlook, and I want other gays to come out. Yes, I am a kind of missionary. It needs missionaries.'

Stephanie, twenty-two

'I'm happy. I do as I like and if other people don't like it they can get fucked. I don't let anybody put me down. I'd throw them through a plate-glass window first. People think if you're queer you've got to be a nancying queen. Well, they couldn't be more wrong. In my case, anyway. I've been in trouble with the police, but only for fighting. I've been in the nick for scrapping, because somebody called me a fucking pouf. I am a fucking pouf, but I'm not having anybody saying it to me in that tone. Put-down tone, you know. The thing is, the more bold you are, the more you get away with. I really enjoy my life. I know how to keep people entertained, especially myself. I go out in drag a lot, and you'd be surprised, the number of straight people I pick up. I generally get them so worked up by the time I get them home that they practically never show any surprise when they find out I'm technically not female. Actually I have decided to have the operation.

'But it just shows, all these people who are so up-tight about their masculinity. When it comes to the point, they've got just as much gayness in them as people who admit they're gay . . . I really enjoy that, sending up the straight world, giving them the come-on, then showing them what I am. That gives me a real kick. But I get all the sex I want, so why should I worry? I'm not scared of anybody, I'll play up to anyone, so that gives me a great advantage.'

He is twenty-two. Regular features, pale, epicene, thinnish blond hair. He says he knew he liked men from the age of seven, and he started his sex-life early. Fifteen years I've been on the scene, so there isn't much I don't know about it.

*

'Of course I'm glad to be gay. Every morning when I wake up I throb with passion and excitement and think "I'm gay." ' James, thirty-six, being ironic.

University Gay Society

A room in a university block; narrow, exiguously furnished, crowded. Members of the University Gay Society, two women, several men who come and go. View over the city, room at the top of building, rainy Sunday afternoon.

JS: 'Do you accept the idea that a few brave and courageous people have broken through the barrier of oppression and dared to proclaim themselves, and that this has been a generally liberating influence on others?'

KATE: 'I think it liberated them, but I doubt very much whether it liberated anybody else.'

VIC: 'I disagree, because I think it has helped a lot of other people. At other times there haven't been many who've refused to accept oppression. The movement over the last ten years has very definitely brought out a whole lot of things that simply didn't happen before. There's no doubt that things have changed, but whether it's a matter of being brave and courageous ... It's often a matter of acting naturally. Often an individual decision is brave ... The effect of people coming out has been to make *Gay News* and gay magazines in general available, and are read by something like forty thousand people who are connected into the world, know what's going on. Perhaps it's only a small segment of the gay community, but there is beginning to be a feeling of community.'

JS: 'It was traditional in industrial society that people were personally repressed. The whole point about the pre-consumer economy was that people internalized the disciplines of the work-place, the productive processes, and that the family reflected this. People learnt personal self-effacement, and this naturally spilled over into their personal lives ... A society that's based on self-indulgence – self-expression if you want to ennoble it – involves a kind of liberation in that people have to consult their needs and wants. As a result gay liberation is merely a spin-off of a changed economic function through which individuals become consumers as opposed to producers.'

CHARLES: 'I think you could put that in a different way by saying that straight people created Gay Lib because they created a need for it. Society is basically straight except for this tiny minority, and it's created a sense of community – admittedly in an artificial way, since gay people are not naturally a community: we just happen to have this one thing in common. If the family hadn't been considered so important, and boosted as the foundation of Western capitalist society, then we wouldn't have needed to organize in the way we have.'

KATE: 'I disagree totally, because there is a natural gay society and it still exists. The only thing is that Gaysoc, CHE, SMG have nothing to do with it. Gay society has always been the ghettos. Gay society is still the clubs and pubs and discos whether we like it or not.'

CHARLES: 'Gaysoc and CHE are still part of the ghetto.'

JS: 'I think there was always a gay subculture, but what I wonder is, whether in spite of the apparent new diversity, in spite of the apparent upheavals, things aren't more or less the same – gayness bears the same subservient relationship to mainstream society that it always has done?'

KATE: 'Yes . . . at times in history it hasn't always been necessary to go down into little tunnels, through gates and grilles or down holes to meet people . . . In Greek times you could be open. At times when society has been tolerant, you didn't get gay ghettos.'

CHARLES: 'Things aren't the same. You have a continuity of clubs, but the people who go to them, their attitude isn't the same, because gay people who were raised in our parents' generation who were apologetic and defensive about it, they never used the word gay, which says something.'

KATE: 'It hadn't been coined then.'

CHARLES: 'But the fact that the word has emerged as a positive word . . . I think the phenomenon of liberation is a spin-off from society. I think we've used the system against itself, that's what it boils down to. We've used this exploitation and commercialism on our own behalf.'

JS: 'Do gay people use the system or are they manipulated by it in an even more subtle way than previously? I remember once talking to an industrialist who, talking of relative affluence and the working class, said "When the pigs are in clover they're not trampling the vines." See what I mean?'

KATE: 'Manipulated by fellow-gays, I have to agree.'

JS: 'You know, with the stress on youth culture, cosmetics, the elixir of youth, the fashion industry . . .'

GRAHAM: 'It's the same with straight men. Any straight man has a virile image which he will try to keep up until he's past it, and women do the same thing and always have done.'

JS: 'Yes; you look in the products in the bathroom of a gay flat, Sabre and Jade and Man Musk and lotions and sprays to render you irresistible, it's the same process and dovetails so beautifully into what the consumer thing is all about.'

KATE: 'We're all part of the main society, as well as being gay. Like someone who's black . . . The same thing's true of cosmetics for black women. But you can't discount a movement like Black Panthers just because someone has brought out a make-up that black women can wear. It's irrelevant. The consumer society has brought out stuff for gays, blacks, that everybody else can use.'

GRAHAM: 'Surely we're more in society now than we ever were before.'

JS: 'Exactly.'

KATE: 'No, that's the illusion.'

JS: 'By identifying gay people, straight society manages to keep tabs on them.'

KATE: 'We identified ourselves.'

JS: 'It's a control mechanism.'

CHARLES: 'I agree with you that it's a control mechanism, but it works to our advantage, because a lot of people don't like being on the fringe of society; and if the alternative is being on the fringe of society, then we'll go back into the closet.'

JS: 'Out of the closets into the boutiques.'

CHARLES: 'I know I wouldn't have come out if I'd had to live completely on the fringe of society . . . So it's paying a price for certain advantages.'

JANE: 'Can't we come out in straight society? Why is it important for us to be gay and almost nothing else? We are something else. I think too much emphasis is put on being gay by people.'

CHARLES: 'By gay people.'

KATE: 'I like living on fringes.'

JS: 'Is being gay a full-time job?'

KATE: 'Yes.'

JANE: 'With some people, yes. Personally, I don't think so.'

VIC: 'One is always gay.'

KATE: 'To a certain extent, Vic, you and I have made a career out of being gay.'

CHARLES: 'But straight people are always straight.'

VIC: 'Exactly.'

KATE: 'The difference is they don't have to scream about it.'

VIC: 'We have to assert our identity, and act for our community, we have to be gay full-time in that sense. Because otherwise we're assumed to be straight.'

CHARLES: 'That's what I meant when I said straights made us.'

VIC: ' 'Cos they get het-up about it [laughter] . . . We have to contest it. Refuse to let them assume we're straight.'

GRAHAM: 'Can't you argue that we manipulate straight society and not the other way round? Because we're the ones who are doing the talking.'

VIC: 'I think so.'

GRAHAM: 'We're doing the active role . . . We have had a condition we're trying to alter, so we must be taking the active role.'

CHARLES: 'We're catering to the mystique, because it's one way of getting straight society to accept us, because if gay people are really boring and there's nothing about them that's interesting, that's a big disadvantage, whereas if there's a mystique . . .'

KATE: 'Straight society's always accepted the extremely camp man . . . It's part of an inbuilt cultural thing . . . There's only one thing worse than being talked about and that's not being talked about . . .'

VIC: 'But this is a standard thing in deviancy theory; that there are two ways of being deviant – one is to flaunt it and make a joke of it and the other is to pass.'

KATE: 'There is a third. Another way.'

VIC: 'Which is?'

KATE: 'Not flaunting it and being outrageous according to the stereotypes, but flaunting it and being outrageous in your own way.'

CHARLES: 'This is our long-term goal.'

KATE: 'Exactly.'

VIC: 'The point is, something is only deviant if it's thought to be deviant. I mean what we're asking for is a society in which the homosexual is not a deviant. Being gay is not a deviant state. You see being left-handed is not deviant, but it is less common than being gay. So deviancy is not concerned with how uncommon something is, it's concerned with being seen to be deviant. Now in Greek society which you mentioned, the point is not that it was tolerant, but that being gay and sleeping with boys – and probably women too – was not seen to be deviant.'

185

KATE: 'This is why we have gay ghettos.'

VIC: 'Exactly. It wasn't a deviant thing; therefore, with deviant behaviour there are only two ways of dealing – flaunting or passing. But what we are trying to do is to cause it not to be deviant, which is the third course. To abolish the deviant aspect.'

KATE: 'We're trying to say "Look, we're everywhere, and we're quite normal otherwise." '

VIC: 'It's not saying we're like everyone else. We're not. It's like saying a left-handed or colour-blind person is like everyone else. They're not. The difference is there is not a *deviant* difference.'

CHARLES: 'Society doesn't put a value-judgement on those things as it does on being gay.'

VIC: 'There is no adverse judgement put on some deviations from the norm as there is on others. We are a larger minority than many of the non-deviant minorities.'

CHARLES: 'And what I think, to come back to the original point, is that we're using straight society, we are doing more manipulating than they are of us, because, even with the cult of gay things, the vast majority of gay men look straight and wouldn't be picked out by the way they dress or groom themselves, so that any special gay market hasn't been used by gay people.'

GRAHAM: 'Look at long hair, how that used to be pouffy. My brother once gave a lift to someone in Wales – and that's about as provincial as you can get – and this person asked him if he were a homosexual because he had long hair. But now that long hair has been adopted by straight people, and they wear platform shoes which at first only gay people did, it's now become less easy to tell gay people.'

JS: 'Yes, what I'm saying is that gay people have been caught up in the main flow of the culture, and for very good reasons.'

GRAHAM: 'I would say that because of certain advantages our condition has, we're able to see society and do things in a way that straight society doesn't normally do. I mean a straight boy or girl doesn't dress in the way which best suits their body, because they're not so aware of the things that are best suited to them . . . That's a reason why a poet is often homosexual, because they felt themselves strange from society. They've felt the agony and the ecstasy of various social situations because they've been forced to delve more deeply into human relations and psychology than anyone else . . . And therefore produced something that's valuable.'

JS: 'You're falling into a traditional homosexual myth, that there's something inherently superior, more sensitive, martyrized, about being gay . . . This merges into the instant emotionalism, "We feel more deeply, more passionately." '

GRAHAM: 'I wasn't saying that. There are obviously great advantages in being straight as well.'

KATE: 'What Graham's basically saying is that everybody knows what the advantages of being straight are . . . he was just listing some of the things about being gay. You only hear the bad things from straight society – perversion, picking up choir-boys sort of thing.'

GRAHAM: 'We merely represent other aspects of society . . .'

KATE: 'It's the same if you read the book of the Soledad Brothers. This is the incredible thing, that so much of the Black Panthers and Black Liberation Movement is so close to our own thing . . . They represent the excesses of repression and correspondingly vehement reaction to it, to the same extent that you get gays sometimes over-reacting.'

CHARLES: 'Just as people assume you're heterosexual, unless you declare otherwise, people assume hetero is bettero.'

JS: 'Do you think there is a gay subculture?'

KATE: 'Yes.'

JS: 'If so, what is it, and how has it changed?'

KATE: 'It's different for everybody.'

JS: 'It can't be if it's a subculture.'

KATE: 'It can. This is the whole point.'

JS: 'How?'

KATE: 'Because it doesn't matter whether people go to discos or are in GLF or sneak out to cottages, that sort of thing, the subculture still exists in that society sees us as a separate group. While some gay people say "Please can I come into your society, please, sir, etc., accept us, accept us," we say we're glad to be gay.'

CHARLES: 'It seems what you're saying is we're separate simply because we've had to cope with a straight world and that gives us a sense of our community, even though we are disparate.'

KATE: 'Just as a black person who's lived in white society that says "White is good" lives in a subculture.'

CHARLES: 'But it's different for everybody, because each person has confronted it in a different way.'

KATE: 'Yes.'

GRAHAM: 'It's been enough to keep people together, just being gay.'

JS: 'One of the most pervasive myths – or perhaps part-truths of the gay world – has been a belief in the democracy of the bed: you never know whether you'll wind up with a . . . costermonger or a movie-star.'

VIC: 'Which is true to some extent.'

KATE: 'It's true in straight society to a point. It's always been easy for a woman to move class because of the person she married . . . Women have had this freedom to marry somebody rich and become a member of that class.'

VIC: 'But what's the chance of meeting someone very rich?'

KATE: 'Look at the romantic fiction that most girls read.'

VIC: 'It represents wishes.'

JS: 'Yes, and some of the last repositories of the most infantile manifestations of that romanticism are to be found in gay literature.'

KATE: 'Yes, but the stories only happen to be gay. They could equally be in *Woman's Own.*'

JS: 'Why is the gay world so romantic in this way?'

GRAHAM: 'Is it because of the starvation of literature which is all oriented towards straight sex? . . . When you look at all the ads on the tube, you're used to it, but it doesn't move you because it's not directed at you.'

JS: 'It's not only in advertising, though, is it, it's in people's own conception of themselves.'

KATE: 'In romantic fiction the boy's always at one end of the room, tall and handsome, the boy looks at the girl, etc., this incredible mystique, blue clouds and they drift together. And the romantic ideal is just as alien to the real straight world as it is to our world. It exists in both. It's a nice idea.'

GRAHAM: 'I'm sure there is a sense of starvation – You pick up any book, whether it's Agatha Christie or Jane Austen or anything, there'll always be a straight romance in it at some point, somebody's always being engaged to someone else. The number of times when you can read in an ordinary work of literature where on page 115 two boys are madly in love, you know, there aren't many.'

JS: 'Because gay people don't have a structure of wife/children, do you think that it's easier to become promiscuous, change partners etc.?'

KATE: 'You get relationships where people have lived together

188

for twenty years, where their domesticity easily surpasses ordinary straight couples.'

JS: 'Is there a danger in the liberation movement that one becomes enslaved to personal appetites and desires once you slough off all conventions, you become consumers of people? Gay people get through a lot of human material in a way that people with structured lives don't. Is that always an unqualified good thing?'

CHARLES: 'Yes, you get some gay people who confuse Gay Lib with just rejection of all existing standards, and say you've got to have anti-standards. Given that the family has always been held up to us for so many years, that there's Daddy who's only had one woman all his life, so you've got to get out and have as many different partners as possible.'

VIC: 'Yes, but there was always the hetero model of Casanova, Don Juan, etc.'

CHARLES: 'Yes, but you're not raised by those standards personally are you? They don't have as great an impact as the immediate family does. The family implants its own attitudes in you, and it takes a hell of a lot of mental effort to break away from that.'

KATE: 'You tend to over-react.'

CHARLES: 'Most of the people who watched say the TV series of Casanova with drooling lips don't live like that, they were relatively monogamous.'

JS: 'Do you believe that gay people with their effortless change of partners do realize the secret desires of many heterosexuals?'

CHARLES: 'Yes, they look at us longingly when they see us camping it up somewhere.'

GRAHAM: 'You have to question the importance of the inherent desire to form lifelong couples. You have to question that, whatever your eventual decision is. Then you have to remember that gay people when they have sex are not concerned with producing children, so in fact it doesn't matter very much as far as society is concerned, because you're not suddenly going to produce a million babies in a week . . . And if you reverse the whole thing, and look at straights from a gay point of view, look at all the marriages and adulteries that are miserable and unhappy, which would have been better if they hadn't married, but where both have been sleeping around when they wished to . . .'

KATE: 'If you imagine straight society without contraceptives, if straight society acted like some gay men do, there'd be such a population explosion. I live among students, who, to a certain extent do hop in and out of bed with each other, most of us do . . .'

GRAHAM: 'The basic point is that promiscuity is a word that has bad connotations in society. Illogically so, because you can argue there's no reason why promiscuity should be bad.'

CHARLES: 'The difficulty is trying to distinguish between doing it because you really want to, and doing it because you think you have to. That's what makes it hard to figure out.'

JS: 'Why is there the compulsion to find so many partners?'

JANE: 'I've been to one gay club, and that was very much a meat-market.'

CHARLES: 'I wonder if women's sexual desires are different from men's? I think men can be more easily aroused by something they read or hear.'

KATE: 'Women listen; men's reaction is more developed to vision. I don't know whether that's society's influence or whether that's people . . . You can't tell. That's why the aims of Women's Lib are so similar to those of Gay Lib.'

CHARLES: 'Surely women get involved with a whole personality, where men can have an orgasm with someone they don't particularly fancy.'

KATE: 'If you're a girl, you can get orgasm with somebody you don't particularly fancy.'

CHARLES: 'You've got to really trust the other person to enjoy sex with them, I think. You've got to be ideologically compatible too.'

KATE: 'Oh come on. I went out with a girl for a year, fascist is the only word to describe her, and the biggest row we had was when I told her I'd slept with someone who was black. That was it . . . She didn't speak to me for two weeks afterwards.'

JS: 'Why are so many gays illiberal?'

KATE: 'You can't generalize . . . Some say all gays are left-wing, others all right-wing.'

JS: 'You're gay, you've got no dependants, you tend to be up-wardly mobile, the image of the aristocratic ideal seems to me very much in evidence; the idea of middle-aged men in baroque interiors drinking Liebfraumilch out of crystal goblets, calling each other by the feminine gender, you know.'

JANE: 'On the other hand, because you're part of an oppressed group, even if you're rich, you feel a companionship with other oppressed groups like blacks, which I do very much . . .'

GRAHAM: 'What I find hard to understand is reconciling being gay with right-wing ideology . . . It usually seems to involve one of the churches and a whole lot of things that seem to me incompatible with being gay.'

JS: 'One of the things is that people's belief-system often bears no relation to their actions, isn't it? . . . I suppose because authoritarian or absolute beliefs impose order and structure where there is none it may be a source of comfort.'

KATE: 'Gays are people, and they have different political views.'

JS: 'But the pressures are still to be conformist.'

KATE: 'There are two pressures -- one to push them into being right-wing and conformist, and the other is because they're gay and out of society and don't believe in some rules, not to believe in any rules.'

GRAHAM: 'If you read Oscar Wilde, he was very conscious of the social order, and prided himself on being in the aristocratic stratum, but his social scene also involved picking boys up off the street.'

JS: 'I think what goes for the whole of society goes for gays. The danger is that in saying "Oh we're part of society at last, isn't that good," and that stops gay people from looking critically at that society, however hideous it may be. The future that's held out to gay people is the same as that which is held out to everybody else.'

VIC: 'You can't say that society is rotten and getting worse and we're going to get out of society. That's not much of an alternative. We have two objectives – one, to abolish the deviant thing of being gay and to join society, not necessarily being absorbed by it, right; and the other, to try to do something about the collapse of our civilization, if it is collapsing; or at least trying to do something to improve it.'

KATE: 'If we ship our political views, instead of making society better for gays, the idea should be to make society as decadent as possible 'cos that'll make it better for us. [Laughter] . . . I think it's just starting to become decadent, I want to push it as far as I can.'

VIC: 'I don't know what decadence means. I think it's a silly word really.'

JS: 'You see I don't think it's decadent at all really; the culture has found a new dynamic, given people a new function in consumption. It's a whole philosophy, a whole informing dynamic.'

VIC: 'Yes but all that's going to have to change, for the simple reason that we're going to run out of resources to consume very quickly; the real question is whether we'll change through catastrophe or planning. Probably catastrophe.'

GRAHAM: 'Yes, but the point is we should be part of society, whether it's going up or down, and not be sitting back, watching it happen. We should be in on society, and not looking at it.'

KATE: 'I disagree, because I'm an anarchist.'

GRAHAM: 'Whatever form society has got to, the whole point about the revolution is that you don't want to be cut out and put down and stamped underfoot. The way not to be is to be in there, as part of society.'

KATE: 'No, there are two alternatives – either within or without society.'

VIC: 'The only way you can be outside society is being dead or dead silent. Because if you are living in the society of other people then you are necessarily reacting to society, whether it's pro or con . . . But I think we've strayed into wider politics.'

JS: 'I think it's difficult not to . . . Do you think gay relationships are more doomed from the start?'

CHARLES: 'Doomed? Do you mean not to be permanent?'

KATE: 'Yes, because of pressures of the society, not something inherently wrong in a gay couple.'

JS: 'How can you be sure?'

KATE: 'You only have to look at the pressures on you. If you go home, and take someone with you, you have to remember you're not allowed to touch the person in your parents' presence. I had a girl-friend who used to live in our house almost, and the ludicrous thing you had to remember was, if her hair was falling over her forehead, you couldn't push it back because your parents were in the room . . . Something completely non-sexual, but touching, running your fingers through her hair is impossible, because you're in straight society, that is, your family.'

CHARLES: 'That should push you together more than pull you apart. I think the pressure on relationships comes from other gay people. There are so many other fish in the sea.'

KATE: 'Somebody else is always trying to grab your partner.'

JS: 'Because individuals are expendable, interchangeable, I think there is a pressure to instability . . . Do you think frequent changes derogate from the quality of relationships?'

192

KATE: 'I don't know about men, but established women couples always go out of their way to make sure everybody knows they're a couple . . .'

CHARLES: 'So that people can't get off with them individually?'

KATE: 'No, so that they can get off individually and still know they're safe.'

CHARLES: 'That's true of gay men I think too, because any couple is bound to have something on the side at one stage or other, but it doesn't necessarily break up the relationship. It can. It may not.'

VIC: 'One of the inheritances from straight society is this thing of fidelity and monogamy, which is entirely irrelevant.'

GRAHAM: 'Monogamy, monotony.'

VIC: 'Not very good monotony either. Some gay couples I know are sensible and honest. They can sleep around and remain couples. Some have to maintain to the other that they're perfectly faithful, which I think imposes a strain.'

KATE: 'Overthrowing the values of straight society of man to woman, we also feel we ought to overturn the value of one to one . . .'

VIC: 'It's a question of the "ought". Why "ought" we to one or the other? What we ought to be aware of is that both are possible. People shouldn't feel peculiar for being monogamous, but people also shouldn't feel we must be the opposite.'

KATE: 'That's what Jeremy was asking – because we're overthrowing the one we must embrace the other.'

VIC: 'People struggle to maintain the romantic monogamy thing, or they can struggle to overthrow everything, which is equally false.'

JS: 'These things have been decided for most people by the social norms and conventions in the past. This means that we're terribly stranded, you have to define yourself from what is within you, and of course, what is in you is only what you get from society, and you get precisely nothing, because if you're in a peculiar doubting situation towards it, how do you construct, fabricate a whole scheme of values, attitudes, behaviour, morality that's valid and true?'

CHARLES: 'By trial and error. Experience.'

VIC: 'And by connecting into the subculture and the different attitudes towards it.'

JS: 'How did you find out you were gay? How did you find your identity as a gay person?'

SIMON: 'The way I realized I was gay was when someone introduced me to it when I was very small and I enjoyed it, and I carried on. I was about seven at the time. And when I went to the swimming baths a couple of years later, the same sort of thing happened again. And I went back for more. And then I never thought any more about it until I was doing my O levels, and then I went out and picked up this black guy from round the corner, and stayed with him for ages and ages . . .'

JS: 'Did you feel guilty?'

SIMON: 'No, not until my parents found out about it. I'm rather sentimental and I kept these letters from my affair, and my brother found them and told my parents. Then I felt guilty, because my mother started being rather nasty – like for instance, yesterday night, I told her I'd probably be staying out all night, and she said "I hope you're going to behave yourself." It's these sly digs that make me feel rather guilty. But it doesn't worry me to that extent. She hopes I'm going to give up the gay life. But once gay, I think, always gay, and I don't want to change, and I'm quite happy at the moment as I am.'

JS: 'Do you find that society weighs on you with a leaden oppressive force?'

GRAHAM: 'No. I think on those occasions when you have to be a little careful, I do so automatically . . . But I don't think so, day to day.'

JS: 'Did you find it hard to acknowledge your gayness?'

GRAHAM: 'Oh, when I'd put a name to it, it took about six months to come to terms with. I didn't want to be for the first six months, then I decided I was, and I made the best job of it . . . It doesn't leave any guilt. I only wish I'd found out earlier. I wasted long enough as it was.'

CHARLES: 'I'd echo that completely. The only difference was, I didn't have any trouble putting a name to it, but putting theory into practice. I felt guilty about that, and it took some time to get round to it.'

VIC: 'I didn't come out till I was twenty-one. I was beginning to face the fact that I wasn't interested in girls I used to take to parties. And round about the same time I realized I was in love with a boy, and this was a bit upsetting because this didn't seem to tally with anything one knew about. And yet I was quite clearly in love and that was that. It took me a while to work out what to do about things . . . As far as sex was concerned, that took much longer. Once I'd registered and allowed the word to seep into my mind, and then read one or two of those ghastly books that we're now trying to get changed and which told me absolutely nothing about myself – then I went on carrying on an absolutely dual thing, knowing I was gay – or camp, because it was Australia – and when I discovered later that a lot of my friends were camp, it was all rather novel and exciting. But I still didn't know what to do with myself. There was no guilt. I was slightly annoyed with myself for having taken so long and having been so naïve. And then when I got to England I discovered sex, which was an excellent thing.'

CHARLES: 'The experience of falling in love with a guy was not frightening; it was a tremendously good experience, and the gender didn't seem to matter so much.'

VIC: 'Yes, because having at the age of twenty-one never fallen in love with anyone was very abnormal, very peculiar. I used to feel very inadequate, you see, because everyone else was busy having girl-friends and falling in love and experiencing deep emotion . . . And when I fell in love with a boy I was much more relieved to learn that I was normal, i.e. could fall in love, than to discover that I was abnormal and had fallen in love with a boy.'

JS: 'Is it the same for girls?'

JANE: 'I just accepted it immediately, because from the age of eight to fifteen I went through crushes on teachers, older women . . . And then when I was about fifteen I felt this tremendous physical attraction to a friend of mine, and I knew about lesbianism obviously, but I'd never connected the two . . . I was always aware – quite wrongly – of the femme/butch thing and I don't think I fitted into that, and then I saw a programme on TV about three years ago, and there were two girls on it, so much of what they were saying related to myself. I thought "Great." It was a TV programme that made me connect the two.'

KATE: 'This butch/femme thing was very much part of the lesbian scene, and to an extent still is . . . But if women have women's lib ideas, they see the butch/femme thing completely divorced from them . . .'

GRAHAM: 'For a long time after I realized I was gay and knew I liked boys, I still hadn't connected the fact that I was neither more nor less like the people on the back page of the local press. That took me a while.'

VIC: 'Discovering that one is normal in fact and that the stereo-types are wrong.'

JS: 'The stereotypes seem to have a seriously disruptive influence on people's self-realization.'

GRAHAM: 'Yes; suddenly you find out that everything everyone's been telling you is false.'

VIC: 'All I had was these books that were obviously not about me. I never came across any of the gay love stories and soppy romances, most of which were very bad, because they had obligatory happy endings in order to get past the censors. They don't now, but they used to . . . There was a book I knew had an unhappy ending, so I never read the last chapter. It was all irrelevant . . . When I discovered my friends were gay I discovered I was connected into society and the things I'd read and heard about were utter nonsense.'

KATE: 'I think the fundamental thing about my upbringing – I'm also an anarchist, but I had all the pressures, all the oppression, the embargo on friends for about two years, all the stereotyped attempts to make me feel guilty, and I've never felt guilty in my life. This has nothing to do with the fact that I'm gay, but that I'm a rebel any-how . . . To a certain extent I played the stereotypes up to the hilt, and still do in a way . . . The first time I slept with a woman I was fourteen and a half and she was then thirty-three . . . I was plunged very much into the lesbian world . . . If I wanted to get out of straight society I could walk round the corner to her flat and I was in a completely different society where everything about me was accepted. So the feeling of oppression passed me by, because I wasn't isolated. There was a stage in the last six months at school, I was isolated because I was the only actively gay person in school, and my reaction to that was I enjoyed myself enormously. I was outrageous. I spent that time completely and utterly in men's clothes in school. Everybody else was walking about in make-up and dresses and I wore suit and tie and shirt. I revelled in it, really enjoyed myself . . . And it was one of the times when I had the most pressure on me from straight society.'

MATTHEW: 'I think my experience is a little different from most people here. I'm a bit older than most, twenty-nine; and I had twelve or thirteen years of absolute agony over being gay. I only came out when I was twenty-six or seven, and I don't feel one recovers from a period as long as that very quickly. I had a marvel-lous feeling of liberation as soon as I discovered the gay movement, but you know the psychological effects of twelve or thirteen years aren't easily overcome.'

CHARLES: 'The first time I remember overcoming guilt was when I first walked into a CHE meeting; there were only about four people there, but that was the first time I'd ever been bolstered by my peer-group instead of having it work against me, and I couldn't believe it . . . The single most important thing aside that they were all gay and would support me, was this thing that none of them fitted to any stereotype.'

KATE: 'Some people get the opposite reaction – if the group they enter is very stereotyped, it's easier to fit in. If you walk into a room full of women, and fifty per cent are wearing suits and ties and the other fifty per cent are in make-up and skirts, you make up your mind which of the two you're going to act up to.'

JANE: 'You leave.'

VIC: 'The only really confusing thing about the whole process of coming out was discovering about the roles. No one will tell you, and I was too shy to ask, and it's not written down . . . Discovering that what people said about the butch/bitch thing didn't have to mean anything. Discovering how to enjoy sex, and not having to worry about whether one was making a fool of oneself, which I did for the first few times, because there's a whole lot of talk about these roles, but as far as I can see they don't seem to mean very much.'

KATE: 'The thing is, with straight society role-playing is so important. A lot of girls who are very intelligent when they're with a boy try to make out they're not intelligent . . .'

MATTHEW: 'There is another role that is generated by the gay world – the pretence that you have no problems. You *had* problems, and you talk at length about those problems you had *before*, but now you don't have any. And I think there's a lot of pressure to sustain that kind of image in the gay movement, and I don't think that's very healthy.'

KATE: 'Yes, "I'm gay and completely happy, there's nothing wrong with me." '

MATTHEW: 'I think people's present problems need just as much airing as their past ones.'

CHARLES: 'I agree with you in that; but I did find, to my surprise, how many things clicked in me and how many things that had been bothering vanished when I came out . . .'

JANE: 'I think the point is very valid, because straight society says being gay is so terrible and awful and so on, so once you've become gay you say "I'm gay and straight society is all wrong, because I'm all happy and smiling and there's no problems or worries, etc." Which is ridiculous. Because if you overcome the hurdle of deciding that you're gay you'll still have problems. Only we feel we oughtn't to say that because it proves to straight society what they've always believed – that gays are neurotic and hung-up.'

JS: 'Do you think arguments about causes and origins are not worth bothering with?'

VIC: 'For curiosity, one is always interested to find out things if possible. As long as the question is the right question. If you can work out why any person is like he is. On the other hand, the question is almost always asked in terms of "If we knew what caused it, then we could stop it." Therefore I say at present I'm against investigating causes in public, because causes mean cure.'

KATE: 'You talk to someone who's gay and he says something that makes you realize he has a mother fixation and you see the stereotype causes coming out.'

VIC: 'But he's probably concentrated on those, because he knows they're stereotype causes.'

KATE: 'Exactly. My father has this thing about Where did we go wrong ... One day I'll sit down and tell him. Basically, I'm lesbian because of my father. He believed in coeducation, he believed girls should have as much right to things as boys have, and he brought me up – English people would say, as a boy. He brought me up to argue and be aggressive and so on. Because I'm aggressive I wouldn't have fitted well into straight society, where I wasn't expected to be aggressive. It's all very anti-women's lib, but it happens to be true.'

VIC: 'I could reinterpret your life completely. What he brought you up to be was a happy lesbian, see? What he brought you up to was not to have to go through a lot of guilt and hiding and so on.'

KATE: 'Yes, I think I've survived because of the things he did. He didn't make me a lesbian. He gave me the ability to fight against oppression.'

VIC: 'In fact, you should be grateful to him for it.'

KATE: 'I am ... I was banned from seeing a teacher at school for two years and then they found out about a girl I was in love with, who incidentally, was straight, the one I went out with for a year ... When they found out, they were horrified, and still are. I think they think I'm reforming. They don't know I'm up to the hilt in the gay world. And their reaction was totally, utterly against. My father at the time was all for rushing down to the school, getting the teacher concerned sacked, because he thought she was encouraging me, which also happened to be correct. The thing that really got me about the whole situation, he found out about the girl, so he knew I was going out with her, and he automatically assumed that this teacher at school who he thought was gay was encouraging the two of us – this was a correct assumption, and he thought I'd slept with the teacher, which was also a correct assumption, but the point was he had no basis for this at all. He just guessed and got it right . . . And because he said "Right, you can't see this girl," I proceeded to do so without him knowing. I spent the first two months violently defending this teacher, telling him he'd got it all wrong, and she wasn't gay, she hadn't been encouraging me, I hadn't slept with her.'

JS: 'Hassle with parents over coming out?'

CHARLES: 'I think there's a tremendous advantage in coming out away from home, whether it's fifty miles or three thousand. It reduces conflict and gives you time to see who you are.'

KATE: 'In my situation, it wasn't a question of coming out; I was found out.'

VIC: 'Forced out.'

KATE: 'I'm much thicker-skinned about it now, having gone through it with such intensity, having been hated for two years and everything I stood for and believed in. Having gone through that, nothing could be that bad again.'

CHARLES: 'You do have to look at yourself and your family, but it helps if you can do it away, find yourself.'

MATTHEW: 'I wonder if anyone can match my mother's remark when I was coming out. I told them of my problems and so on, and my mother said "Why don't you go along to some of these gay clubs and get it out of your system." ' [Laughter.]

KATE: 'It's the values behind that remark that are so staggering. The point is, if you had gone to gay clubs under those circumstances, you'd've been so horrified and sickened . . .'

VIC: 'My first visit to a gay club, it was in Melbourne. It was full of stereotype people. In the two years I've been in London the types in gay clubs have changed, and this is longer ago, it was frightening. All those puffy queens.'

199

JS: 'Do you think those stereotypes will disappear over time? Will they get weaker, or do they correspond to something ineradicable?'

VIC: 'I think this is part of the deviant thing. I think it has been obvious and will continue to be so, because there has been no break in the culture . . . the obvious blatant reaction to being cast as sexually deviant.'

KATE: 'If women's lib movement helps to stop role playing in the straight world, you won't have anything to react against. If the idea that a female is feminine disappears, then a gay man as a young boy can't start putting on make-up and acting in a way that everyone can see as feminine. Same too for a girl . . . It'll be jokes in history books in two thousand years' time. I think it'll be that timescale . . . That's how they used to act, how funny and silly, just because a man has five or six more inches of skin there and a woman has breasts, made such a total difference . . . If it doesn't change in the majority world, the straight world, real world, whatever you like to call it, if it doesn't change there, it won't change in the gay world, because we are reflecting that society . . . Some of us don't mind, we like living on the fringes.'

JS: 'Is old age the spectre for gay people which is sometimes claimed?'

CHARLES: 'I feel sorry for people who are old now who are just coming out. They've missed out. Look at old people now. I've thought "How can I avoid getting into that situation when I'm sixty?" But it'll be different because everyone here will be sixty at the same time, and we'll have each other as a boost for each other.'

KATE: 'There is this fear, especially with gay men, that they might be left on their own, because you get the cracks about dirty old men.'

CHARLES: 'Tatty old queens.'

VIC: 'There's also the thing that you won't be married, you won't have children to look after you. In fact, it's usually women who become widows rather than men widowers, because men die earlier and marry older anyway, so the average married man is going to die before his wife, and isn't going to be alone in old age, and anyway there's children . . . In our society there is sufficient family feeling to keep most men, straight men that is, in some degree of being cared for, although it leaves a lot out. Is it going to be the same for us because we don't have children? History seems to suggest we shan't have such long-lasting relationships, although this may also be changing, and it is a slightly worrying sort of thought, only as Charles said, it is going to be different for us because we've grown up in a different society. We've got our friends . . . There are plenty of old men nowadays who can be reasonably happy.'

JS: 'Show me them.'

VIC: 'Some of my priestly friends . . . They're not too badly off. They have the consolations of religion, but more important is the consolation of all their fellow-priests, of the same age and younger.'

JS: 'Will you be able to establish secular monasteries for unbelieving gays of a certain age?'

CHARLES: 'Isn't CHE already a kind of secular church?'

JS: 'I sometimes feel there's an unhappy resemblance between the new liberated gay world to that of older unliberated gay world.'

VIC: 'The difficulty is the small reach so far of ideas of liberation. The alternative society altogether has touched only a fairly small segment of the society.'

JS: 'The alternative society can't come to terms with old age, because it's a product of youth culture and hedonism.'

KATE: 'This reflects society in general.'

VIC: 'I'm not worried. I feel I shall continue to make friends who'll continue to be friends all my life . . . I do have a lot of straight friends. Although I've made hardly any straight friends in England . . . I'm not much exposed to straights [Laughter] . . .'

Homosexuality has passed within a few years from being a subject not to be mentioned without horror and revulsion, through acceptance (admittedly with an amused kind of pity by 'straight' society), to a position where it is contemplated by many young people with the same sort of *frisson* associated with current flirtations with Satanism or necromancy. It isn't that the 1967 Act released a wave of tolerance and sympathy; rather the Act legitimated attitudes already evolving, and which sprang from reasons far more compelling than the growing militancy of gay groups – from reasons that are primarily economic. By releasing homosexuality from its pall of secrecy and silence, a new and well-defined group has been identified which is highly consumer-oriented.

Gay people tend to have more money to spend on themselves and more leisure than people with dependants. The removal of the stigma, the lessening of the sense of shame, coincide with the identification and extension of new consumer markets. In this way the consumer society anticipates and neutralizes groups of people formerly thought to constitute a threat to morality and order. And the irony is that even those groups who are felt to be in the vanguard of an alleged moral revolution are often doing no more than helping to signal the existence of a once-submerged though substantial minority, in a way that has more to do with the exigencies of the economy than with personal liberation. Such seems to have been one of the principal effects of the proselytizing of the Gay Liberation Front (GLF) and the more sedate attack of the Campaign for Homosexual Equality (CHE).

The discrepancy between what we think we're doing and the social function we actually fulfil, is nowhere more clear than at the meetings of some of the gay organizations.

A London meeting of GLF

A distempered room in Central London; stone floor, platform at one end; tubular chairs with green canvas seats and back-rests. Although the meeting of GLF is advertised for 7.30, at eight o'clock there are no more than a dozen people in the room – all newcomers, because the initiated know that nothing starts before half past eight or nine, or even not at all. Of those who have come for the first time, several are tourists, a few are students; an American with shoulder-length blond hair surveys the pitifully small effort with an amused disdain.

Most people are slightly nervous; it is a bit like a revivalist meeting, where people expect to be called on to testify, and they are silently rehearsing their testimony. Occasionally, a face is seen through the dusty pane of the swing doors; anxious and interrogative, but, daunted, retreats and does not enter. There is something unequivocal about attending a meeting specifically for gay people; people can visit gay bars or discos and not feel so exposed. There is always an alibi for being in a pub – you can delude yourself you're only there for the beer; to go to a meeting requires a directness and self-honesty that many homosexuals are not ready for.

Although everybody insists that there is no structure in GLF, no officials, no organizers, it immediately becomes clear that there are cognoscenti and novices. Some of the former are going round, carefully instructing new arrivals in the ways of GLF, probing, proselytizing. The approach is direct and friendly. 'Do you feel oppressed, or do you feel that you're free to do as you like?' 'Do your friends know, do the people you work with know? Could you tell them?' Most of those catechized are only too anxious to defer to those who, in spite of everything, seem to be in control, welcoming, instructing. Among those present for the first time there is little conversation. They are so anxious not to appear to be doing anything so vulgar as scraping up an acquaintance or picking each other up, that a kind of paralysis prevents even the most innocuous small talk. Most people in the room are under thirty-five; many under twenty-five. One or two men in dark suits, who have come straight from work.

By nine o'clock there are perhaps fifty people in the room. The air of expectancy remains unfulfilled. No one makes any attempt to do anything. Here and there small groups are talking together. 'I feel more oppressed by the economic structure than I do by my homosexuality,' a young man in an anorak is saying. 'But it's part of the same thing, surely.' 'How do you mean?' 'Women, gays, blacks, we're all oppressed by a white male-dominated capitalist economy.' Someone comes round with a jam jar for contributions towards the hire of the hall; a man who refers to himself as 'the tea-lady' brings a tray full of mugs.

Of the people present, ninety per cent are male. There are many in jeans or boy-blue overalls; one or two in sequined jackets; some with make-up, glitter on the eyelids; but for the most part the fashion seems to be a carefully neglected stylishness. From time to time somebody asks for silence – which he gets almost immediately, because everybody thinks something is going to happen; but it is only to announce a demonstration against the editor of a local North London newspaper, who has said disparaging things about gay people in his paper. A friend from Canada says a few words and is given in return fraternal greetings from GLF London. Somebody says 'Who wants to talk about sex?' Laughter. Then somebody asks 'Well, what are we here for? What do we think we're here for?'

At last a generalized discussion begins; it is dominated by nine or ten people, all articulate, passionate and middle class. The rest look from one to another of the speakers, relieved that someone has at last taken the initiative; but the atmosphere remains tense, and even those who contribute to the discussion seem to be as anxious about the impression they are creating as about the quality of their remarks. An Australian girl talks about abortion, and declares fervidly that thousands of her sisters all over the world are being murdered by the system. Someone else says that to him oppression means going into gay bars and being charged extortionate prices for a pint of beer. 'But that's only one insignificant aspect of the whole thing.' 'It's not insignificant to me. I drink a lot of beer.' This leads to a discussion about the gay ghetto, the traditional homosexual subculture, the furtiveness of the freemasonry. 'Look what happens – we imitate some of the most oppressive features of straight society, playing male/female roles; anxiety to conform and be accepted makes us often act out those things we have no need to.' A man of about thirty talks scornfully of homosexual *ménages*, which are like a caricature of suburbia, all shopping bags and vacuum cleaners and hairdressing appointments. 'It's these stereotypes of the gay world which straightjacket and oppress us; stereotypes that make us harmless, good for a laugh. There is a half-awareness about homosexuality in society that in many ways is almost more dangerous than ignorance.'

There then follows much talk about 'coming out' – of telling the people at your place of work, telling your friends and your family that you are gay. Someone who did this recently says that everybody was wonderful about it. He felt reborn; it had caused him agonies before daring to take the plunge; now he wondered at his own pusillanimity. 'Well what about teachers? I'm a teacher, I couldn't tell my colleagues.' 'The ILEA doesn't sack people for being gay.' 'No, but the kids could make your life a misery.' 'Or their parents.' A teacher says that he wears a GLF button to school, and nobody took exception to it. 'But coming out in teaching, even if they didn't chuck you out, you'd ruin your chances of promotion.' 'Who wants promotion? Happiness is more important than promotion.' 'If all the gay teachers in the ILEA were thrown out,' someone says grimly, 'they'd have a *real* staffing crisis on their hands.'

There are some more testimonies of how easy it is once you've plucked up the courage to admit you're gay. 'I told my parents, and they said "Well, you're still our son, and if that's the way you are, so be it." Graham and I are completely accepted; our parents visit each other.'

'What's the difference though between being accepted and being patronized?' This is felt to be too academic a question, and is shouted down. First things first.

'I couldn't tell my mother, it'd kill her.'

'Everybody thinks that. But I never heard of it killing anybody. In the end, mothers are pleased. It means they can have you all to themselves.'

'Good God, they caused it. Why should they be protected from knowing what they've done?'

An explosion of anger at this: more vulgar stereotypes about mother/son relationships.

'You simply cannot generalize. Anyway, the *causes* are irrelevant – we're dealing with situations and how to react to them. We don't want endless debates about what makes people gay – that's capitulating to straight society again. Gay is good, and that's all there is to say.'

Most individual accounts of coming out are like confessions of faith. 'I doubted until I declared myself, and now I feel free.' Some are heroic. There is talk of pushing back frontiers, opening doors, liberation, self-assertion, joy and pride in finding one's gay identity. The enemy is felt to be capitalism, role-playing, middle-class white male oppression.

Yet somehow, among these young people, metropolitan, jubilant, it is difficult to believe in this oppression. There are certainly cases of people being persecuted for their homosexuality (see the closing section of this book). In smaller communities and among older age-groups the stigma remains often and the lives of many are corroded by guilt and shame. But for this group to talk in impassioned tones about oppression is an exaggeration. Here they are, being themselves, trying to defy a society that looks on benignly. More than benignly. In fact, what they are doing is carrying out the demands of changed economic conditions. It is the relaxation of traditional disciplines that allows them – even demands of them – that they be as they are. More than this, it gives great latitude for self-expression, permitting even revolutionary incantations, the illusion of personal heroics. The gay community has been discovered in the early seventies in much the same way, and for the same reasons, that teenagers were discovered in the fifties.

Before that time there were children, adolescents and adults, but the creation of a teenage identity developed an awareness of belonging to an interest-group which made it easier for the opening up of new markets in fashion, cosmetics, records, etc. And after the rich vein of teenagers, who were part invented, part discovered, like a lost race who had been among us all the time without anyone having noticed their presence, it is inevitable that when gay people have announced their existence, they should be wooed and courted as adolescents were. With over two million homosexual people, it promises to be a lucrative process. Gay people are some of the most avid consumers of clothing, holidays, theatre and cinema, restaurant meals, cosmetics, as well as of household goods. And if there is an illusory combat in the gay community's struggle for recognition, this can only strengthen the function which that community is required to serve.

There are now gay groups based on all kinds of common interests – travel, cricket, badminton, theatre, football, photography, tennis, cinema. There are meetings for teachers, transvestites, Jews, Marxists, even librarians. If the consumer economy depends upon individuals consulting their needs and wants and then striving to fulfil them, it is inevitable that a liberation in the area of sexual behaviour should be set in train; and the crusading of gay groups can only occur in this context.

There is a danger that the gay movements, instead of being the radical or reformist force which they claim to be, may merely institutionalize yet another area of 'freedom' that has been opened up by consumerism.

CHE meeting in a Midland town

Most people don't have access to the London gay world; although most industrial towns and cities of any size have their gay pub; a club possibly; and London is felt to be of easy access to most people for a weekend. The pressures of community are far greater on those who live in small towns, and even in some large cities many feel that they are observed, commented on in a way which doesn't happen in London. The gay pub in most towns is likely to be a cocktail bar at the side of one of the bigger hotels, plush, discreet, and most of the habitués will soon get to know each other. I met a young man who spends much of his time at weekends visiting the gay pubs in the Midlands and North, because 'they're so thankful to see a new face it doesn't particularly matter if it's not a very pretty one, and you can have the pick of the crop.'

A summer evening in a Midland town. The Friends' Meeting House, an early nineteenth-century building behind the main shopping centre, a place of calm and quiet behind the ravages that are transforming the town from its red-brick and sandstone country-town tradition into a twentieth-century 'complex' of precinct offices and underpasses. The neat row of gravestones behind the building are more recent than they appear – some of the names engraved in the plain ogival stones are as recent as the nineteen-fifties. The grass is high around the graveyard, overrun by cranes-bill and willowherb. A meeting of the local group of the Campaign for Homosexual Equality has been arranged; but the door is locked, and somebody has to go and fetch the caretaker from his place of work, which is the telephone exchange. In the meanwhile we wait outside, talking politely. Somebody makes a joke about 'unholy communion', talking of a relationship between two members of the group; a man in a clerical collar says 'You can't expect me to find that funny.' He apologizes, and somebody awkwardly changes the conversation. 'I think that's called larkspur, or is it a dwarf delphinium?'

Somebody arrives with the key. We file, perhaps fifteen people, through the building, through the areas used by play-groups, which are littered with plastic transparent pink and blue horses and duck-lings, into a plain room with sedate chairs with imitation straw bottoms, and a plain walnut table. On the carpet, a felt horse on a metal frame with wheels which a child from the play-group has left there. Someone removes it unobtrusively. The chairs are arranged in a circle. A young man nervously says it all reminds him of Sunday School. Much time is taken up with announcements about future meetings, which all sound so much more interesting than this one: all the heads of local schools have been written to, with a view to a discussion with sixth-formers. They talk of a recent treasure-hunt in cars that had been organized: somebody had had a burst tyre and had had to go home. The vicar shows some photographs of his church on a council estate, in red dawn light, a fifties geometrical building against a lurid, pink sky.

At last a discussion gets going. There are certain people who contribute far more substantially than others, including the vicar, who has to leave early anyway, because he is supposed to be at a church meeting; and he gives a conspiratorial and collusive smile of apology. Looking round at those assembled, I have a curious sense of

207

time, not only in the oddly correct room, the flush of the dying sun on the red-brick, the cranes outside, heaving together the bulk of a new office block, but in the styles of the people in the room. It is a bit like a parish council meeting; a village cricket team. A few of the occupants of the room are in their late twenties, but most are older; and it seems, in their anxiety to conform outwardly with their idea of 'straight' society, they have slightly exaggerated the conservatism of dress and style, so that, instead of looking unremarkable, there is a distinctly anachronistic air: traditional masculine style, lovat green, tweed sports-coat, sandals and flannels. A striped shirt and flared trousers look quite conspicuous by contrast. The hair is short in almost every case. A similar assembly of people could have met here fifteen years ago, with scarcely any alteration in detail. For the most part they are cowed by the norms of provincial life. They agree that they are compelled to lead double lives; they are constantly aware of the vigilance of peers, neighbours and fellow-workers. One girl says that if anybody at work asked her if she were homosexual, she would say yes, but that such a question would itself be quite unthinkable on the part of those she worked with; even if they suspected it, they would not know how to broach the subject; it would lie between them like an insurmountable barrier. 'Not married? Oh,' would be the nearest anybody might come to indicating what they felt. I discover that I know someone known to the vicar. 'For goodness' sake don't say you've met me here.' Among those present are a security guard, a social worker, a head teacher, a factory worker, a man who is unemployed, a civil engineer, a physicist – almost an allegory of the incidence of homosexuality in the population; a kind of gay Canterbury Tales welded together by an improbable yet all-embracing faith. Nobody here was actually born in the area. Most are from other parts of the country, although a few do come from a neighbouring town, where the meetings are held alternately. That in itself is significant – all have been in some way uprooted. They could not imagine belonging to CHE at home – in Stockport, Frome or Bangor. Most of the people here have accepted that their life lies in this small community, and they accept the frustrations that accompany their choice. A few of the younger ones are obviously more mobile. One or two say they want to go to London, it's only a question of time before they bow to the inevitable. Because they know that this is the place where they will spend the rest of their life, or because they are professionally vulnerable and don't want to jeopardize their prospects of promotion, they prefer to subordinate their sexual life to their profession or to respect for the views of the community. Indeed, there is a strong sense of mild persecution, of attenuated conspiracy in the way they talk about being found out; the nightmare of the importance of their sexuality to other people.

We then talk about the positive value of living in a place like B—. At least, in a place like this, people take more interest in each other ('Too much'); people put more into relationships here than they do in London, individuals are not so easily replaced by others; more effort is made to get on with each other. Individuals are less expendable. There is less indifference towards people. On the other hand, you get to know them too well, there is a danger of exhausting each other's company too quickly for lack of diversity and lack of external stimulus. New faces are eagerly sought, each newcomer avidly incorporated into the group. I had the impression that individuals tend to leave the group to split up in twos, and then contritely return to the group when that breaks up. The comradeliness is essentially a product of isolation and the lack of a much-desired personal relationship. Very few are in it out of idealism or for ideological reasons.

A contempt for the local gay bar is expressed. It is run by an eccentric and capricious woman who will arbitrarily throw people out if she doesn't like the look of them. This means that the bar tends to be filled only with pretty young men. The subject of cottaging is raised – not called that, but 'picking up people in public lavatories'. But the subject is not pursued. Nobody is actually admitting to anything. Even within the group there is a strong feeling that it is necessary to keep one's pride, self-respect: presumably, if anyone does anything he will feel ashamed of, a trip will be made to a neighbouring town or city. So how do people cope? Brief periods of intense activity in London tend to alternate with the long provincial exile. Holidays. Occasional weekends. Parties. Most of those present live alone; in lodgings, bed-sitters, sometimes in their own homes on private estates with a wife or mother. There has not been a tradition of sharing flats in this town. Traditionally, you leave home to get married, and you go from the parental home into your connubial one. Flats, rooms were felt to be, in this working-class community, places for itinerant labourers, tramps, common lodging houses; or places of impossible luxury where the wives of manufacturers drank cocktails and kept exotic pets in the central heating which dried the air up. Anybody sharing flats now would be expected to stop doing so in their early twenties; it might be regarded in the new liberal climate as an adolescent indulgence; not something to prolong into maturity. I can remember two girls I knew who moved into a flat when I lived in Northampton in the early sixties. 'Flats. Girls of nineteen!' cried their mothers. 'What do girls of nineteen want to do in flats that they can't do at home?'

There is some discussion about whether there is such a thing as the 'homosexual condition'. Most seem to think that with gay people the sex drive is nearer the surface than with most heterosexual (which the vicar pronounces 'heaterosexual') people, and that must be why there is a tendency to give way to it in dangerous places.

By ten o'clock everybody is wondering whether they will have a chance to get a drink before the pubs close. 'Oh, if we all go, that'll make it a gay pub!'; a stolid drinking place in the town-centre. Oh well. Thank you, it's been very interesting. Thank you for talking to us. I never said a bloody word. I had the impression that everybody who spoke had said more or less the same thing at the previous meeting. It was all inhibited, formal and rather polite; static, in fact. It has a secretary and a treasurer and a chairman. It seemed isolated, over-anxious and deferential, testing the moral water with a big toe. The dying light hesitates on the dusty windows of the meeting-house; and then the street-lamps start to be a little brighter than the Western sky.

Harry, twenty-four

'I'm a drop-out from university, twice, which is something of a record. First I was in Swindon, engineering students [grimace]. I had absolutely nothing in common with them. The second time I was in Bristol, reading Physics, but I seemed not to relate to the people in the Physics department at all. My parents are Northern Irish, and have all the prejudices that you might expect. I'm a Tory, I have my own business now, computers; I suppose I'm fairly ambitious . . . I think I need to prove myself. I'm a fairly well-balanced person. I'm not promiscuous, though, and I know that not being promiscuous isn't really part of the gay scene. I can't bring myself to go and pick up people if I know it's only for a one-night stand. I go to the Catacombs, I'm half-fascinated and half-repelled by it. I think when you're with one person you should be faithful to him.

'Twice I've had really deep relationships with boys. The first one got drowned. It was in Bristol, and I've always been keen on sailing, and it was a calm day, and he said he thought he'd go for a swim . . . He went as far as a buoy some way off, and then I simply never saw him again . . . I got some friends from the University Flying Corps. We searched the area for hours and hours. They finally found his body, a week later, all eaten by crabs and things; it wasn't a very attractive sight. I had to go and identify him. I recognized him by the swimming trunks . . .

'It was strange, I went to see his parents after it happened, and they were very nice to me, but when they realized what our relationship had been, they wouldn't even let me go to the funeral . . . I remember his mother saying to me "Are you sure you did everything you could?" . . . I'm a very emotional person, I just burst into floods of tears. I was sharing a flat at the time with three straight guys, they didn't understand what it was all about. Two of the happiest months of my life, and that's how it ended.

'Then I met Steve, and that gave me a year of happiness. I knew that he was going out with other boys after about the first six months, but that didn't bother me. Well, I didn't like it, but I was prepared to put up with it for the sake of our relationship . . . I was keeping him for six months of that time, and then a few months ago he just threw me out. He was very intelligent, he got a First, and I was really happy with him. I'd like to go back to him, but I know it can't happen.

'At the moment I'm going through this terrible conflict. I feel in one way I'd like to be terribly promiscuous, and at the same time I'd rather have a stable relationship with just one person. I don't know if I'm unusual in that. My family have been very understanding. My father was a marine commando, and so is my brother, but they've never said anything disparaging or made me feel in any way ashamed. My father commanded the cliff assault in Normandy . . . I've not really found my way around the gay scene. I dislike it, actually, the meat-market aspect of it.

'My job is important to me, I've a partner, actually; he's straight and he's one of my very best friends, both him and his wife. Thank God I'm not involved with him, I couldn't bear that.

'I like nice things. I collect glass, actually, Victorian, Georgian.

There wasn't much cut glass before early Victorian . . . I like to give dinner parties. I specialize in onion soup and soufflé; that's the way I prefer to lead my social life. I've always found being gay very natural. I don't think I feel guilty about it; but I do have this feeling of duality – in some ways I'm afraid to plunge in, because of what it can do to people, and at the same time I feel a strong urge to be promiscuous. I have a great admiration and respect for my father. My mother too, only she doesn't have his intelligence . . . I was brought up a bit all over the place. I went to eleven schools. I suppose that had quite an influence on me – you're just beginning to settle down, make friends, and then you're off again. My father was always present in my life; he was in Egypt for the first two or three years, and I remember, on my fourth birthday, he wrote me a poem from Egypt; something quite trivial, but it's funny how you remember these things as important. After that he was always there, very dependable . . . When I was younger I was rather fat, and this gave me incredible feelings of inferiority. I don't think I'm attractive; it always slightly surprises me when people tell me I'm attractive. I suppose I'm vain. I don't like to think that being gay is a full-time occupation. I like to think my work is more important but being gay is something you can't deny. It would be stupid to try. I think what I want is for gay people to be accepted by society. I'm not in favour of banner-waving and proclaiming yourself like Gay Lib, but I don't believe in trying to conceal yourself all the time and leading a double life.'

Len, early thirties

Disabled, he lives with his elderly mother in a privately rented flat in South London; he has his own room, which he has carefully furnished and decorated in a way that contrasts strangely with the old-fashioned chintzy feel of the rest of the flat; multicoloured lighting, mobiles, typing desk, units for hi-fi, records, small Japanese colour TV, large teddy bear. Len works; he does a clerical job for a Local Authority department, but this seriously under-occupies his mind. His mother is anxious and mild, and, to her son's embarrassment, tells everybody he takes home that she is worried about what will happen to him when she is gone. She brought us in some coffee and cakes on a tray with a paper doily; and her deferential goodwill was painful. Len noticed my discomfort, and said 'It's all right, she thinks everybody who comes here is a potential successor to look after me. Don't worry, I shan't make any demands on you.

'I find all the talk about gay liberation a bit of a laugh, frankly. How can I be liberated? There's only one liberation I shall ever get and that'll be a liberation from life . . . I've been to some of their meetings; when you hear them talk, I feel I ought to do a Lazarus act, you know, take up your bed and walk . . . I'm bitter, sure I'm bitter . . . I'm bitter, not only about being disabled, but it's their insensitivity to people who are in a situation like mine . . . It isn't only me. I don't feel particularly sorry for myself; but really, all that, it's only for people who are young and pretty . . . What about all the poor sods who are disabled mentally, those who are too old, how do you think they feel about being liberated? Come and liberate me from old age – it makes you weep. I know I'm a special case, but you know, that gives you the chance to see things that other people might miss sometimes. I refuse to spend my time being bright and pretending everything is just fine. It isn't. I'm not like you. I'm excluded. I have been given sex by people, out of pity . . . Sex is something you can't give as a charity. Charity is worse than prostitution. I'd sooner pay somebody . . . I have met people who want to have sex with me; or they've said they wanted to. But then, because of what I am, I'm always there, waiting to see the feeling of revulsion, the gritted teeth, all that; and then I over-react and reject people, so I don't give them a chance. I suppose I ought not to think about all the people I can never have, but as that includes about a hundred per cent of the human race, it's not easy . . . That sounds like self-pity, I'm sorry, I'm only trying to tell you what it feels like . . . Having to depend on people for everything; it's bad enough, without having them on about liberation . . . You see, it gives you a sense of detachment. My life is like everybody else's, only more so: they've all got their disablement within them, but I carry mine like a gravestone and they don't want to sit and look at epitaphs, unless they're necrophiliacs, and that's not normal . . . do you see what I mean? Everybody's life is limited; but they go on as if they could be free of everything about themselves. You're still lumbered with your disabilities whatever kind they are. Being homosexual is part of you that should be neither strength nor weakness, or both. Sure you accept it. I accept being gay; but I don't accept my disability. Now then. Am I liberated? Should I be liberated?

How can I accept something that is so incapacitating, that limits me so? I believe in being in a state of war with life, with all the things that hurt and limit people. Sexuality is an endless, insatiable urge in people. It is quite ludicrous. It can be beautiful (not for me); but because it is necessary to keep the species going (for some obscure reason), it's never satisfied ... Or I've never met anybody who ever admits to being satisfied ... not just gay people, that's general ... It's an absurdity, to look for some kind of self-fulfilment in something that can't be fulfilled ... I mean, it's that absurd clash between our aspirations and our humanity. So I find it hard to believe in these things that everybody gets so excited about ... I don't know why I am gay ... Perhaps it was because I was overprotected. I had to be. So what?'

Bernard, twenty-eight

'There's nothing *pansy* about me ... I've seen men killed, and it didn't have any more effect on me than killing a chicken ... I've worked on trawlers, oil-rigs, buildings, skyscrapers ... I worked tunnelling on the Victoria Line; I've been a miner ... I've seen men crushed by falling rock, I've seen them helpless under a ton of earth, just their eyes, scared, pleading not to leave them, with the roof caving in, and you know you had to save your skin or die with them. I wouldn't give it a second thought; I'm away like a bullet from a gun ... I was on a trawler, in a force nine gale, two blokes got pissed and started fighting, knives; one of them, he just stuck a knife in his gut, you could hear it tear like a sack, and he went straight overboard. You just learned not to see things it's best not to see; you have to learn to be blind, deaf and dumb; if you don't, somebody'll do it for you. Like on the buildings, I've seen people fall a hundred feet, sometimes just get up and walk away ... It's happened to me. I fell off some scaffolding, never said anything to anybody; I had a bit of a shooting pain in my leg, went back to work without a thought. Later I thought I'd better go and see what was the matter, doctor said "You've broken your leg in three places." I didn't even know it had happened. I didn't care. I don't care about pain. I think you've got a duty to be a man, you know, act like a man, even if you've got warped tastes in sex.'

JS: 'Why warped?'

BERNARD: 'Well it is warped isn't it? It's not natural, normal . . .
If I've been with a bloke, I hate him afterwards . . . I hate the bloke,
because he reminds me what I am. I know it's not his fault . . .
sometimes I've had to hit him, especially if he's very nancy like,
know what I mean? . . . Silly that is . . . I don't go in for sex much
though. I drink a lot, and then you know, you can't get it up . . .
You can swill it all out of you, see. I'll drink thirteen or fourteen
pints a night, then I don't know where I am . . . You don't know
who you are after that amount. I'm bent. I can face that . . . I don't
mind saying it; but if anybody else said it to me, I'd knock their
face so they squinted out the back of their neck . . . I'd kill anybody
who called me a queer. I'm not pansy . . . I live like a man, I want
to be treated like a man . . . I've got one tattoo, look, "Mum and
Dad". I mean it. They live in Sunderland. I don't see them much.
But that tattoo is the only thing that means anything to me.'

Gay Catechism

JS: 'What do you most want from life?'
  ADRIAN: 'To be happy.'
JS: 'Is that possible?'
  ADRIAN: 'How do you mean? It must be.'
JS: 'Do you believe in love?'
  ADRIAN: 'Of course.'
JS: 'Have you ever been in love?'
  ADRIAN: 'Yes. Lots of times.'
JS: 'What went wrong?'
  ADRIAN: 'I met the wrong person.'
JS: 'But you're still hopeful?'
  ADRIAN: 'Yes.'
JS: 'How are gay people different from straights?'
  ADRIAN: 'They're more sensitive.'
JS: 'In what way?'
  ADRIAN: 'We suffer more.'
JS: 'Because of being gay?'
  ADRIAN: 'No, because of what society does to us.'
JS: 'What does it do?'
  ADRIAN: 'It tells you it's something to be ashamed of.'
JS: 'Are you ashamed of it?'

ADRIAN: 'No I am not. I'm proud of it.'

JS: 'Do your parents and friends know?'

ADRIAN: 'Some do. I don't feel I need to go shouting all over the place about it.'

JS: 'But if you're proud of it?'

ADRIAN: 'I've got no time for Gay Lib and all that loud-mouthed nonsense. It does gays a bad turn.'

JS: 'Do you enjoy life?'

ADRIAN: 'I love every minute of it.'

JS: 'Do you think gay people are more emotional than others?'

ADRIAN: 'They feel things more deeply. One minute you're on cloud seven and the next you're in the depths of despair. But it's all part of the same thing.'

JS: 'Are you promiscuous?'

ADRIAN: 'Well I am. But not from choice.'

JS: 'Why then?'

ADRIAN: 'Until I can find a lasting relationship.'

JS: 'And what then?'

ADRIAN: 'I'll settle down.'

JS: 'Why are gay people promiscuous?'

ADRIAN: 'You have to prove to yourself you're still attractive, you can still get what you want.'

JS: 'What are you most afraid of?'

ADRIAN: 'Getting old . . . That terrifies me. Literally, I wake up in the night sometimes, and it's a nightmare.'

JS: 'How old are you?'

ADRIAN: 'Twenty-six. Past it really.'

JS: 'Past it?'

ADRIAN: 'Well I think you're always aware of the next generation. To be old if you're gay is to be nowhere.'

JS: 'What is your greatest ambition?'

ADRIAN: 'To travel . . . And have a relationship . . .'

JS: But you've had some relationships?'

ADRIAN: 'Yes.'

JS: 'What went wrong?'

ADRIAN: 'I'm too trusting . . . They turned out to be on the make, deceitful. I told you, I've always met the wrong person.'

Gordon Fraser, thirty-four

Dark hair, receding slightly, mobile openness that belies inner uncertainty. He has been teaching French at an independent school in a cathedral town in the North of England. At the age of thirty-two he became deeply involved with one of his pupils, a boy of seventeen. The boy's parents came into possession of some letters written by the teacher to his pupil, and have threatened him with exposure, prosecution. Gordon was suspended from school, his case investigated by the Department of Education and Science, and he was sent to a psychiatrist. When I met him, he was in the midst of the drama of suspension, social obloquy and uncertainty.

Gordon was the son of an official in the diplomatic service. His mother died when he was a child, and he was fostered by friends of the dead woman. He knew all the time that he was not their child, although they were very kind to him. He attended a day grammar school, and went up to Oxford in the late fifties. He had one or two relationships with undergraduates, but they all seemed unsatisfactory, and he never related the abstraction of homosexuality to his own needs and relationships. He assumed that he would grow out of it. When he left university he got married, and now has three children. The relationship with his wife has never been very deep: there was very little communication, and he was for a long time aware of a deep sense of lack of fulfilment and a denial of his own needs. It was not until he had been teaching for some time that he met and became attracted to Andrew, then in the first year sixth form. Since the school was small, and friendships were quite common between pupils and members of staff and their families, it was not long before Andrew became a regular visitor at the house. Gordon's wife was doing an external degree, locked herself away for long periods of time in her study, and left Gordon and Andrew together. The relationship was quite reciprocal; Gordon emphasizes that he did not seduce the boy, but that there was a real sense of mutual discovery. It was not until he was thirty-two that Gordon realized the nature of his desire and of his sexuality, and Andrew once said to him that it was ironic that they should both be discovering themselves at such disparate ages. He was grateful to Gordon, as Gordon was to him; only rueful that he had not known himself better many years previously. Although his wife knew nothing conclusive, the sterility of their own marital relationship

217

may have made her suspect. In any case, she herself had a lover. If the discovery of Gordon's relationship with Andrew had one positive by-product, it was that it abridged the unsatisfactory ritual that he was enacting with his wife. In a way he feels that he was indiscreet in writing to the boy in the first place. Andrew was always interested in Gordon's children, and was almost, in an ironic and irregular fashion, part of the family. And indeed, Gordon feels that he was a father figure for Andrew. Not that Andrew didn't have a father; but his father was possibly overpunctilious in his regulation of every aspect of the boy's life. An immigrant from Eastern Europe, he exercised a very rigorous control over his son's life; letters from home were always full of exhortations to work, not to waste time; because Andrew was being formed to continue the family business. Gordon suspects that the parents knew there was a relationship between their son and his teacher. During the holidays Andrew was always telephoning, writing letters; was restless and unhappy without him.

The drama erupted during the summer holidays. Andrew had been to France for a holiday, and as soon as he returned home, he was either confronted with evidence (notwithstanding that he had taken the tell-tale letters with him), and, possibly in a moment of adolescent self-will had admitted it. The father got in touch with the headmaster, who sent an urgent wire to Gordon, himself on holiday in Germany with his family. The headmaster was obliged to suspend him; and meanwhile, his case was investigated by the Department of Education and Science, who directed him to have a psychiatric diagnosis, while further consideration was given to his fitness to teach in the future. Gordon was for a time so frightened that he returned to Germany, in an attempt to get a teaching job there. The boy was taken away from the school, and sent to a day school. Gordon says it is ironic that one of the ideas of sending children to boarding schools – partly to toughen them up – should involve a certain abrogation of parental responsibility; which only exacerbates the anger when anything is found to be amiss.

Of course Gordon has not seen Andrew since that time. The revelations seriously incommoded his wife, because they exposed her relationship with another man, himself married. The father of the boy has threatened prosecution, but as yet there appears to have been no police investigation. The headmaster felt betrayed and vulnerable, and of course fears for the reputation of the school.

Gordon came back from Germany and has been applying for other jobs unconnected with teaching. He is not sorry that his career in teaching has been ended; but of course the disturbance and anxiety have depressed him deeply. What he regrets most of all are the years spent without any knowledge of what he regards as his true nature. The self-denial, the self-repression, the desperate attempts to conform, the failure to understand his own needs, despite the education he received, the continuing *naïveté*, the failure to recognize himself. That he was discovering his true nature at the same time that Andrew was discovering his own is not in doubt. What he says he most needed at seventeen was someone like himself to help as a self-defining image for the process of development. Although Gordon had met Andrew's parents, and indeed, he, his wife and the parents had all been out to dinner together earlier in the summer, when the knowledge of what had happened emerged, there was no question of any further contact, no attempt at explanation. Gordon feels that the threat of prosecution has been held over him and the school, as a kind of blackmail; in any case, it is perturbing not to know what is going to happen; to be in a twilight world of ignominy, anxiety and fear is very debilitating. Gordon says he has no doubt that it was the kind of relationship he had always wanted, yet had been unable to attain. The boy is now under constant surveillance; has been sent to a day school where he has had to start the sixth form all over again, although he is now almost eighteen. He has a talent for design: not the sort of thing his parents would recognize as a suitable career – for them that is the kind of thing one does with one's leisure. They are orthodox, right thinking, and are convinced that with Andrew it was simply a phase; whereas they are equally convinced of Gordon's total depravity. By severing all contact they are able to create for themselves a sense of his monstrous nature, without having their conception of him contaminated by any actual personal contact. In this way they are themselves absolved from any guilt in the processes that have caused their boy to stray so flagrantly from their ideas of what is normal. The father is hard-working, strict, puritanical.

Gordon says that everyone has been very kind, even his wife – for one moment he broke down and was able to talk to her and cry openly, although this period of intimacy and understanding between them did not last. His foster mother was kind and understanding, and wondered only why he hadn't told her earlier. His friends have been uniformly liberal. Only the headmaster, whose school has been indirectly 'tainted', has been angry. When Gordon was offered the 'I-don't-know-what-came-over-me' cliché, he scorned it. That was when the headmaster insisted he see a psychiatrist. His wife would have played the role open to her – the mitigating circumstances, pressure of work, money worries, etc., but Gordon, being himself rather puritanical, refused the easy alibi. He said that in fact this relationship had been the best thing that had ever happened to him. He is at present living with his foster mother in the country; waiting. His own father, married now for the third time, has been civilized and urbanely liberal about it. Gordon's only hope is that the father of the boy will not proceed, inhibited possibly by what he would consider reflections upon his own stern sense of rectitude and propriety. A kind of angry social stalemate, with people who can only resent and despise each other, and to whom a way to understanding and explanation is barred.

Colin Enderby, early thirties

'I was born in Sunderland, youngest of five. My father was a miner. I went to local grammar school and then to Hull University, where I did English and history. I had a struggle to admit that I was gay. I was brought up with the morality of the *People* and the *News of the World*, intimacy taking place, indecent assault, and all that. It's not the most propitious atmosphere for acknowledging that you're deviant. I had a few affairs with people when I was at university; not students – boys in the town. Then when I left university I went straight into teaching. That was in 1961, when you could still go into teaching without being teacher-trained. I went to a Secondary Modern School, and I was in my element. I loved teaching. I taught for seven years, without ever getting involved with my kids in any way. I did like young boys, fifteen, sixteen, seventeen, but I was never tempted at school.

'I had an affair with a married man, actually, and that went on for . . . oh, a matter of years. I used to visit him and his wife, and he used to come and visit me in my flat, cook my tea. That was very good. But in the end his wife found out: she guessed. We went to a youth-club dance, and somebody put his arm round me, in a friendly way, you know, and she said to him "I think Colin's a queer," and I suppose he got mad and it all came out; and she set about divorcing him. Then he moved in with me. I was cooling a bit, because I really preferred younger people, but he seemed to get more dependent on me.

'Anyway, before this happened, I'd seen this boy around town; very young and obviously rather effeminate. I'd seen him walking round town on Saturday afternoons among the shopping crowds, walking always with another boy, the same one. And then in 1968 I changed my school; I went to a Comprehensive. I was doing well in my career and everything seemed to be fine. Then this boy came into the school, and I found I was teaching him history. I was very attracted to him; he was very pretty, thirteen at the time. I talked to my friend about him, and as I was really enthusiastic Mark (that was the guy who I lived with) asked me to point him out to him at this youth-club dance, which I did. Anyway, the boy came up to me after one lesson – he'd already made one or two allusions. I remember one day: he'd come in to bring some money for some excursion or other, and I was sitting at my desk, collecting the money, and I said to him "I feel like the king in his counting-house with all this money." And he said "The queen more like." There was nothing of the innocent child in him. Anyway, after school I was at my desk one day, and he came in, and he threw down the metal label of a bottle of Brut after-shave in front of me, and said "Guess where I spent last night." He said he'd been with Mark – actually his name was Bill, but he thought Mark sounded more glamorous; and it was quite obvious he wasn't bluffing; he really had spent the night with him. I was very uncomfortable; appalled, in fact. And immediately after work I went rushing home and said to Mark "Look, this can't go on"; because of my job and everything. And at first he said why not, etc., but in the end he agreed that I was right. He said he'd meet the boy and tell him the whole thing wasn't on. It was funny. They'd agreed to meet in a Wimpy Bar in the city centre, and I just happened to be walking past and I saw them in the window. They sat there, very romantic, pouring with rain, most charming setting for such a touching scene. I went in and sat down with them, and we sat talking about things, and then I invited them back to my flat for coffee, which was a mistake. Mark had agreed to give him up and all that, but of course, by even taking the boy into my flat, I'd let him know where I lived. Then the damage was done. That was that. He was falling in love with me anyway, and that's how it all started. It was in many ways a very good relationship. He came from a big family, he was the eldest. His mother was very young when she had him; she's only thirty-something now.

'Anyway, my relations with Mark became more and more difficult. I had a nice time with the boy, and then the summer holidays came, and that sort of put a stop to it. Meanwhile Mark was getting divorced, and there was a danger that my name might be quoted in the divorce courts, so that was a worry. Then Mark took a post in Saudi Arabia – things had become impossible between us. We slept in single beds in the same room, I couldn't bear to have him near me after all this. We used to quarrel terribly. One day we even had a fight in the street. We'd been out – we'd had a nice evening, as a matter of fact, one of the few nice evenings we had had together, and then as we were passing some police houses, he started yelling and carrying on and said "You're not the first fucking queer that's broken up a happy marriage." It wasn't happy; it would've broken down anyway . . . So I hit him. He didn't hit me back at the time, but he started again a bit later, swearing and so on, and I hit him again. This time he hit me back, and he damaged my nose, I had to go to hospital . . .

'He threatened to murder me . . . I used to hear him, talking apparently to himself, but obviously for my benefit. "I can't do it, not that. But I must." Sometimes, lying in bed, he used to say "It's the only way, I can't do it . . . But I'll have to kill him." He used to write letters and then crumple them up and leave them lying where I could pick them up and read them. He knew a quite famous film actress, and he would write letters that began "Thank you, M," or whoever it was, "for your advice. I'm afraid that you're right. It's the only way out, to get it over with." That was all pretty unnerving. In the end I slept with a knife under my pillow, just in case.

'Anyway, the storm broke in May 1969. I got home one night and found a note saying would I please contact Bristol CID. I didn't know what it could be; I'd witnessed an accident some weeks previously, so I thought it might be that. Anyway, I went to the station, and I knew something was wrong straight away. I was put into a room, and the detective looked at me and said "So you're Enderby, are you?" So I knew it was nothing to do with the accident. He just glared at me, glowered, I don't know a word to describe it, straight in the eyes, and after a long silence he said

"We've been investigating your homosexual activities," and he mentioned Gary's name, and he said "You've been under surveillance for the past three weeks," and he mentioned a whole list of names of kids I'd known in Plymouth . . . Of course, I panicked, and admitted the thing with Gary. I didn't realize that was a trap. I could probably have got away with it if I'd denied everything. It appeared later that they'd been going on some anonymous letters. I could have brazened it out, but of course that's part of the way of getting you . . . Anyway, I can't tell you how shattering it all was. I'd never really thought about the law and the police and all that. In fact I'd always been fairly law-abiding. I was always a Labour man, coming from a working-class area, but I'd never given much thought to the workings of society or justice. I kind of believed in justice, as an idea, I suppose. Anyway, I went to a solicitor next morning, and told him what had happened, and then of course it was too late to retract what I'd said, so I made a statement at the police station the same evening. I didn't write it, the detective wrote it for me, I couldn't have written anything at that time, I was too scared and trembling . . . And there was always the threat that if I didn't admit to it, there would be other charges, all these boys I'd known in Portsmouth, because I'd never been active in Bristol, I'd always been very careful, and anyway, the gay scene is very poor in Bristol, much better in the Portsmouth/Southampton area, there are lots of boys there on the game, it's amazing. So they gave me all the routine about how it'd be better for me, it'll look better and all that, and of course I bought it. They said if you plead not guilty, you'll have to go before a jury, if you plead guilty it'll be easier, it won't take so long.

'Anyway, I was advised to get myself some treatment before the court case came up, because that also helps you and makes things look better if you're contrite about it. I went to my own GP at first, who was very unsympathetic; and then, at last, I got sent to a psychiatrist . . . That was the strangest interview. He kept pouring himself soup out of a flask, didn't really seem interested. He said "You're not the kind of person who hangs round public lavatories, are you?" I said "No," which was true. He said "Good, because I come through the park sometimes, and I see them and I think it's disgusting." Then he said "You could go into hospital. That would help your case." He said "Private hospital, how much can you pay, it's £35 a week.", and that was in 1969. I said "Well not long at that rate, three or four weeks, I guess." And then he said "Well, there are about twenty NHS beds there, I'll see what can be done." That was on the Wednesday, and then on Friday morning I was told there was a place for me at The Retreat near Cardiff. It was a beautiful place. Lovely summer. I played tennis a lot of the time, I could go out when I wanted. I had boys, even in Cardiff. They asked me if I wanted treatment, and I refused. I said "It isn't an illness." I had a lot of visitors . . . so many of the staff of the school came, and they were very kind. It was a bit of a problem about my family, because I usually went down to Plymouth for the holidays to stay with a sister who'd been widowed. And I carried on writing to them, and getting the letters posted from Bristol so that it looked as if I was carrying on as usual. But in the end somebody sent my sister a cutting from the newspaper after the trial, the anonymous letter writers got busy again doing their social duty; that was the worst moment, when she rang the hospital. She rang all the hospitals in Cardiff, and when I got in from tennis one afternoon and found her letter . . . They came to see me. That was an awkward moment too. They didn't know what to say. They said "Well you're still our brother; even if you'd committed murder, we'd still stand by you." But they didn't really understand. How could they?

'Anyway, in the court, it was all very bizarre. There was a policeman on duty who was one of the boys I used to teach. A man came in to bring my QC some notes, and he saw me in the dock and said "Good God, what are you doing here?" It was funny; at one point the policeman said "What the hell did you want to go and get mixed up with a kid like that for?" because he'd been with men before; there was a taxi driver who'd been on a charge for the same thing, and so the recorder said he was satisfied that I hadn't corrupted the kid. If I had, apparently, that would have been much more serious. It was funny, the police report, the language they use; it looks so stark and horrible written down. I remember the detective at one point using the expression "They played with each other's tails", that's an old-fashioned working-class way of putting it; the whole thing seemed so dissociated from the experience. They tried to make me admit to having buggered the kid. I said no I hadn't, and they said "No, but you tried though, didn't you?" You know, casting doubts on my manhood sort of thing . . . Anyway, they fixed on two charges in the end, I don't know how they work them out. And I was found guilty and sentenced to two terms of imprisonment, two years each, to run concurrently and suspended for three years. My friends who'd stood by me were convinced I'd go to prison; but I hadn't really thought it was possible. I was in a daze, I suppose. Anyway, afterwards I went up to Manchester, and although this was hanging over me, I had more boys in Manchester than I'd ever had before. I knew that any offence of any kind, and I'd have to go to prison. But I didn't care. I stayed with these people who had been so good to me, and who were living in Manchester at the time. They tried to warn me, but I was quite reckless . . . At a certain level of shame, you get installed in it . . .

'I was banned from teaching. I had to go before a panel at the DES, a psychiatrist and two others, and they asked me why I wouldn't have treatment . . . They grilled me for one and three-quarter hours, and then they said that my teacher's certificate would be withdrawn. They said "Do you know what that means?" I said "I can't ever teach again?" They said "Oh no." But I couldn't teach again until such time had elapsed in which I could prove myself to have been rehabilitated. So I've been rehabilitating like mad. I couldn't get a job at first. Nothing I wanted to do. All the jobs I applied for, often there was simply no answer. Then, in the end, I got offered a job in a hostel, but because it was partly paid for by the local education authority, that was out. Another one, under the auspices of the Home Office, that was out. They have a black list, and I'm most definitely on it. In the end I got a job with a private charity in a hostel for compulsive gamblers. Now I work as a hostel visitor co-ordinating policy in different hostels up and down the country.

'I really do miss teaching though. There's nothing else I really want to do. The minimum period for being banned is five years, I think . . . I've got lots of people who will speak up for me, say that it was only a momentary aberration . . . I've got an affair now; met him in a cottage in Strawberry Lane, Newcastle. He's at Huddersfield Poly . . . He depends on me quite a bit. His father's a miner. He's going to be an interior designer. He's coming to London in the summer, and we hope to get a flat together.

'It has made me bitter . . . I wake up in the night sometimes, in a cold sweat, and can hardly believe what has happened.'

James, forty-six

He is slight, balding, dark hair, timid. Large brown eyes, rather scared. He lives in a small Midland town, with his parents, who are in their late seventies. He left school when he was fifteen, and has worked in shops all his life. For the past eight years he has worked in a chemist's.

'My life I've lived like a rat in a hole. I've never had any real life of my own. It's my own fault. I'm not looking for sympathy. I'm not trying to blame Mum and Dad. I think that's too easy . . . I think it was me, the way I am. I've always been a dreamer, ever since I was ever such a kid. I used to dream my life instead of living it. If I even saw somebody in the street who I liked the look of, I used to go home and imagine all sorts of things about him . . . I'd pretend I was in all sorts of situations with him, where he needed me. It was like home-movies, I used to make my own, in my mind, and in the last reel I ended up in his arms . . . Corny, I suppose, but that was all my life amounted to for years and years. And I never thought of it in any other way. I never thought I would actually know anybody, meet anybody to touch or anything like that. I always thought of myself as never having anybody to have friend-ship with. But I've always been on the lookout, I suppose, without realizing it. Everybody who used to come into the shop, if he was young, I used to tremble almost in giving him whatever he'd bought, and if I happened to touch his hand it was like getting an electric shock; I had to snatch my hand away so he shouldn't think I'd done it on purpose.

'But as time passed, I noticed something. I was getting older, but the people I was most attracted to stayed the same age. When I was thirty I went on holiday with my parents to Torquay, and staying in the same hotel there was a boy about fifteen with his mother and father. And it was sort of understood that I should go out with him, look after him, keep him out of the clutches of . . . people like me, I suppose. He liked me. We went out, trips, walking . . . Nothing happened, but I'm sure he was, you know, that way. When I left I gave him my address and said "You must come over and see us," and he said he would, but I never heard from him again.

'That was the nearest I ever came to . . . knowing anybody. But it had a very unsettling effect on me. It gave me a taste for something more. When I got back home, I felt I was a new person. I could talk to people, it gave me the confidence to talk to people, young people. I felt I'd really come out of my shell. I joined the church choir. Harmless enough . . . And there was a boy, oh he was lovely. I fell in love with him. I can't tell you what pleasure it gave me, just to be with him, singing with him, listening for his voice among the others . . . just watching him. Nothing happened, I don't want you to think I'd do anything like that. It would have had to come from him, but he was much too innocent, too nice a boy for anything of that . . . I think for six months I was happy, just to know that I'd see him on choir practice nights and on Sundays . . . He was nice to me; he talked to me about his parents, and I was thrilled that he didn't seem to put me in the same category as them. I think I was a sort of older brother.

'But then they moved. People always move. Why don't people stay in the same place? I always have, and there's nothing so terrible about it. He came in one day and said they were going to Bradford . . . It was like the end of the world. He was everything to me. I thought about him at home, at work, when the television was on, I just sat there thinking of Danny, I don't think I registered anything that was going on around me at that time.

'It shattered me, that . . . I even thought of going up to Bradford, to be near him. I couldn't, obviously. I don't know how I got through it, the separation. The last time I saw him, it was Whit Sunday. On the evening he was going, I said "I shall miss you," and he smiled at me, but he didn't say anything. I wanted to say "Can I write to you, or will you write to me?" but I couldn't get the words out . . . Men don't write to boys of that age if they're not related to them. Although I was more than related to him, I loved him . . . But I kept the hope he might write to me. He knew where I lived. And I watched the postman every day for months, until hope faded. I really did despair. I think I must have been on the verge of a breakdown. I couldn't concentrate. I used to cry. I once went to Bradford, but I had no idea of where he lived. I spent three days there, then came home and spent the next three days crying my eyes out.

'But that cured me. It cured me of thinking I could ever get to know anybody as a real friend. But I can still look at them. I see them when I'm going home from work, standing outside the factory gates or the pubs or the cafés, and I look at them, and I just store up the pictures of them in my mind, and I can't wait to get home. I know it's unrealistic. I ought to get out and meet people. But I've never made friends. I don't even go to choir now. I regard my life as finished. I believe in God, and He has been a great help to me ... I expect my parents will die, and then I'll be alone. But I've had a lot of practice.

'But these boys ... I look at them, and all I can do is wonder what they think about, what they can be like, as people to know ... I wish I was like them. If I could have my time again, now, perhaps I'd be like them, laughing, carefree, riding a motor bike, showing their teeth, their hair blowing in the wind ... But I know it's silly. I don't talk to people about it, it's so silly. You're the first person I've spoken to like this ... Ten years ago, I wouldn't even have done that. But now I think, what does it matter? I've been chaste, I've had to be, but I haven't taken a vow of silence.'

Melvyn, fifty

'What do you do, when you're my age and you know that you're basically homosexual, and you've got a wife and two adolescent children? ... It never occurred to me when I was young; I enjoyed sex with my wife, I may have thought "Oh is that all there is to it," and I realize now that I was never truly excited by her; but as for affection and warmth, I'd never find anyone like her. But I can't jeopardize all that, can I? If I told her, it would make our relationship, I don't know, it would rob her of the years we've had together ... I don't doubt that she'd be understanding; she'd probably say "Oh that's all right, darling," and get on with whatever she was doing. But you can't do that to people. Even if her intelligence told her it didn't matter, what might it do to her emotions? What about the children? Could you tell a fourteen-year-old girl, Oh by the way, Daddy's gay ... It sounds ridiculous ... As for all the social thing, that doesn't matter, because we've got a circle of close friends, we don't go to polite dinner parties or play bridge and all those things that most of the people around us do; I could dispense with all that. As a matter of fact, we're already considered a bit bizarre, because we don't do all the things they do; our car is dirty, our garden a bit scruffy; only they can't quite dismiss us, because I have a responsible job in local government. But they disapprove ...

'How can it happen? Not being gay, I can understand that, that doesn't stretch my imagination at all; it's just the way you can go so long denying it, suppressing it . . . When I look back, it must have been there always, sometimes in abeyance, sometimes sublimated . . . When I was young I was attracted to boys at school; but then I assumed that was one of the famous phases we're supposed to go through . . . But what to do about it? Time has eroded my ability to do anything. I'm a prisoner of my circumstances . . . I'm not going to jeopardize the security of my family; they are my responsibility . . . At present I lead very much a double life. But that has its anxieties, because I'm not by nature a deceptive person . . . All the people I meet, I can't tell them my real name, I try to act lower class than I am. Do you know what I do? I go into a public lavatory to change, and carry my office clothes in a carrier bag . . . It's absurd, talking about it I want to laugh, but when I'm doing it, it's so serious, the grim determination with which I set about the change in my personality, although I suppose you would hardly consider the change of clothing very different from my office clothing; but to me, it means a whole new personality. It consists only of a casual jacket and some slightly more fashionable trousers and a red sweater . . . To me that's really daring . . . Fortunately I'm quite well preserved, and I haven't grown fat. That is something to be thankful for . . . But I regard the life I lead now as unrealistic. Something will have to give somewhere. I only hope it isn't me who cracks up . . . Because it is a strain . . .'

Postscript

Most people who discover themselves to be wholly or partly homo-sexual do so without reference to any of the official agencies to which the upbringing and education of children is entrusted – family, school, peer-group; but are left to come across their self-knowledge quite fortuitously, by chance, by a random encounter, sometimes after years of guilt and self-disgust. One of the results of this *laissez-faire* process in the search for identity is that many people see their lives entirely in terms of personal dramas, a long journey towards self-understanding, sometimes spanning years or decades of their lives. It is a deeply isolating experience; it severs individuals instead of uniting them. It denies the fact that the processes taking place are in fact quite often similar, and that communication is possible between individuals who cower within themselves, jealously guarding their suffering, their isolation, their problems. Many people do not have access to others with whom they could share and minimize guilt and anxiety. This isolation is a natural outcome of a society that has so atomized its communities and so destroyed its network of kinship obligations – brushed away by individual con-sumption like so many importunate cobwebs – that nothing is per-ceived but individual dramas, personal tragedies, unspeakable and incommunicable suffering, private grief. The individual homosexual looks at the road he has travelled, and having installed himself in the gay scene – or the gay counter-scene, having established a *ménage* or lasting relationship, or having suppressed things about himself which he cannot face, or having concealed what he considers his ugly deviancy, he may well think there is no more to be said. Everybody is anxious to assert the uniquely searing experience that is his own; whereas it is far less of a personal drama and far more a result of *social* experience than most people can or will admit. When poverty, hunger, unemployment were still the principal deter-minants upon the lives of most people, we could look at social forces and say 'That is the cause of our pain.' But society appears to many people to have retreated: it no longer breaks the body in factory or mill; it no longer denies us subsistence; it no longer punishes in the same way that privation and want punished. And accordingly, social forces have become invisible, ghostly things, that only lurk in phan-toms like cancelled holidays or motorway pile-ups. All that is left for the purposes of everyday living is a great stranded piece of sea-wrack left behind by the ebbing away of the obvious social influences of the past; something called the Individual.

What you know about yourself is denied everywhere in the bland façades and official functions of our social institutions. The individual may be able to monitor his needs, but finding them everywhere negated, turns in upon himself, and accepting the weight of evidence against him, may well accept the mutilation of his sexuality. Even the process of loving others can be seen as aberrant and impossible of reciprocation, a deadening and crushing experience instead of the most hopeful and fulfilling of which human beings are capable. That is a cruel and ugly process. But there is something no less cruel about the process by which it is being supplanted. A society that permits, within a controlled and limited area, the expression of sexuality, because it can be harnessed for the gain of others, may well prove to be an exploitation as damaging to individuals in body and mind as the kind of human usury represented by the mines and mills of the nineteenth century.

I can remember my own initial sexual fantasies as being without guilt. At first undifferentiated, during adolescence they became focused on males. I felt then that by a kind of magic, no doubt conjured forth by the intensity of feeling, my love would be reciprocated, and I serenely accepted that it must be within the order of things that love is automatically returned. I was born into a culture that had taught me that self-gratification is the purpose of our existence. When I discovered it was not, I was so shocked that it took fifteen years to recover. The belief that one had only to want for something for it mysteriously to appear succeeded a hopelessness, a conviction that I must be the most monstrously perverted creature on earth. I was quite unaware that there might exist other people with whom it might be possible, not only to communicate, but even to develop some sort of reciprocal relationship. The result of this was a series of endogenous and morbid, unrequited passions, which convinced me that I must be quite repelling and unloveable – conviction never far from introspective adolescence – and delayed for many years the development of an affective and sexual life. At the same time I was caught up in a process called higher education (which it emphatically was not); and as people who have been robbed of one of their senses are said to develop those that remain more effectively, I was invited to bloat compensatory areas of my mind as a consolation and, if I chose to accept it, as a public proof of my worth and merit. I think I must have been almost thirty before I was able to restore the repressed and mutilated emotions, in a relationship with another person; although I do not believe the damage can ever be made good completely.